Computers and Education

Computers and Education
E-Learning, From Theory to Practice

Edited by

Baltasar Fernández-Manjón
Universidad Complutense, Madrid, Spain

Juan Manuel Sánchez-Pérez
Universidad Extremadura, Cáceres, Spain

Juan Antonio Gómez-Pulido
Universidad Extremadura, Cáceres, Spain

Miguel Angel Vega-Rodríguez
Universidad Extremadura, Cáceres, Spain

and

José Bravo- Rodríguez
Universidad Castilla – La Mancha, Ciudad Real, Spain

 Springer

A C.I.P. Catalogue record for this book is available from the Library of Congress.

ISBN 978-1-4020-4913-2 (HB)
ISBN 978-1-4020-4914-9 (e-book)

Published by Springer,
P.O. Box 17, 3300 AA Dordrecht, The Netherlands.

www.springer.com

Printed on acid-free paper

TABLE OF CONTENTS

v

PREFACE

Computers have long been used in education and today their use is having an ever greater impact on society thanks to the increasing educational success of the Internet and easier access to it. This broad field, which may include any kind of learning process aided by Information and Communication Technologies, is usually referred to as e-learning. E-learning is commonly recognized as a powerful and valuable extension to traditional educational initiatives and Learning Management Systems (LMS) are key tools that support these new educational models. For this reason a significant amount of research and development on both technological and educational issues in e-learning has been taking place with striking results. The field is beginning to come of age and is making important advances in the development, reusability and interoperability of educational content fostered by maturing standards and specifications (e.g. IMS, ADL/SCORM).

Nevertheless, even if we take these advances into account, more research and application work is needed in order to produce more cases of success and to generalize e-learning in industry, universities and schools. Certain problems have been identified such as those regarding costs, the knowledge needed to effectively apply this approach, or the fact that in many cases traditional LMS sometimes lack the required flexibility and adaptability to implement innovative educational models that need to be addressed. There are other issues also open such as how to involve learners further in the instructional process, how to stimulate the collaborative creation of educational contents, how to ease the creation and reuse of contents for non-experts, how to make more open and collaborative environments, or how to put into practice the effective integration of mobile devices in educational settings.

This book attempts to reflect several different views and efforts of the computers in education use. The book collects a set of selected and improved papers presented in the 4th International Symposium on Educational Informatics (SIIE in Spanish) hold in Cáceres (Spain) on November of 2004. The book includes also contributions of well known researchers in the

Educational Informatics field. The book chapters present experiences not only from the research point of view but from a practical point of view as well.

Cáceres, Spain, November, 2006

Baltasar Fernández-Manjón, UCM
Juan Manuel Sánchez Pérez, UEX
Juan Antonio Gómez Pulido, UEX
Miguel Ángel Vega Rodríguez, UEX
José Bravo Rodríguez, UCLM

ACKNOWLEDGEMENTS

The editors thank the Spanish Ministery of Science and Education for grant TSI2004-20279-E towards the edition of this book

Chapter 1

A HISTORY OF E-LEARNING
Echoes of the pioneers

Paul Nicholson
Faculty of Education, Deakin University, 221 Burwood Highway, Burwood, Australia 3125
pauln@deakin.edu.au

Abstract: In many contemporary sectors, E-learning is often regarded as a 'new' form of learning that uses the affordances of the Internet to deliver customized, often interactive, learning   materials and programs to diverse local and distant communities of practice. This view, however, is historically disconnected from its antecedent instantiations, failing to recognize the extensive links between developing educational theories and practices that had shaped the use of E-learning over the past 40 years. In addition, the historic divide between Education and Training has led to both the concurrent development of different notions, foci, and labels for technology-enhanced learning in different contexts and situations, and different conceptual origins arising in acquisitive and participatory learning metaphors.

Key words: E-learning; history; theory; practice.

1.   PARALLEL HISTORIES AND TERMINOLOGY

With the historian it is an article of faith that knowledge of the past is a key to understanding the present (Stampp in Szasz, 2006). In the history of E-learning, it is important to note that there is no single evolutionary tree and no single agreed definition of E-Learning: since the 1960s, E-learning has evolved in different ways in Business, Education, the Training sector, and the Military (for a military perspective see Fletcher & Rockway, 1986), and currently means quite different things in different sectors. In the school sector, 'E-Leaning' refers to the use of both software-based and online learning, whereas in Business, Higher-Education, the Military and Training sectors, it refers solely to a range of on-line practices. (Campbell, 2004)

1

B. Fernández-Manjón et al. (eds.), Computers and Education: E-learning, From Theory to Practice, 1–11.

The history of E-learning across all sectors is best summed up as: *'Opportunities multiply as they are seized.'* (Sun Tzu, 410bc) as for the past 40 years, educators and trainers at all levels of Education, Business, Training and the Military made use of computers in different ways to support and enhance teaching and learning. (Charp, 1997; Molnar, 1997) Consequently, the contemporary use of the term 'E-learning' has different meanings in different contexts (Campbell, 2004). In the Higher Education, Business, and Training sectors it relates particularly to Internet-based flexible delivery of content and programs that focus on sustaining particular communities of practice. E-learning in business and training can be characterised as being driven by notions of improved productivity and cost reduction, especially in an increasingly globalised business environment, with a focus on content delivery and online course management. These sectors initially employed the limited learning models extant at the time, but have since moved to incorporate a diverse range of learning models and foci. (Nicholson, 2004) Campbell (2004, p1) argues that:

> 'Broadly, in industry settings, E-learning reflects an emphasis on informal and non-formal, just-in-time learning where the emphasis is on collaborative productivity. Whilst, in higher education settings, best-practice online learning emphasises the development of metacognitive skills, where the emphasis is on reflective and collaborative learning.'

In the context of the wider education community, the use of the term E-learning has historically had wider connotations that embrace a diverse range of practices, technologies, and theoretical positions. It is not only focused on online contexts, and includes the full range of computer-based learning platforms and delivery methods, genres, formats and media such as multimedia, educational programming, simulations, games and the use of new media on fixed and mobile platforms across all discipline areas. It is often characterised by active learner-centred pedagogies. (e.g., Harel, 1991; McDougall & Betts, 1997)

The growth of E-learning in Business and Higher Education, and its marketing as a 'killer-app' (Friedman, 1999), has led to concerns about the influence of quality assurance driven models on the structure and quality of these programs (e.g., King, 2002; McGorry, 2003). Related concerns about its ability to deliver meaningful pedagogically structured learning experiences, or to have a clearly identifiable learning paradigm have also been raised (Gillham, 2002; Stone Wiske, Sick *et al.*, 2001; Suthers, Hundhausen *et al.*, 2003). Recently, driven by such concerns, its focus has expanded to accommodate the incorporation of learner engagement and social-learning models (e.g., Mortera-Gutiérrez, 2006; Schroeder & Spannagel, 2006). Since its inception, technological advances in computers and networks facilitated advances in E-learning as educators seized on new features in an attempt to adapt them to their needs, to accommodate new educational theories, or looked for the promise of enhanced functionality. Curiously, many of these were foreseen by the pioneers of E-learning.

2. ORIGINS

The origins of E-learning as currently practiced in Business, Higher Education and the Military stem from the insightful work of Patrick Suppes at Stanford and Don Bitzer at the University of Illinois. While others such as Porter (1959) and Uttal (1962) were also active early in this field (Fletcher, 2002), only Suppes and Bitzer clearly situated the use of technology within a broader educational agenda (e.g., Suppes, 1964, 1966, 1986).

2.1 Patrick Suppes

In the 1960s, there were few educational applications of computers in universities, with most performing routine computational tasks. It was thought that the high cost of technology would prevent its ubiquitous uptake as an educational tool. In 1966 Suppes argued that '... in the future it would be possible for all students to have access to the service of a personal tutor in the same way that ancient royals were once served by individual tutors, but that this time the tutors would be in the form of a computer.' (Suppes, 1966). He argued that the single most powerful argument for the use of computers in education is individualized instruction and the dialogue that it supports. This was not an idle conjecture, but was based on Bloom's research that demonstrated that one-on-one tutoring improved student achievement by two standard deviations over group instruction – the equivalent of improving the performance of 50th percentile students to that of 98th percentile. (Bloom, 1984) Individual tutorials, Suppes argued, were also a core aspect of the university and computers would embrace and extend this through the use of virtual learning environments.

Driven by a belief in the educational potential of computers, Suppes founded the Computer Curriculum Corporation at Stanford as part of his ongoing inquiry into the nature, benefits and effectiveness of computer-enhanced learning. In accordance with prevailing psychological paradigms, he developed a Computer Managed Instruction system and used it widely in his courses. Suppes also provided elementary school children with individual CMI tutorials in mathematics to supplement teacher instruction. The results were inconclusive but led to suggestions for improved practices.

Suppes work and teaching was confined to structured fields and views of knowledge, with 'drill and practice' approaches being typical for such fields. He was concerned with both producing better learning, and learning how to be a better teacher with computers.

Contemporary critiques of his approach often overlook the lack of viable alternative paradigms at that time, something that Suppes was aware of. For example, in 1971 he noted that there was (then) a shallow understanding of how to use CAI effectively, and that it would take a long time to develop the necessary deep theoretical understandings that would underpin better practises. His research found that CMI produced profound effects on learning, and identified changes in students' understandings ranging from simple to complex. While his use of computers was essentially as a tool, he foresaw the potential for wider applications of computers in education. His research led to the following (amongst other) items for consideration:

- In 1971 the technology was not up to the tasks that he envisaged for it.
- The impediments to individual CAI were pedagogical not technological.
- CAI can track & follow each student, providing the potential for customised learning pathways.
- Richer learning theories were needed to inform design and practice.
- In the future, large numbers of students using CAI will be an important part of the mainstream university.
- There was a tendency to assess the product (of CAL) with simple studies using simple statistics when more complex measures might have led to more incisive conclusions.
- Students learning styles needed to be considered when developing CAL.
- How would more complex questions and responses be developed and handled as students increasingly engaged with higher-level content?

2.2   Don Bitzer: PLATO

In the early 1960s, Don Bitzer at the University of Illinois created PLATO, a timeshared computer system, to address concerns about student literacy. PLATO could be used to develop and deliver computer-based education, including literacy programs. It allowed educators and students to use high-resolution graphics terminals and an educational programming language, TUTOR, to create and interact with educational courseware and to communicate with other users by means of electronic notes – the forerunner of today's conferencing systems (Bitzer, Braunfeld et al., 1962). Woolley (1994) argues that as well as PLATO's advances in Computer Assisted Instruction, its communication features were equally innovative and were the foundations of today's conference and messaging systems:

'Two decades before the World Wide Web came on the scene, the PLATO system pioneered online forums and message boards, email, chat rooms, instant messaging, remote screen sharing, and multiplayer games, leading to the emergence of what was perhaps the world's first online community.' (Woolley, 1994)

When PLATO was eventually commercialised, it became the direct ancestor of today's E-learning systems such as Blackboard™ and WebCT™. It's interesting that what are widely touted as the key features of such systems are exactly those that Woolley identifies in PLATO! Like Suppes, Bitzer appears to have created the technology mainly as a tool, but also oversaw its operationalization in other dimensions.

3.   FROM SIMPLICITY TO COMPLEXITY

When Dan Watt took the first computer terminal into a Boston school in 1969 , he could hardly have envisaged the subsequent changes that would occur – in particular the shift from localized 1:1 computing to distributed many: many models that occurred with the rise of constructivist and social-constructivist theories in the 1990s, and the related notions of situated and distributed cognition. To accommodate these cognitive and social learning theories required a major epistemological shift to embrace active learners, and indeed active communities of practice (Wenger, McDermott et al.), that were both knowledge consumers and knowledge creators (e.g., Papanikolaou, Grigoriadou et al., 2002).

3.1   Paradigm shifts

The eclectic history of E-learning means that constructs and paradigms in and across fields of use have merged and developed as part of the following trends in a progressive and incremental manner rather than being a new 'killer app' or 'a new way of learning'. The two interrelated trends examined briefly below (Figures 1 and 2 below) are the pedagogical focus of learning environments, and changes in the psychological foundations of learning. The size of the circles in those figures is meant to imply increased adoption or implementation over previous items, and is indicative only – they are not based on particular data. These meta-level characteristics of E-learning environments represent key lenses into what educators and developers were attempting to build and achieve with educational computing.

One of the most obvious trends in all areas of educational, business and training applications has been the increased scale of adoption of constructivist

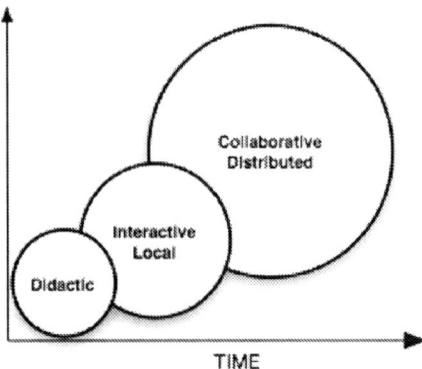

Figure 1-1. Trends in pedagogical stances over time. (Nicholson & McDougall, 2005)

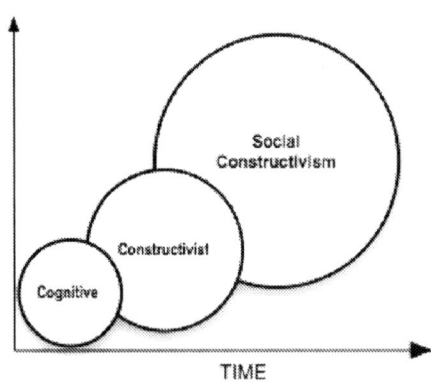

Figure 1-2. Development of learning paradigms over time. (Nicholson & McDougall, 2005)

paradigms, particularly social constructivism (Palincsar, 1998), distributed constructivism (Resnick, 1996), and the uptake of constructivist pedagogies (Forman, 1988; Ridgway & Passey, 1991). However, some care needs to be taken not to see this focus as being new or somehow being linked to the rise of ubiquitous networks etc. because its origins can be seen in both Bitzer's and Suppes' work, and because constructivist computing has been a key aspect of the use of computers in schools from the 1980s. However, in regard to the non-school sector, the constructivist trends shown below are arguably based more in the notions of communities of practice and computer-supported collaborative work (CSCW) than in constructivist psychology focus in schools.

3.2   Historical phases

Since its inception, E-learning has assimilated a diverse range of pedagogical practices, but the defining aspect of E-Learning—the trend towards collaborative online learning environments—is not only a result of the increasing adoption of constructivist paradigms, but is also a consequence of the affordances of ubiquitous global networks that have facilitated the realisation of individualised learning and interpersonal interactivity on a large scale, perhaps far exceeding the expectations of Suppes and Bitzer in its scale and scope.

3.3   A framework for comparison

Comparing E-learning practice over time is problematic and fraught with a host of methodological concerns. While Table 1 below provides an historical perspective based on macro-level features, it says little about the processes and agency occurring under the various categories. In order to make detailed comparisons of technology-based learning systems and paradigms over time it is necessary to explore complex interactions and

Table 1-1. The changing focus of educational technology over the past 30 years (after Charp, 1997; Herrington, Reeves et al., 2005; Leinonen, 2005; Mortera-Gutiérrez, 2006; Nicholson & McDougall, 2005; Pilla, Nakayama et al., 2006; THOMSON, 2005)

Era	Focus	Educational characteristics
1975-1985	Programming; Drill and practice; Computer-assisted learning – CAL.	Behaviourist approaches to learning and instruction; programming to build tools and solve problems; local user-computer interaction.
1983-1990	Computer-Based Training; Multimedia;	Use of older CAL models with interactive multimedia courseware; Passive learner models dominant; Constructivist influences begin to appear in educational software design and use.
1990-1995	Web-based Training	Internet-based content delivery; Active learner models developed; Constructivist perspectives common; Limited end-user interactions.
1995-2005	E-Learning	Internet-based flexible courseware deliver; increased interactivity; online multimedia courseware; Distributed constructivist and cognitivist models common; Remote user-user interactions.

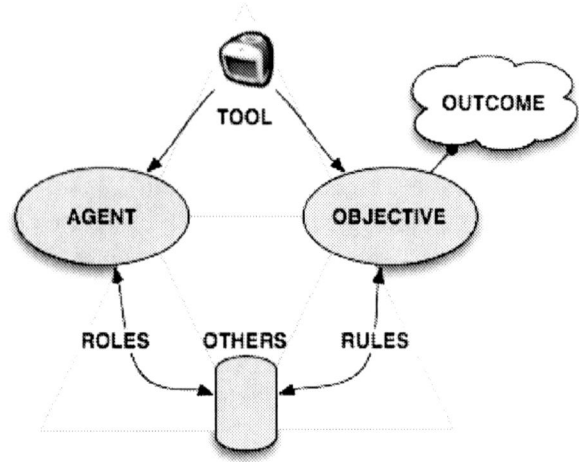

Figure 1-3. Activity Theory model for use with educational technology
(after Nardi, 1996; Roschelle & Pea, 2002)

contexts. The nature of some of this complexity is revealed in Figure 3 – an adaptation of Nardi's Activity Theory model for use in technology-based learning contexts. The value of this model is that it provides a plausible, fruitful and comprehensible framework for use in exploring E-learning environments—as in Table 2 below. As an example of its use, Roschelle & Pea note that '…the tutor, tutee, tool debate (Taylor, 1980), …has largely focused on the topmost agent-tool-objective relationship of the diagram' (Roschelle & Pea, 2002, p.8). A focus on 'the others' and their couplings may include distributed and collaborative learning, social-constructivism and learning communities. Using agency as a probe makes it easier to examine and compare the nature of E-learning environments through better articulation of the nature and purpose of the Tool, its efficacy, and impact.

Table 1-2. Agency in Taylor's (1980) models of use. (Roschelle & Pea, 2002)

Model	Agent	Objective (goal)	Tool
Tool	Student	Semiotic tool	shared-knowledge
Tutor	Computer	student problem-solving behaviour	model-tracing
Tutee	Student	student-created program	microworlds

4.   CONCLUSIONS

The contemporary claims for E-learning being 'new or different' arise in the different and independent development of the application of computers to educational needs in the business and education sectors, as well as from the 'lost history' of educational computing. It is clear that early pioneers such as Suppes and Bitzer, though confined by the dominant paradigms and technologies of their time, were striving to move beyond their contemporary practices to better engage learners and to enhance teaching and learning: at the inception of the field, PLATO contained features that pre-empted, and now characterise, cutting-edge third generation E-learning systems.

What we find by inspecting the past is that the notions of agency in contemporary E-learning systems can be found scattered heavily throughout past endeavours; the need to develop knowledge and skills, creating and interpreting texts (in the post-modern sense), synthesising and making sense of data, and creating new knowledge. Their model also highlights the need for such a model! It is difficult to begin to interrogate the diverse field of technology-enhanced learning without the aid of such a meta-level model.

While the hyperbole surrounding E-learning is not surprising given its origins in the business and training sectors, it is a concern that it has been so readily accepted as fact. While recent events have celebrated its rich history, the distillation of the 'lessons learned' and the developmental pathways has not been widely published or publicised.

The lesson of History has been that societies that don't understand their history are fated to repeat the mistakes of the past, suggesting that there is a need to make the history of the development of technology-enhanced learning more widely available and perhaps to consider its uptake as an element of professional development programs.

A focus on the Roschelle and Pea model may well be an important part of such programs as professional educators need to have appropriate tools with which to interrogate their field. Without such intellectual tools of inquiry to use in developing an historical perspective, we may well better appreciate William's caution...

History, history! We fools, what do we know or care?
(William Carlos Williams)

REFERENCES

Bitzer, D. L., Braunfeld, P. G., et al. (1962). PLATO II: A multiple-student, computer-controlled, automatic teaching device. In J. E. Coulson (Ed.), *Programmed learning and computer-based instruction* (pp. 205-216). New York: John Wiley.

Bloom, B. S. (1984). The 2-sigma problem: The search for methods of group instruction as effective a one-on-one tutoring. *Educational Researcher, 13*(6), 4-16.

Campbell, L. (2004). *What does the "e" stand for?* (Report). Melbourne: Department of Science and Mathematics Education. The University of Melbourne.

Charp, S. (1997). Some reflections. (the 30-year history of computers in education). *T H E Journal (Technological Horizons In Education), 24*(1), 8-11.

Fletcher, J. D. (2002). is it worth it? Some comments on reearch and technology in assessment and instruction. *Technology and Assessment: Thinking Ahead. Proceedings from a Workshop (2002)* Retrieved 07/07, 2006, from http://darwin.nap.edu/books/0309083206/html/26.html

Fletcher, J. D., & Rockway, M. R. (1986). Computer-based training in the military. In J. A. Ellis (Ed.), *Military contributions to instructional technology* (pp. 177-222). New York: Praeger.

Forman, G. (1988). *Constructivism in the Computer Age.* Hillsdale, New Jersey: Lawrence Erlbaum Associates.

Friedman, T. L. (1999, November 17). Next, It's E-ducation. *New York Times,* p. 25 (Section A).

Gillham, D. (2002). Web resource appraisal process (WRAP): A framework to establish critically appraised nursing knowledge--an active web based learning exercise. *Nurse Education in Practice, 2*(4), 257.

Harel, I. (Ed.). (1991). *Children designers: Interdisciplinary constructions for learning and knowing mathematics in a computer-rich school.* Norwood, NJ.: Ablex.

Herrington, J., Reeves, T., et al. (2005). Online Learning as Information Delivery: Digital Myopia. *Journal of Interactive Learning Research, 16*(4), 353-367.

King, K. P. (2002). Identifying success in online teacher education and professional development. *The Internet and Higher Education, 5*(3), 231.

Leinonen, T. (2005). (Critical) history of ICT in education - and where we are heading? [Electronic Version]. *FLOSSE Posse. Free, Libre and Open Source Software in Education,* 23 June. Retrieved 31-08-2006 from http://flosse.dicole.org.

McDougall, A., & Betts, J. (1997). *Learning with the media of their time: a snapshot of infrastructure, policy and practice in a technology immersion school.* Melbourne: Computing in Education Group of Victoria.

McGorry, S. Y. (2003). Measuring quality in online programs. *The Internet and Higher Education, 6*(2), 159-177.

Molnar, A. (1997). Computers in education: a brief history. *T H E Journal (Technological Horizons In Education), 24*(11), 63-69.

Mortera-Gutiérrez, F. (2006). Faculty Best Practices Using Blended Learning in E-Learning and Face-to-Face Instruction. *International Journal on E-Learning, 5*(3), 313-337.

Nardi, B. (Ed.). (1996). *Context and Consciousness: Activity Theory and Human-Computer Interaction.* Cambridge, MA: MIT Press.

Nicholson, P. S. (2004). E-Training or E-Learning? Towards a synthesis for the knowledge-era workplace. In P. S. Nicholson, Thompson, J., Ruhonen, M., Mulitsilta, J (Ed.), *elearning solutions for professional organizations* (pp. 360). New York: Kluwer.

Nicholson, P. S., & McDougall, A. (2005). eLearning: 40 Years of Evolution? In IFIP (Ed.), *The eighth IFIP World Conference on Computers in Education [ISI 1571-5736].* Stellenbosch, ZA: IFIP.

Palincsar, A. S. (1998). Social Constructivist Perspectives on Teaching and Learning. *Annual Reviews of Psychology, 49*(1), 345-375.

Papanikolaou, K. A., Grigoriadou, M., et al. (2002). Towards new forms of knowledge communication: the adaptive dimension of a web-based learning environment. *Computers & Education, 39*(4), 333-360.

Pilla, B. S., Nakayama, M. K., et al. (in press). Characterising E-learning practices. In *Proceedings of WCC2002, Santiago, Chile, July 2006 [ISSN: 1571-5736]*. New York: Springer.

Porter, D. (1959). Some effects of year long teaching machine instruction. In E. Galanter (Ed.), *Automatic teaching: The state of the art* (pp. 85-90). New York: John Wiley.

Resnick, M. (1996). Distributed Constructionism. In D. C. Edelson & E. A. Domeshek (Eds.), *International Conference on the Learning Sciences: Proceedings of ICLS96, Evanston, IL July 25-27, 1996* (pp. 280-284). Charlottesville, VA: Association for the Advancement of Computing in Education.

Ridgway, J., & Passey, D. (1991). A Constructivist Approach to Educational Computing. *Australian Educational Computing,, 6*(2), 4-9.

Roschelle, J., & Pea, R. (2002, Jan 7-11). *A walk on the WILD side: How wireless handhelds may change CSCL*. Paper presented at the CSCL2002: Computer Supported Collaborative Work, Boulder, Colorado.

Schroeder, U., & Spannagel, C. (2006). Supporting the Active Learning Process. *International Journal on E-Learning, 5*(2), 245-264.

Stone Wiske, M., Sick, M., et al. (2001). New technologies to support teaching for understanding. *International Journal of Educational Research, 35*(5), 483.

Sun Tzu. (410bc). *The Art of War*.

Suppes, P. (1964). Modern learning theory and the elementary-school curriculum. *American Educational Research Journal, 1*, 79-93.

Suppes, P. (1966). The uses of computers in education. *Scientific American, 215*(206-220).

Suppes, P. (1986). Computers and education in the 21st century. In W. Neilson & C. Gaffield (Eds.), *Universities in Crisis: A mediaeval institution in the twenty-first century* (pp. 137-151). Toronto: The Institute for Research on Public Policy.

Suthers, D. D., Hundhausen, C. D., et al. (2003). Comparing the roles of representations in face-to-face and online computer supported collaborative learning. *Computers & Education, 41*(4), 335.

Szasz, F. M. (2006). Quotes about History. from http://hnn.us/articles/1328.html

Taylor, R. (Ed.). (1980). *The computer in the school: Tutor, tool, tutee*. NY: Teacher's College Press.

THOMSON. (2005). History of E-Learning. from http://www.knowledgenet.com/corporateinformation/ourhistory/history.jsp

Uttal, W. R. (1962). On conversational interaction. In J. E. Coulson (Ed.), *Programmed learning andcomputer-based instruction* (pp. 171-190). New York: John Wiley.

Wenger, McDermott, et al. *Cultivating Communities of Practise: A guide to Managing Knowledge*.

Woolley, D. R. (1994). PLATO: The Emergence of Online Community. Retrieved 30/12, 2004, from http://www.thinkofit.com/plato/dwplato.htm

Chapter 2

.LRN: E-LEARNING INSIDE AND OUTSIDE THE CLASSROOM

Supporting Collaborative Learning Communities using a Web Application Toolkit

Carl Robert Blesius[1], Pablo Moreno-Ger[1], Gustaf Neumann[2], Emmanuelle Raffenne[3], Jesús González Boticario[3], Carlos Delgado Kloos[4]

[1]*Harvard Medical School - Massachusetts General Hospital, Laboratory of Computer Science, 50 Staniford St. MA 02114 (USA);* [2]*Vienna University of Economics and Business Administration (Austria);* [3]*Universidad Nacional de Educación a Distancia-UNED (Spain);* [4]*Universidad Carlos III de Madrid (Spain)*

Abstract: .LRN is an Open source Web portal and Web application toolkit designed to support both large and small communities of practice and learning inside and outside of educational institutions and the enterprise. .LRN has the features of a complete Course Management System, but is focused on supporting collaborative online learning communities that often go beyond the typical institutional or course based setting. This chapter describes the main features of .LRN, gives an overview of its modular and adaptable technical architecture, includes case studies from projects the authors are directly involved with (which help highlight the benefits of the platforms open source nature and its high performance capabilities), and concludes by giving a quick summary of the future direction of .LRN and the not-for-profit corporation that has formed around the software.

Key words: Collaborative Learning, .LRN, OpenACS, LMS, CMS, Web Portals, Software Consortia, Open Source, E-Learning.

1.   WHAT IS .LRN?

.LRN is a fully internationalized open source portal and application framework built to support online collaborative learning communities and blended learning environments. .LRN is based on the tenet that learning is a

B. Fernández-Manjón et al. (eds.), Computers and Education: E-learning, From Theory to Practice, 13–25.

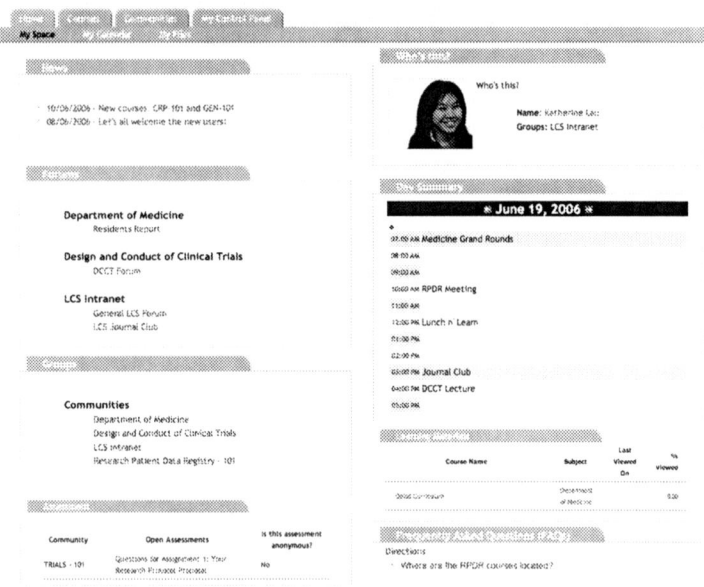

Figure 2-1. A screenshot of the .LRN personal portal page. It aggregates information from community and class portal pages. End users can customize this page as they please

social experience (Wegerif 1998), that effective learning usually takes place in the context of communities (Alavi 1994; Wenger 1998), and that administration of these communities should be distributed. Each learning community has its own stakeholders and needs to define its own unique set of interactions, so the software is designed to be flexible and allow delegation of administrative roles as close to the learners as possible. While some e-learning environments are built around a course catalog (course management systems, CMS) and other are built around a content management system (learning content management systems, LCMS) .LRN focuses on online communities (learning community system, LCS), with course management and content management applications as an added value. This contrasts with the more content-centric approaches of most of the key systems in the e-learning arena, like the commercial WebCT (Goldberg and Salari 1997) or the Sakai (Farmer and Dolphin 2005) opensource project and taking the community oriented approach of Moodle (Dougiamas and Taylor 2003) to the extreme.

From an e-learning perspective, some interesting samples of .LRN applications are the Learning Object Repository System (LORS) that supports the IMS Content Packaging Specification (allowing packaging, organization, and import/export of learning objects), the Assessment tool (tests, quizzes, surveys, evaluations, etc.) that supports the IMS QTI import

Table 2-1. A rough order of magnitude estimation of the .LRN development cost based on lines of source code

Total Physical Source Lines of Code (SLOC)	487,182
Development Effort Estimate, Person-Years (Person-Months)❶	132.77 (1,593.26)
Schedule Estimate, Years (Months) ❷	3.43 (41.19)
Estimated Average Number of Developers (Effort/Schedule)	38.68
Total Estimated Cost to Develop (average salary = $56,286/year, overhead = 2.40).	**$17,935,662**
❶Basic COCOMO model, Person-Months = 2.4 * (KSLOC**1.05) ❷Basic COCOMO model, Months = 2.5 * (person-months**0.38) Data generated using David A. Wheeler's 'SLOCCount'	

and export, Gradebook, Homework (an assignment drop box for course facilitators), User Tracking (allows administrators to track what users have or have not seen), the ePortfolio package (allows individuals to keep track of their personal learning progress and share their interests and accomplishments with others) and, optionally, E-Commerce support (e.g. credit card based course registration).

.LRN is about learning communities and these are supported by applications such as the Forums and News applications (with email and RSS subscription options), a WYSIWYG Wiki system (which can be used in the context of the .LRN Learning Object Repository or as a simple content management system), Photo Album, group and individual calendaring (with Outlook synchronization), Weblogger, and Web-based group/personal file storage with WebDAV support.

The first version of what would become .LRN was created by ArsDigita Corporation (which has been sold to RedHat) for the Sloan School of Management (MIT's business school) and was based on software ArsDigita built for corporate knowledge management, intranets, and dynamic database backed websites. The system that was created for Sloan was called the *"ArsDigita Community and Educational Solution (ACES)"* (Meeks and Mangel 2000) and was released under the GNU Public License. The system was built to run on Oracle, but in 2001 a group of volunteers started the work required to support the PostgreSQL open source database.

Simplistic development cost calculations (Table 2-1) give a very rough estimation of the amount of development (~133 person years) and investment (~$18,000,000) that has gone into the software.

2. TECHNICAL BACKGROUND

.LRN is built using OpenACS (Calvo and Peterson 2002; Hernández 2005), a mature enterprise toolkit for building scalable web applications. OpenACS follows a multi-tier software design pattern (Web server, application server, and database) and depends on AOLserver (Reuven 2002) (an application/Web server), which was built from the ground up as a tool for building highly scalable database-backed web applications.

2.1   General architecture

Based on almost 10 years of experience, the .LRN platform has evolved into a modular web application, with the goal of providing a sustainable and rich architecture, which promotes extensibility and adaptability without sacrificing maintainability. This is achieved with an organization in which functionality is divided into *packages* that can be designed, maintained, and distributed independently.

A default installation of the platform includes the core packages that provide the infrastructure of the system, a portal infrastructure (Fig. 2.1) and the basic set of .LRN packages (Fig. 2.2) necessary to support a typical E-Learning scenario, however there are dozens of official packages that can be added to the default installation. In addition, a mature package development process allows numerous non-official packages to be created by third parties. This allows institutions to create their own additions to the basic OpenACS/.LRN installation and encourages them to share their creations. This is similar to the Building Blocks program around Blackboard's open architecture (Blackboard Inc 2006), although the distribution of the packages as open source applications is more common in the OpenACS/.LRN community.

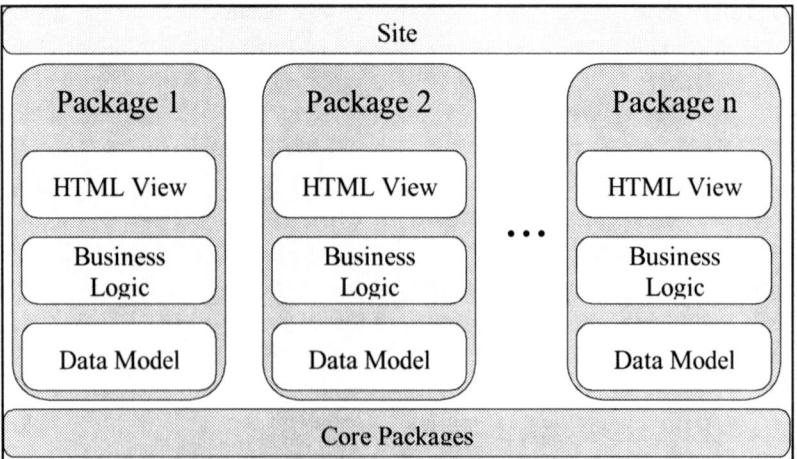

Figure 2-2. General architecture of the OpenACS/.LRN platform. The "site" layer is a common entry point for all the packages, where the look and feel of the site is defined.

Generally packages are designed following a Model-View-Controller pattern that separates the view (HTML syntax), the business logic (Tcl scripts), and the data model. Typically the resulting packages are web-based software applications that take advantage of base functionality provided by core packages and can be distributed independently.

2.2   Separation of the View and Business Logic: The Templating system

Decoupling the view from the functionality itself provides a number of advantages in the development of web applications, most of them derived from the fact that neither web programming nor HTML design are trivial tasks and that both require a different set of skills. In fact, the first benefit obtained from this separation is the definition of two separate roles: The web *programmer* and the web *designer*.

The .LRN platform provides such a separation by means of the Templating System. Every request that the server receives is handled in two steps. First, a Tcl script (Ousterhout 1994) is executed. This contains the business required to attend to the request, like checking for permissions, accessing a database, modifying some data or preparing some data for display. The actual rendering of the page is postponed until the second step, the execution of an ADP page (AOLserver Dynamic Page), which is a simple document containing HTML markup and special tags. The key idea is that creating an ADP page does not require special programming skills (other than HTML).

2.3   Implementation of the Business Logic: The Application Server and the Web Application Programming Interface

The evolution of the .LRN platform and its backing software (namely, OpenACS and AOLserver) provides a number of programming APIs that facilitate the implementation of the business logic layer with different level of abstraction. At the core of the system, AOLserver provides a highly efficient multithreaded back-end, which is based on resource pooling and a caching mechanism, with a throughput capable of sustaining sites such as www.aol.com and www.mapquest.com. AOLserver provides a fully featured API for application programmers that can be called using Tcl.

However, it is not common to have to deal with this low-level API, as .LRN provides a rich API that facilitates development with high-level constructs for database access and management, creation of data structures, and flow management. The power of this API is an important factor in .LRN platform development, because it simplifies the development and maintenance of packages by third parties.

2.4   The Data Model and the Object System

The .LRN architecture is enhanced by an abstraction in the underlying data model: the Object System. Initially, all the data objects defined by the different packages are stored in their respective package-specific data model which contains the tables and views necessary to properly store and manage those objects. But the .LRN implementation suggests the registration of these objects in a centralized listing. This centralized system stores references to all the objects and keeps track of the packages responsible for their management.

One of the most obvious advantages of this approach is exemplified by the Permissions System. The management of a healthy learning community often requires moderation and permission based contribution that may require a complex and fine-grained authorization mechanism. Instead of re-writing code to support varied and complex permissions a developer can simply register the objects needed in their applications (e.g. a blog post) in the centralized repository. The .LRN Permissions System will then detect any calls to that content (regardless of the package) and act consequently. This approach also facilitates the integration with other services or applications offered by the platform (e.g. adding support for comments to the blog post by integrating with the comments package), versioning (a core feature), and categories (another package/application).

Another benefit of registering all objects in an Object System is the ability to display content objects in multiple contexts. An example of this can be found in the .LRN Learning Object Repository System (LORS) designed for the maintenance of content in the form of Learning Objects (Koper 2003) and compatible with the specifications proposed by IMS (IMS Global Consortium 2004). LORS takes advantage of both Wiki Package content objects and .LRN IMS QTI (IMS Global Consortium 2004) compatible Assessment Package objects to allow end users to create sequenced learning modules (e.g. a self test made up of sequenced content and questions). As long as all objects are properly registered in the central repository, various combinations of these objects can be used in different contexts with relative ease and limited development overhead.

3. SUCCESS STORIES AND SELECTED USE CASES

The high performance implementation and the open source nature of the platform has been a key factor in the adoption of .LRN by a number of institutions in different countries. These are some examples.

3.1 E-LANE

E-LANE is one of the projects funded by the European Commission under the @LIS Programme (Alliance for the Information Society 2006). @LIS is a European Commission project aimed at reinforcing the partnership between the European Union and Latin America in the field of the Information Society. E-LANE (E-LANE 2006) is one of the projects focused on e-Learning. Its objective is the deployment of courses for digital literacy and life-long learning in partner countries in Latin America, namely Mexico, Guatemala, Colombia, Chile, and Brazil.

For the selection of the e-learning platform, it became clear from the very beginning that it had to be one based on an open source license. With .LRN, E-LANE found a solid foundation on which to build. In the context of the project, the platform was extended to support detailed learner tracking and e-learning specifications, such as IMS-QTI (IMS Global Consortium 2005) as mentioned previously and IMS-LD (IMS Global Consortium 2005).

Pilots have been rolled out with more than 1000 students, in scenarios such as basic and graduate courses in Guatemala, digital literacy courses in Mexico (in collaboration with the local government), courses in schools in Chile, and basic courses for indigenous people in their own languages in Colombia.

3.2 Vienna University of Economics and Business Administration: Learn@WU

The Vienna University of Economics and Business Administration (Wirtschaftsuniversität Wien, abbreviated WU) is one of the largest business universities worldwide, with more than 22,000 students and ~2,000 courses offered each semester. The Austrian university system offers unlimited access to all students who pay a tuition fee of 350 €. This admission policy leads to high enrollment. Up to 4,000 freshmen enroll in a business-related study program per year.

High interest in the programs caused severe resource problems at the university. Therefore, in 2001 the university started Learn@WU (Alberer,

Alberer et al. 2003) as a content project with an initial 2 year budget of 3,4 Mio € to provide full coverage of the first-year courses and to provide an E-Learning alternative to classical university style lectures.

Some requirements of the university did not fit well the standard feature portfolio of other course management systems evaluated:

- A student should be able to visualize the topics that have been already covered within a "concept space map", and see how his or her scores compare with other students.
- The system must be able to represent a very detailed organizational structure for permission management. Since up to 50 parallel classes are offered per semester per course, multiple institutes host the same classes, and external lecturers teach many courses. The requirements for the rights management system were quite complex.
- The system should be integrated with the existing Kerberos authentication databases.
- More than 40,000 exams are evaluated per year for the first year of study only. The system should provide support for the integration of a mark reader and exam feedback system for students.

None of the evaluated environments were able to address these needs, nor was it feasible to modify them appropriately. The decision to use the framework turned out to be very effective, and the university used it as the base on which to develop a highly tailored system according to these requirements, continuously working with the collaboration and support of the .LRN community.

Learn@WU has been highly accepted by the students and faculty, with more than 30,000 learning resources online available to students and more than 25,000 registered users. It delivers up to 35 GB of data per day and handles up to 4.3 Mio requests (hits) per day. Students solve up to 350,000 interactive exercises per day during preparations for exams. Even at peak times, when more than 1,200 users are concurrently active, the response-time of the system (an IBM power5+ server running 64-bit Linux) is below 0.4 seconds. At the university the system is regarded as a very successful project, having halved the number of beginner classes. Most of all, it helped the university provide a high quality learning experience with limited personnel and room resources. "Without Learn@WU, the operations of our university would not have been possible", says Christoph Badelt, president of WU. Triggered by Learn@WU, E-Learning became a strategic goal of the university. As of summer 2006, there are 25,474 .LRN users, 405 open courses in 135 subjects, and 820 communities.

3.3 National University for Distance Education in Spain

The National University for Distance Education in Spain (UNED) is the biggest governmental Spanish university for distance teaching education with national and international coverage. From its beginnings in 1972, it has proved its quality and solidity both as an educational and as a research institution. As one of the ten largest Universities in the world by number of students, UNED is providing IT services for over 180,000 students, 1,500 faculty staff, 5,000 tutors, 1,200 administrative personnel, and 120 study centers. UNED has more than five years of experience in delivering online courses for over 140,000 students per year, supporting a task-based learning approach, where students no longer deal with the question-and-answer model and loosely coupled contents, and they choose .LRN for its robust architecture, scalability, and modularity.

The flexibility and open source nature of .LRN allowed UNED to create a customized solution, called aLF (Boticario, Gaudioso et al. 2001), which provides a wide set of tools for supporting courses and collaboration communities of varied nature (departments, faculties, administrative units, research projects, user groups, study communities, etc.). The system has evolved over the last four years to integrate E-Learning and collaboration utilities with the rest of the IT services provided at UNED. As of summer 2006, there are 42,000 .LRN users, 130 courses, and 160 communities.

3.4 Partners Healthcare Systems (PHS) and Massachusetts General Hospital (MGH)

Partners Healthcare Systems is a not-for-profit corporation with 9 large institutional members and 35,000+ full time employees. It is the major teaching affiliate of Harvard Medical School and is fully dedicated to enhancing patient care, teaching, research, and leading the world in integrated healthcare.

MGH is a member of PHS and is the largest hospital-based research program in the United States, with an annual research budget of more than $450 million. It is the oldest and largest teaching hospital of Harvard Medical School and nearly all of the hospital's active staff physicians are on Harvard Medical School faculty. At MGH ~1.5 million patients are seen each year and teaching and just-in-time knowledge access is recognized as a key part of providing the best possible care.

Within the Harvard system there are multiple in-house E-Learnig solutions available in addition to purchased commercial systems. MGH was interested in a system that would help facilitate clinical research by connecting staff, support online courses for both regulatory requirements and continuing education, and help with the administration and reporting needs of educational units. .LRN was proposed in response to an internal request. After evaluation of .LRN, existing local solutions, and proposals by closed source commercial providers, .LRN was selected. Major factors in the choice were: the modular open source architecture, which allowed MGH to create custom packages, the high speed and low cost of required additions, and available commercial support.

MGH added a number of applications for local use, tying them into the preexisting .LRN data model. These modules included administrative tools to facilitate course registration workflow, attendance tracking, reporting, PDF certificate generation, and improvements to the assessment package. The system ties into the local MS Active Directory user management system (using LDAP) giving all the MGH staff easy system access. MGH also implemented a data collection infrastructure and reporting mechanisms for course registration so that people can be targeted by administration with tailored information and offerings.

The initial pilot/development phase (initially circa 1500 users in the context of clinical research and regulatory training) was successful and the second pilot has begun. This portion of the work includes a focus on just-in-time access to clinically relevant resources (E-Learning in the context of patient care), clinical learning modules, ePortfolios, and integration of assessment with collaboratively created learning content for physicians in training. This allows the residency program to test key knowledge, create a virtual space for exchange, and focus on covering any identified deficiencies in medical training on an individual basis.

4.   GOVERNANCE AND FUTURE DIRECTION

4.1   The .LRN Consortium

The .LRN software is backed by the .LRN Consortium, a non-profit corporation founded by users of the software, which is committed to advancing innovation in educational technology through open source principles. Consortium member institutions work together to support each other's deployments and to accelerate and expand the adoption and development of .LRN. The Consortium ensures software quality by certifying components as .LRN-compliant, coordinates software development plans, and maintains ties with OpenACS.

The .LRN Board of Directors, representing Consortium members, sets broad strategy and has ultimate oversight responsibilities for the project, while the .LRN Leadership Team is a group of .LRN experts who are responsible for the evolution and management of the .LRN project. The .LRN Leadership Team decides what goes into releases and works with the OpenACS technical release management to help manage implementation, testing, and documenting new features and bug fixes.

4.2   Future Direction

Currently that OpenACS/.LRN repository contains more than 200 different packages. While this is a great achievement, there is significant organizational and technical overhead involved in maintaining these packages. The code base is developed by more than 100 developers in total, who provide more than 2,000 contributions per quarter. This is substantially more than the average source forge project, which has about 600 contributions per quarter (Koch 2004). From the code management point of view it is desirable to reduce the number of packages on the one hand and to increase the flexibility of the packages on the other hand.

The OpenACS community has voted to base the forthcoming versions of OpenACS on the object oriented scripting language XoTcl (extended Object Tcl), see (Neumann and Zdun 2000). The development of the XoWiki system (Neumann) is a case study to explore some of the functionality in the context of .LRN and OpenACS. XoWiki provides functionality of a wiki-system and of a content management system (revisioning, inclusions, cate-gorization), while providing a range of "Web 2.0" functionality (Weblog, RSS, AJAX, COMET) through a single package.

Another short term goal that has been earmarked by .LRN Leadership Team, (partially funded through a government grant) is to fulfill level 1 and level 2 accessibility success criteria (as defined by the W3C Web Accessibility Initiative) (W3C 2006) over the next 2 release cycles. .LRN is committed to helping provide users with special needs access to E-Learning services and is positioned to achieve this.

.LRN provides a highly flexible set of tools that can be customized for individual needs and scaled upward as local usage dictates. .LRN is actively under development, both formally and informally guided by its users through an inclusive governing process, and a flexible foundation to cultivate innovative learning environments.

ACKNOWLEDGEMENTS

Special thanks go out to the <e-UCM> Research Group (www.e-ucm.es) for their support, Katherine Lau from the Lab of Computer Science in Boston, the National Library of Medicine for supporting this work through a Medical

Informatics Training Grant (T15-LM-007092), the Regional Government of Madrid by supporting this work through the FPI Scholarship Program (4155/2005), the European project E-LANE (C-ALA2002/48-264/208), and the MOSAIC project (TSI2005-08225-C07) funded by the Spanish Ministry of Education and Science for supporting software development for .LRN.

REFERENCES

Alavi, M. (1994). "Computer-Mediated Collaborative Learning: An Empirical Evaluation." Management Information Systems Quarterly 18(2): 150-174.

Alberer, G., P. Alberer, et al. (2003). The Learn@WU Learning Environment. 6th International Conference on Business Informatics, Dresden, Germany.

Blackboard Inc. (2006). "Blackboard Building Blocks." Retrieved June 14th, 2006, from http://www.blackboard.com/extend/b2/.

Boticario, J. G., E. Gaudioso, et al. (2001). Towards personalised learning communities on the web. First European Conference on Computer-Supported Collaborative Learning, Maastricht.

Calvo, R. A. and D. Peterson (2002). The OACS web application framework. Ausweb 2002, Australia.

Dougiamas, M. and P. Taylor (2003). Moodle: Using Learning Communities to Create an Open Source Course Management System. World Conference on Educational Multimedia, Hypermedia and Telecommunications 2003, Honolulu, Hawaii, USA, AACE.

E-LANE. (2006). "The E-LANE Project." Retrieved June 14th, 2006, from http://www.e-lane.org.

Farmer, J. and I. Dolphin (2005). Sakai: eLearning and More. 11th European Univeristy Information Systems (EUNIS 2005), Manchester, UK.

Goldberg, M. W. and S. Salari (1997). An Update on WebCT (World-Wide-Web Course Tools) - a Tool for the Creation of Sophisticated Web-Based Learning Environments. NAUWeb '97 - Current Practices in Web-Based Course Development, Flagstaff, Arizona (United States).

Hernández, R. (2005). OpenACS: robust web development framework. Tcl/Tk 2005 Conference, Portland, Oregon.

IMS Global Consortium. (2004). "IMS Content Packaging Specification." Retrieved June 14th, 2006, from http://www.imsproject.org/content/packaging/.

IMS Global Consortium. (2005). "IMS Learning Design Specification." Retrieved June 14th, 2006, from http://www.imsproject.org/learningdesign/index.html.

IMS Global Consortium. (2005). "IMS Question & Test Interoperablity Specification." Retrieved June 14th, 2006, from http://www.imsglobal.org/question/index.html.

Koch, S. (2004). "Profiling an Open Source Project Ecology and Its Programmers." Electronic Markets 10(2): 77-88.

Koper, R. (2003). Combining re-usable learning resources and services to pedagogical purposeful units of learning. Reusing Online Resources: A Sustainable Approach to eLearning. A. Littlejohn. London, Kogan Page: 46-59.

Meeks, C. and R. Mangel (2000). "The Arsdigita Community Education Solution." Arsdigita Community Journal.

Neumann, G. (2006). "XoWiki." Retrieved June 14th, 2006, from http://media.wu-wien.ac.at/download/xowiki-doc/index.html.

Neumann, G. and U. Zdun (2000). XOTcl, an Object-Oriented Scripting Language. Tcl2k: The 7th USENIX Tcl/Tk Conference, Austin, Texas, USA.

Ousterhout, J. K. (1994). Tcl and the Tk Toolkit. Reading, MA, Addison-Wesley

Reuven, M. L. (2002). "At the forge: introducing AOLserver." ACM Linux Journal 2002(101): 12.

W3C. (2006). "Web Accessibility Initiative." Retrieved June 14th, 2006, from http://www.w3.org/WAI/.

Wegerif, R. (1998). "The Social Dimension of Asynchronous Learning Networks." Journal of Asynchronous Learning Networks 2(1): 34-49.

Wenger, E. (1998). Communities of Practice: Learning, Meaning, and Identity. New York, Cambridge University Press.

Chapter 3

EDUCATIONAL MODELING LANGUAGES
A Conceptual Introduction and a High-Level Classification

Martinez-Ortiz, I.[1], Moreno-Ger, P.[2]; Sierra, J.L.[2], and Fernandez-Manjon, B.[2]

[1]*Centro de Estudios Superiores Felipe II, C/ Capitan, 39, 28300 Madrid, Spain;* [2]*Facultad de Informática, Universidad Complutense de Madrid, C/ Prof. Jose Garcia Santesmases, s/n, 28040 Madrid Spain*

Abstract: Creating good quality learning resources is not sufficient for an optimum learning experience. Equally important is having a more enabling learning process involving not only the delivery of learning materials but also other activities that the learner must carry out to meet the learning objectives proposed by the instructor (tutoring, tests, reading books, etc.). Educational Modeling Languages (EMLs) are the cornerstone of e-learning because they provide a language that can be used by the instructors to formalize their own teaching process so that it can also be interpreted by computers. In this chapter we provide a conceptual introduction and a high-level classification of some of the proposed EMLs.

Key words: Educational Modeling Language (EML), Learning Design (LD), learning process, activity, learning object.

1. INTRODUCTION

In the past few years the popularity of the Internet has facilitated new ways of learning, numerous educational tools and applications have appeared and e-learning has come into being. In this context, the idea of reusable resources (i.e Learning Objects, LO (Downes 2001; Koper 2003)) appeared, leading to the development of several specifications and standards to represent learning content (IEEE-LOM 2002), as well as educational resources, and methodologies to facilitate the development of learning materials (Fernandez-Manjon and Sancho 2002; Martinez-Ortiz, Moreno-Ger et al. 2005). The aim of these initiatives was to decrease the total cost of producing and maintaining good quality LOs, thereby promoting their

B. Fernández-Manjón et al. (eds.), Computers and Education: E-learning, From Theory to Practice, 27–40.

reutilization among companies and institutions. To allow this interchange, different initiatives have arisen (e.g. Instructional Management Systems - IMS-, Advanced Distributed Learning -ADL-, Aviation Industry CBT Committee -AICC-, etc). In the past and also in the present there has been an ongoing and active research into how to get the most out of LOs and regarding how to create LOs that can be adapted to different learner needs (Martinez-Ortiz, Moreno-Ger et al. 2005), or how to enhance motivation and engagement among authors is underway. For instance, in our research group we are betting on game based learning (Moreno-Ger, Martinez-Ortiz et al. 2005; Martinez-Ortiz, Moreno-Ger et al. 2006) providing teachers with a set of tools and a methodology to develop their own small games that can replace an LO inside a unit of learning.

However, most recent works (Koper 2000; Weitl, Süß et al. 2002; Paquette, de la Teja et al. 2005) show that creating and reusing good learning materials, although important, is only one aspect of the whole story. In the words of Prof. Koper (Koper 2000): *"providing adequate knowledge is not enough: it has to be learned"*, meaning that the learning process is not only a simple transfer of knowledge. When a course is being designed, it is necessary to decide not only what learning material will be used, but also in which order this material will be shown, and which other *activities* are needed (i.e. self-assessment, problem resolution, tutoring, class discussions, etc.) during the *learning process*. Therefore, one of the most prominent trends in the development of e-learning software is to provide means for describing these learning processes. As introduced in this chapter, this can be done by using suitable Educational Modeling Languages (EMLs).

The rest of the chapter is structured as follows: Section 2 provides a general overview of the concept of EML. Section 3 proposes a three-category high-level classification for EMLs, and summarizes the most relevant ones. Section 4 surveys the *de-facto* EML standard (IMS Learning Design -IMS-LD-). Finally, section 5 closes this chapter.

2.   EDUCATIONAL MODELING LANGUAGES

The generalization of the term *Educational Modeling Language* (EML) in e-learning comes from the work developed at the *Open University of the Netherlands* (OUNL). They analyzed the diversity of Learning Management Systems (LMSs) in use and tried to address the shortcomings of e-learning systems derived from the lack of application of instructional and pedagogical theories. As a result they designed and put into practice the language called EML-OU.

In a study of Educational Modeling Languages made by the CEN/ISSS WS/LT Learning Technology Workshop, (Rawlings, van Rosmalen et al. 2002), the concept of EML was defined as a: *"semantic information model and binding, describing the content and process within a 'unit of learning' from a pedagogical perspective in order to support reuse and interoperability"*.

From this definition the following concerns stand out:

- **Semantic information model.** Like an ontology or a schema, it is a meta-model (conceptualization) of a particular domain of discourse. In this case it is a meta-model of the teaching/learning process.
- **Information model and binding.** The "binding" of an EML is a linguistic formalization of the semantic model. Usually, this formalization is done using a Domain Specific Language (DSL) based on XML technologies, and therefore this binding is machine readable.
- **Units of learning**. This concept is the key point of an EML. As defined in (Koper 2001) a *unit of learning* (also known as a *unit of study*) *"is the smallest unit providing learning events for learners, satisfying one or more interrelated learning objectives"*. Therefore, a unit of learning can not be divided without losing its semantics and its effectiveness towards the attainment of learning objectives. A *unit of learning* can be a course, a workshop, a practice, a complete study program, etc. The unit of learning defines the model of training/teaching, and the *environment* where this activity is done. Such an environment is characterized by the resource material and the services (e.g. forum, chat, videoconference, e-mail) that will be used during the performance of the unit of learning.
- **Pedagogical perspective.** An EML should be relatively independent of teaching theories, so the teacher or the learning designer could decide which of these theories he/she applies.
- **Reuse and interoperability**. Just as with LOs, the idea behind an EML its not only to allow computer applications to interpret an EML script, but also to promote the reuse of successful units of learning descriptions and also to allow the exchange of these units between different e-learning applications without taking into account how the target information system implements the semantics of the EML.

In (Koper 2000) several desirable characteristics for an EML are identified. The main ones can be summarized as:

- An EML must be defined formally and be machine-readable, so the script created with the EML can be interpreted by a computer application.
- An EML must be pedagogically neutral so different trends of teaching can be applied in a unit of learning using the same EML.
- An EML must allow designers to create complete units of study that include the *activities* to be done by the learner (what to do), the people

involved in the activity (with whom), and the environment where the activities will be performed (which learning materials are needed, which software tools, etc.).

- The units of learning created using an EML should be resilient to technical changes, evolution, and platforms, since their purpose is to facilitate reusability between systems and tools.

To sum up, EMLs are used to describe units of learning that in turn describe the learning process. But they also provide a mechanism of communication between technical and non-technical staff inside an organization during the operationalization of such units of learning.

3.   A THREE-CATEGORY CLASSIFICATION OF EDUCATIONAL MODELING LANGUAGES

From the different initiatives developed based on the principles of the EMLs described in the section above and the EMLs described in (Rawlings, van Rosmalen et al. 2002), it is possible to classify the EMLs to be studied (this classification can also be found in (Vantroys 2003)):

- **Evaluation Languages**. This category is formed by languages allowing designers to describe the stages of the learning process in which problem-solving or question-answering are involved in an abstract way.
- **Content Structuring Languages**. This category is formed by languages allowing designers to arrange the learning resources in sequence, always taking into account the learner's needs and performance in order to improve the learning experience.
- **Activity Languages**. This category is made up of languages focused on the activities in general (using computers or not) during the learning process.

Table 3-1. High-level classification of some Educational Modeling Languages

Type of Language	EML
Evaluation Languages	Tutorial Markup Language (TML) http://www.ilrt.bris.ac.uk/netquest
	IMS Question & Test Interoperability (IMS-QTI) http://www.imsglobal.org/question/index.html
Content Structuring Languages	TArgeted Reuse and GEneration of TEAching Materials (Targeteam) http://www.targeteam.net
	Learning Material Mark-up Language (LMML) http://www.lmml.de

Type of Language	EML
	ARIADNE Course (Curriculum) Description Format (A-CDF)[1] http://www.ariadne-eu.org/en/publications/references/index.html
	AICC Course Data Model http://www.aicc.org/
	IMS Simple Sequencing (IMS-SS) http://www.imsglobal.org/simplesequencing/index.html
	ADL Sharable Content Object Reference Model 2004 (ADL SCORM 2004) http://www.adlnet.gov/scorm/index.cfm
Activity Languages	Educational Modeling Language – Open University of the Netherlands (EML-OU) http://eml.ou.nl
	IMS-Learning Design (IMS-LD) http://www.imsglobal.org/learningdesign/index.html
	PALO http://sensei.lsi.uned.es
	Educational Environment Modeling Language (EEML) http://www.istituti.usilu.net/botturil/web/e2ml/index.htm
	Méthode d'ingénierie d'un système d'apprentissage (MISA) http://www.licef.teluq.uquebec.ca/gp/
	XEDU

In Table *3-1* several EMLs are classified according to these categories. The next points give several details about these languages.

3.1 Evaluation Languages

TML/Netquest (Brickley 1995) uses the Tutorial Mark-up Language (TML), which is an extension of HTML intended to produce questions. TML was designed to separate the semantic content of the layout from the question content itself. The TML files are in text format, and can be generated from other formats or other questions in a database.

IMS Question & Test Interoperability (IMS-QTI) is an ongoing effort of the IMS initiative to produce question banks and test banks (IMS-QTI-ASI_INFO 2002; IMS_QTI2-INFO 2006). The principal aim of IMS QTI is to allow the interchange of test and test data between LMSs. An IMS-QTI test decouples the questions themselves (what is being asked) from how to display the questions and how the questions are graded. IMS-QTI allows interactive tests to be created, which allows hints to be included inside questions. It is also possible to create test templates that will be instantiated when students take the test, creating different tests from the same templates.

---

[1] The A-CDF specification is not available at the moment (July 2006), but can be retrieved using the Web Archive service at http://www.webarchive.org

3.2   Content Structuring Languages

Targeteam enables the production and maintenance (use and reuse) of learning material (Koch 2002). This EML allows the use of material in different learning situations and pedagogical domains (primary, secondary and higher education). Using Targeteam, it is possible to create course notes and other contents such as explanations, motivation, and examples. It is focused on the use of an XML-based language, TeachML, and uses the concept of *issue* as a unit of study.

LMML is based on a meta-model that can fit into different application domains. LMML relies on XML for the description of e-learning material (Slavin 1995), and comprises various learning material modules, each one containing other sub-modules. Focused on a conceptual, modular and hierarchical structure of e-learning content, LMML can be adapted to different learning situations and students. It uses the concept of *course* as a unit of study.

ARIADNE Course Description Format (A-CDF) is an EML for the description of learning objects (Verbert and Duval 2004). A course in A-CDF consists of XML documents along with a course generator LMS (Durm, Duval et al. 2001). It places special emphasis on the content and its aggregation, but it is expressive enough to describe the learning process in accordance with a pedagogic model. The didactic material that can be managed through CDF is restricted to text format. It uses a combination of tools developed by the ARIADNE consortium (curriculum editors, LMS, KPS (Duval, Forte et al. 2001)) and establishes the concept of *course* as a unit of study.

IMS Simple Sequencing (IMS SS) (IMS-SS 2003) defines a method for representing the intended behavior of an authored learning experience so that any learning technology system (LTS) can sequence discrete learning activities in a consistent way. A learning designer or content developer declares the relative order in which elements of content are to be presented to the learner and the conditions under which a piece of content is selected, delivered, or skipped during presentation.

AICC Course Data Model (AICC/CMI_CMI001 2004) contains all of the information needed to describe a course. This format may be passed from one LMS system to another through a course import/export process and has Assignable Units (AUs) as its components. Data in this format is also stored internally by the LMS system and is used by the CMI in determining values of the communication data model elements sent to AUs in the course at runtime. The sequencing within a course is controlled using *prerequisites*, which are requirements that must be satisfied by a student before entering a new AU. It uses the concept of *course* as a unit of study.

ADL SCORM (SCORM_OVW 2004) represents a coordinating model intended to give a collection of standard practices that can be generally accepted and widely implemented. Indeed, ADL SCORM can be considered as an application profile of these practices. The SCORM initiative puts into practice different technological developments from groups such as IMS (IMS), AICC (AICC), ARIADNE (ARIADNE), and the IEEE LTSC (IEEE_LTSC); all within a single reference model to specify consistent implementations that can be used throughout the e-learning community. SCORM defines the technical foundations of a web-based LMS, describing:

- A "Content Aggregation Model" (CAM) that describes the components used in a learning experience, how to package those components for exchange, and how to describe those components to enable search and discovery (i.e. metadata). It also defines requirements for building content aggregations (e.g., course, lessons, modules, etc).
- A "Runtime Environment" (RTE) for Learning Objects (LO) to support adaptive instruction based on learning objectives. It describes the Learning Management System (LMS) requirements for managing the run-time environment (i.e communication between content and LMSs). The RTE covers the requirements of Sharable Content Objects (SCOs) (smarts LO) and their use of the API and the SCORM RTE Data Model. The purpose of the SCORM RTE is to provide a means for interoperability between SCOs and LMSs. SCORM provides a means for learning content to be interoperable across multiple LMSs regardless of the tools used to create the content.

In addition, in SCORM 2004 (formerly SCORM 1.3) a "Sequencing and Navigation" model was introduced to allow the dynamic presentation of learning content taking into account learning needs. It is based on IMS Simple Sequencing and describes how SCORM conformant content may be sequenced through a set of learner-initiated or system-initiated navigation events. The branching and flow of that content may be described by a predefined set of activities, typically defined at design time. Also described is how a SCORM conformant LMSs interprets the sequencing rules expressed by a content developer along with the set of learner-initiated or system-initiated navigation events and their effects on the run-time environment.

3.3 Activity Languages

PALO is a modeling language that has been developed by the UNED (Universidad Nacional de Enseñanza a Distancia, Spain) (Rodriguez-Artacho, Verdejo et al. 1999). PALO describes courses organized into modules that contain learning activities, content, and an associated teaching plan. Using PALO the designer can create templates to define types of learning scenarios. Using the features of the language, it is possible to sequence the learning tasks and modules. In addition course constraints can be created, defining deadlines and dependencies between modules and tasks. It uses the concept of *Module* as a unit of study.

Educational Environment Modeling Language (E^2ML) (Botturi 2006) is proposed as a visual modeling language for the design of educational environments in Higher Education. E^2ML is a visual modeling language, which allows an explicit definition of the learning process and of the educational activities.. In particular, it addresses the following issues:

- It facilitates the communication between the different stake-holders involved in the process (unit of learning designers, technical staff, teachers, etc.) by having a visual representation of the design like the "blueprints" of a building that is going to be built.
- The design of a UoL can be used as basis for another UoL, not only by the same designer, but also by the community.

XEDU (Buendía-García and Díaz-Perez 2003) is oriented towards offering instructional designers a framework for the specification of any instructional application from both instructional design theories and software engineering points of view. The main entities defined in XEDU are: *learner profile*, which stores all relevant information about the learner, including the outcome of the learning process; the *learning scenario* that comprises the activities and the conditions in a specific learning context; and finally the *didactic structure* that organizes educational content with a specific didactic purpose. The concept of *didactic structure* represents a unit of learning in XEDU.

MISA (Paquette, Crevier et al. 1997; Paquette 2004) is a new approach called *instructional engineering* (IE) (Paquette 2001). IE is based on *instructional design* (ID) theories (Reigeluth 1983; Merrill 1994; Dick, Carey et al. 2000) plus software and cognitive engineering. The IE provides a methodology to support the planning, analysis, design and delivery of a learning system, sharing the principles of the EMLs. MISA enables the design of a learning system through 35 tasks, producing 35 main deliverables called documentation elements (DE). The creation of these DE is divided into six well-defined phases. The concept of *learning scenario* represents a unit of learning in MISA.

Finally, among the different proposed specifications, IMS-LD (IMS-LD-MOD 2003) has emerged as the *de-facto* standard for the representation of any unit of learning applying any pedagogical theory. This language is detailed in the next section.

4.   IMS LEARNING DESIGN

Based on OUNL-EML, the IMS Learning Design (IMS-LD) specification was drawn up by the IMS/LDWG work group extracting its main concepts and adapting those parts that overlap with other IMS specifications like the packaging for interchange. In this way, an IMS-LD design is embed inside a content package distributed following the IMS-Content Packaging specification. Additionally, some parts of OUNL-EML have not been reused, like the XML syntax (a DocBook (Walsh and Muellner 1999) dialect) for developing the educational content itself.

In addition, one of the aims of IMS LD has been to integrate and work together with other IMS specifications. For example, IMS Simple Sequencing content can be used as a LO inside an activity of IMS LD. Moreover IMS QTI can also be part of an IMS LD activity so that the learner's grades on the test can be used to select the learning activities that will be delivered to the learner.

The high-level structure of a learning design according to IMS LD is sketched in figure *3-1*. Also, to facilitate understanding and the implementation of the specification, it is divided into 3 levels (A, B and C) where each level is built on top of the model and the semantics defined at the previous level:

- Level A contains the core model components of IMS-LD. When a learning design is created, two distinguished parts need to be created: a static and a dynamic part (the dynamic part will be described later). Inside the static part we find: *roles* (that define the type of participants in the learning process), *activities* (what should be done during the learning process), and the *environment* where each activity will be carried out (providing the learning content, LOs, and service tools needed). Also as a header we find: prerequisites (previous knowledge required), learning objectives (what is intended to be learned), some related metadata, and finally the title of the unit of learning.
- Level B introduces *properties* and *conditions*, where properties define a user data model and conditions are used to personalize the presentation of the unit-of-learning, based on if-then-else rules that usually query the values of the learner properties.
- Level C adds notifications behavior. A notification happens after an event and should be emitted by the runtime environment. Notifications can be triggered as an activity is completed or an expression proves to be true.

The dynamic behavior of IMS-LD, where the learning process is defined, can be seen as a theatrical metaphor. A *method* consists of one or several *plays* that are performed in parallel. Each *play* (see figure *3-2* (a)) is made up of one or more *acts* that will be performed in sequence. The acts serve as the synchronization point between the people (roles) involved in the learning design. Inside an *act*, different *role-parts* are found, each one indicating an *activity* and a *role*. These components are references to entities that should have been defined in the static section. During runtime, each user that has the referenced *role* will perform the *activity*. A *role-part* can be seen as a swim lane of a UML Activity Diagram which can only contain simple activities or structured activities (see figure *3-2* (b)).

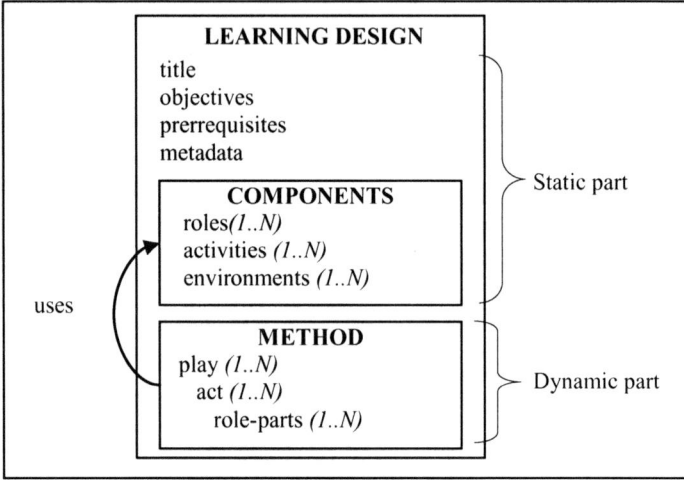

Figure 3-1. IMS-LD Structure

Using Levels B and C more complex dynamic sequencing can be created, in particular dependencies between activities. For example, a tutor could be required to grade an essay after it has been submitted by a learner.

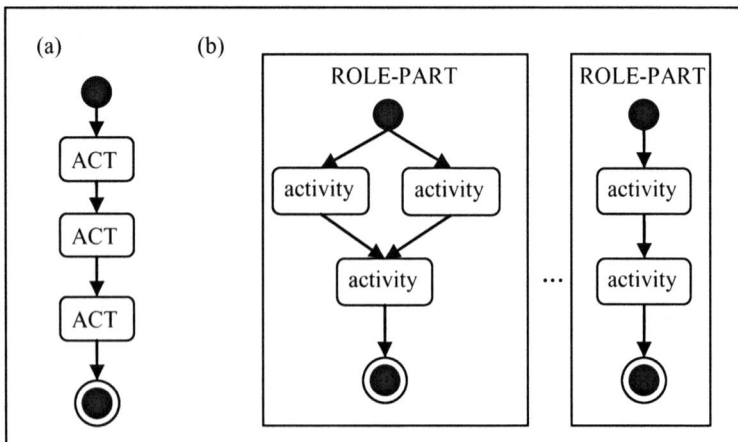

Figure 3-2. UML Activity diagram: (a) A play made up of three acts, (b) An act made up of two role-parts, where the activities are selected as user choice (left) or in a prefixed sequence (right)

5.   CHAPTER CONCLUSION

Educational Modeling Languages enable instructors and educators to build and exchange courses based on the general concept of units of learning and taking into account the whole learning process. These learning designs can be part of a repository for their reuse in similar situations. For this purpose, the concept of *learning patterns* applied to LMSs (Avgeriou, Papasalouros et al. 2003) can be useful. The origin of this kind of pattern is from the concept of Object Oriented Programming design patterns (Gamma, Helm et al. 1994): *"Design patterns describe simple and elegant solutions to specific problems [...]. Design patterns capture solutions that have developed and evolved over time. [...]They reflect untold redesign and recoding as developers have struggled for greater reuse and flexibility"*. Therefore these patterns can also be exchanged, used and validated by the community, reflecting proven pedagogical approaches for certain contexts.

In addition, an EML serves as a communication language between technical and educational staff. The Educational staff is responsible for the description of the learning experience while the Technical staff is responsible for the implementation of the engine that interprets the EML and the development or integration of the tools used inside the learning process. Therefore, a LMS that supports an EML can be seen as a meta-LMS, enabling non-technical staff to define the behavior of their own LMS without any programming knowledge.

Although IMS-LD is becoming the *de-facto* standard EML, there are a few matters that IMS-LD does not resolve such as the support for groups of learners, who are usually needed in peer-to-peer education, and collaborative learning in general. Also, the specification does not allow the dynamic role changing again needed in peer-to-peer education, where sometimes the learner becomes the teacher/coach of other learners in the group or the class. In addition, it is not usually possible to design an entire course completely and sometimes planning may also have to be adapted to fit the learner level during the course. It must be said that IMS-LD specification deals almost exclusively with static design and does not care about dynamic aspects, so the e-learning community may have to wait for a specification that particularizes IMS-LD like ADL-SCORM does for IMS-Content Packaging. For now IMS-LD only includes four types of service tools that can be used in an environment (mail, conference, monitor, index search), however there are usually more services available in a LMS that might a be useful to launch inside a learning design as well. IMS is concerned with this issue and there are subsequent specifications such as IMS Enterprise Services, IMS General Web Services and IMS Tools Interoperability Guidelines that will hopefully be included in the next versions of IMS-LD.

Finally one of the issues that teachers who want to use an EML come up against is that there are few software developments on EMLs and also few LMS that support EML. IMS-LD may be the exception thanks to the development of Coppercore (a IMS-LD engine) (Martens and Vogten 2005; OUNL 2005) and partially in LAMS (an LMS and authoring environment based on activities) (Dalziel 2003; LAMS 2005). However, some problems have been found (Barrett-Baxendale, Hazlewood et al. 2005): (1) The integration of all the software tools involved (LMS, IMS-LD engine, authoring tools) needs to be facilitated, (2) the usability of these tools must be improved to disguise the fact that at the present time IMS-LD and XML are behind the scenes, (3) the reliability of the software tools should be improved.

These considerations raise potential lines for future research into enhancing the current EML arena. These lines include the development of graphical tools for IMS-LD-based authoring (UML graphical notation is an interesting starting point) and the application of existing mature technologies and tools regarding workflow systems (Dumas, Aalst et al. 2005) in the context of running dynamic content. At the moment our group at the Universidad Compluentse de Madrid is engaged in these lines of research.

ACKNOWLEDGES

The Spanish Committee of Science and Technology (TIN2004-08367-C02-02 and TIN2005-08788-C04-01) and the Regional Government of Madrid (4155/2005) have partially supported this work.

REFERENCES

AICC. "Aviation Industry CBT Committee." Retrieved July 1, 2006, 2006, from http://www.aicc.org.
AICC/CMI_CMI001 (2004). CMI Guidelines for Interoperability AICC revision 4.0, Aviation Industry CBT Committee - AICC Subcommittee: 241.
ARIADNE. "Alliance of Remote Instructional Authoring and Distribution Netoworks for Europe (ARIADNE)." Retrieved July 1, 2006, 2006, from http://www.ariadne-eu.org.
Avgeriou, P., A. Papasalouros, et al. (2003). "Towards a Pattern Language for Learning Management Systems." Educational Technology & Society 6(2): 11-24.
Barrett-Baxendale, M., P. Hazlewood, et al. (2005). SliDe, SLeD Demonstrator - Final Report v 1.0. Hope Park (United Kingdom), Liverpool Hope University: 13.
Botturi, L. (2006). "E2ML: A Visual Language for the Design of Instruction." Educational Technology Research and Development 54(3): 265-293.
Brickley, D. (1995). "Towards an open question-interchange framework." Retrieved June 1, 2006, from http://www.ilrt.bris.ac.uk/netquest/about/lang/motivation.html.

Buendía-García, F. and P. Díaz-Perez (2003). "A Framework for the Management of Digital Educational Contents Conjugating Instructional and Technical Issues." Educational Technology & Society 6(4): 48-59.

Dalziel, J. (2003). Implementing Learning Design: The Learning Activity Management System (LAMS). 20th Annual Conference of the Australasian Society for Computers in Learning in Tertiary Education (ASCILITE 2003), Adelaide, Australia.

Dick, W. O., L. Carey, et al. (2000). The Systematic Design of Instruction (5th Edition), Allyn & Bacon.

Downes, S. (2001). "Learning Objects: Resources For Distance Education Worldwide." The International Review of Research in Open and Distance Learning 2(1).

Dumas, M., W. M. P. v. d. Aalst, et al. (2005). Process-Aware Information Systems: Bridging People and Software through Process Technology, Wiley-Interscience.

Durm, R. V., E. Duval, et al. (2001). Extending The ARIADNE Web-Based Learning Environment. World Conference on Educational Multimedia, Hypermedia & Telecommunications (ED-MEDIA 2001), Tampere, Finland.

Duval, E., E. N. Forte, et al. (2001). "The ARIADNE knowledge pool system." Communications of the ACM 44(5): 72-78.

Fernandez-Manjon, B. and P. Sancho (2002). "Creating cost-effective adaptive educational hypermedia based on markup technologies and e-learning standards." Interactive Educational Multimedia 4: 1-11.

Gamma, E., R. Helm, et al. (1994). Design Patterns: Elements of Reusable Object-Oriented Software, Addison Wesley.

IEEE-LOM (2002). IEEE Standard for Learning Object Metadata: 39.

IEEE_LTSC. "Institute of Electrical and Electronics Engineers (IEEE) Learning Technology Standards Committee (LTSC)." Retrieved July 1, 2006, from http://ltsc.ieee.org/.

IMS-LD-MOD (2003). IMS Learning Design Information Model Version 1.0 Final Specification. IMS Specifications, IMS Global Learning Consortium.

IMS-QTI-ASI_INFO (2002). IMS Question & Test Interoperability: ASI Information Model Specification, IMS Global Learning Consortium.

IMS-SS (2003). IMS Content Simple Sequencing Information and Behavior Model Version 1.0 Final Specification, IMS Global Learning Consortium.

IMS. "IMS Global Learning Consortium." Retrieved July 1, 2006, 2006, from http://www.imsproject.org.

IMS_QTI2-INFO (2006). IMS QTI and Test Interoperability Assessment Test, Section, and Item Information Model, IMS Global Learning Consortium.

Koch, M. (2002). "Interoperable Community Platforms and Identity Management in the University Domain." International Journal on Media Management 4(1): 21-30.

Koper, R. (2000). From Change to Renewal: Educational Technology Foundations of Electronic Learning Environments, Open Univerity of the Netherlands: 41.

Koper, R. (2001). Modeling units of study from a pedagogical perspective : the pedagogical meta-model behind EML., Educational Technology Expetise Centre (OTEC, Open University of the Netherlands: 40.

Koper, R. (2003). Combining re-usable learning resources and services to pedagogical purposeful units of learning. Reusing Online Resources: A Sustainable Approach to eLearning. A. Littlejohn. London, Kogan Page: 46-59.

LAMS. (2005). "LAMS v 1.0.2." Retrieved July 1, 2006, from http://www.lamsfoundation.org/.

Martens, H. and H. Vogten (2005). Reference Implementation of a Learning Design Engine. Learning Desing: a Handbook on Modelling and Delivering Networked Education and Training. R. Koper and C. Tattersall, Springer: 91-108.

Martinez-Ortiz, I., P. Moreno-Ger, et al. (2005). Using DocBook To Aid in the Creation of Learning Content. New Trends and Technologies in Computer-Aided Learning for Computer-Aided Design. A. Rettberg and C. Bobda, Springer: 147.

Martinez-Ortiz, I., P. Moreno-Ger, et al. (2006). Production and Deployment of Educational Videogames as Assessable Learning Objects. First European Conference on Technology Enhanced Learning (ECTEL 2006), Crete, Greece, LNCS.

Merrill, M. D. (1994). Instructional Design Theory, Englewood Cliffs.

Moreno-Ger, P., I. Martinez-Ortiz, et al. (2005). The <e-Game> Project: Facilitating the Development of Educational Adventure Games. International Conference on Cognition and Exploratory Learning in the Digital Age (CELDA 2005), Porto, Portugal.

OUNL. (2005). "Coppercore v 3.0." Retrieved July 1, 2006, from http://www.coppercore.org.

Paquette, G. (2001). "TeleLearning Systems Engineering - Towards a new ISD model." Journal of Structural Learning 14: 1-35.

Paquette, G. (2004). Educational Modeling Languages, from an Instructional Engineering Perspective. Online education using learning objects. R. McGreal. London, Routledge/Falmer: 331-246.

Paquette, G., F. Crevier, et al. (1997). "Méthode d'ingénierie d'un système d'apprentissage (MISA)." REview Informations In Cognito 8.

Paquette, G., I. de la Teja, et al. (2005). Using an Instructional Engineering Method and a Modeling Tool. Learning Desing: Modelling and Implementing Network-based Eduation & Training. R. Koper and C. Tattersall, Springer-Verlag.

Rawlings, A., P. van Rosmalen, et al. (2002). Survey of Educational Modelling Languages (EML), CEN/ISSS WS/LT Learning Technologies Workshop: 79.

Reigeluth, C. M. (1983). Instructional Design Theories and Models: An Overview of Their Current Status, Lawrence Erlbaum Associates.

Rodrıguez-Artacho, M., M. F. Verdejo, et al. (1999). Using High-Level Language to Describe and Create Web-Based Learning Scenarios. IEEE Frontiers In Education FIE '99, San Juan, Puerto Rico.

SCORM_OVW (2004). SCORM 2004 Overview 2nd Edition, Advanced Distributed Learning: 57.

Slavin, R. E. (1995). Cooperative Learning: Theory, Research and Practice (2nd Edition), Allyn & Bacon.

Vantroys, T. (2003). Du langage métier au langage technique, une plate-forme flexible d'exécution de scénarios pédagogiques. Laboratoire TRIGONE - Équipe NOCE, Université des Sciences et Technologies de Lille: 182.

Verbert, K. and E. Duval (2004). Towards a Global Component Architecture for Learning Objects: A Comparative Analysis of Learning Object Content Models. World Conference on Educational Multimedia, Hypermedia and Telecommunications 2004, Chesapeake, VA, AACE.

Walsh, N. and L. Muellner (1999). DocBook: The Definitive Guide. Sebastopol, CA, USA, O'Reilly.

Weitl, F., C. Süß, et al. (2002). Presenting Complex e-eLearning Content on the WEB: A Didactical Reference Model. Proceedings of E-Learn 2002 world conference on E-Learning in Corporate, Government, Healthcare, & Higher Education, Montreal, Canada.

Chapter 4

REPRESENTING ADAPTIVE AND ADAPTABLE UNITS OF LEARNING
How to model personalized eLearning in IMS Learning Design

Daniel Burgos, Colin Tattersall and Rob Koper
Open University of The Netherlands, PO Box 2960, 6401DL, Heerlen

Abstract: In this chapter we examine how to represent adaptive and adaptable Units of Learning with IMS Learning Design in order to promote automation and interoperability. Based on a literature study, a distinction is drawn between eight types of adaptation that can be classified in three groups: a) the main group, with interfaced-base, learning-flow and content-base; b) interactive problem solving support, adaptive information filtering, adaptive user grouping; and c) adaptive evaluation and changes on-the-fly. Several sources of information are used in adaptation: user, teacher and set of rules. In this paper, we focus on the core group a). Taking the various possible inputs to an eLearning process, we analyze how to model personalized learning scenarios related to these inputs explaining how these can be represented in IMS Learning Design.

Key words: Adaptivity; adaptability; adaptation; personalized learning; IMS Learning Design; Unit of Learning.

1.   ADAPTIVITY, ADAPTABILITY AND ADAPTATION

1.1   What is adaptation?

Recent research has addressed the definitions of adaptivity and adaptability, both focused on personalized learning (Ahmad et al., 2004; Cristea, 2005; Chen and Magoulas, 2005; Burgos et al., 2006). In summary, adaptivity is the ability to modify e-learning lessons using different parameters and a set

41

B. Fernández-Manjón et al. (eds.), Computers and Education: E-learning, From Theory to Practice, 41–56.

of pre-defined rules. In contrast, adaptability is the possibility for learners to personalize an e-learning lesson by themselves. These two approaches go from machine-centered (adaptivity) to user-centered (adaptability). However, we contend that there are a vast number of stages in between which define a gray area, with some adaptivity and some adaptability. In practice, it is quite difficult to isolate one from the other due to their close relationship (Klann, 2003). Furthermore, all the in-between stages are also personalized learning as they enable the dynamic adaptation of several features in a course, a lesson plan or a Unit of Learning. As a result, we view the concepts not as two opposite corners from which to look at personalized learning, but as describing a wide range of approaches taking the best of each. Hereafter, we use the word *adaptation* to cover the various approaches.

1.2   Adaptation by whom?

The Adaptive Hypermedia Systems approach indicates that the best adaptation is the one that a user cannot see; the one where the cognitive load of the user is reduced to the minimum or even zero (Klann, 2003; De Bra et al., 2005). For example, a user is able to follow an introductory section in a course only the first time he logs-in, since that section is hidden from the second login onwards. This means that the adaptation must be done by the system automatically, depending on the user's performance. From this point of view, mainly based on adaptive hypermedia Web systems, there are two well-defined inputs: user and set of rules This approach is focused on *micro-adaptation*: monitoring the learning behavior of the student while running specific tasks and adapting the instructional design afterwards, based on quantitative information (Park and Lee, 2003; Mödritscher et al., 2004). On the one hand, there is a provider of some information based on behavior (the student). This means a non-voluntary action where the information is collected from the provider without his knowledge or agreement. On the other hand, there is a decision maker (the set of rules) who takes the collected information and decides further movements based on it.

Although this is an interesting approach, there are some drawbacks on this view of the involved inputs. First, the input of the student as a decision maker, who progresses from one side, being a non-voluntary provider of information, to the opposite side, stressing the cognitive load in the final decisions about the learning process. We agree that sometimes a student cannot decide what is the best or the most convenient for him at a certain moment, because of lack of training or of a broader vision on his studies (Snow, 1980). But we also hold that, leaving apart his interests and opinions, this approach dismisses his motivations, wishes and personal drives (i.e. feelings and emotions). All of them are important parts in the learning process. Second, the input of the teacher as one of the participants involved while building adaptive courses is something to take into consideration. His inputs, feedbacks and contributions do not end when the course is delivered. A teacher can and should modify the learning flow of a student or a group of students as long as the course takes place. He should make a good balance between the time and the effort invested and the actual outcome, though.

Furthermore, we count up to four inputs in a balanced formula for adaptation: a) the user, when some information is taken from his behavior and performance (Tennyson, 1980, 1981); b) the user, when he contributes with his/her own personal decision (Bell and Kozlowski, 2002); c) the teacher, when he also contributes with his/her personal decision (Van Rosmalen et al., 2006); and d) the set of pre-defined rules made by the learning designer/author (usually, the same teacher); a kind of adaptation engine (Wasson, 1997). The inputs a) and b) provide some personal needs and drives to learn; the inputs c) and d) take care of the didactical quality and of the learning efficiency.

2. ELEMENTS IN IMS LEARNING DESIGN TO REPRESENT ADAPTATION

IMS Learning Design (IMSLD, 2003), or simply IMS LD, is a specification focused on the modeling of Units of Learning (UoLs). IMS LD augments other well-known e-learning specifications, like SCORM (ADL, 2000), IMS Content Packaging (IMSCP, 2001), IMS Question and Test Interoperability (IMSQTI, 2000) or IMS Simple Sequencing (IMSSS, 2003). IMS LD has also a good understanding with some e-learning systems like Moodle (Dougiamas, 2003). IMS LD provides a language to describe the teaching and learning process in a Unit of Learning. It describes among other things the roles, the activities, the basic information structure, the communication among different roles and users; and all these under the pedagogical approach decided by the teacher and/or the learning designer.

IMS LD is technically structured in three levels: Level A provides the basic definition of the Unit of Learning, meaning learning activities, support activities, environments, roles, role-parts, learning flow and activity structures. Level B adds some important elements to Level A: properties, conditions, calculations, monitoring services and global elements, and Level C adds the use of notifications.

Level A provides a basic and larger information structure and the guidelines to assign activities to roles and to define learning acts and plays. Level B provides a more flexible use of these elements since it allows for the modeling of alternative learning itineraries, dynamic feedback, run-time tracking and collaborative learning, amongst others (Koper and Burgos, 2005). Level B is the key to the most expressive adaptation in IMS Learning Design as it provides some powerful resources and elements to model personalized Units of Learning. The elements in Level B that can be used for adaptation are explained below: Properties, global elements, monitoring service, conditions and calculations.

2.1   Properties

Properties in IMS LD are variables that are declared in the learning design (in the *imsmanifest.xml* file) and are used and viewed using global elements written in XHTML files. They can also be used inside the learning design, in conditions or calculations. We deal with the global elements, the conditions and the calculations in the next sections. The values inside of a property can be of different types like Integer, Boolean, text, float, file, etc.

There are five types of properties in IMS LD:

1. *Local properties*. Only accessible in the instance of a Unit of Learning (the *run*) (Tattersall et al., 2005). They have the same value for every user in that instance. For example, a question in a questionnaire.

2. *Local personal properties*. Only accessible in the instance of a Unit of Learning but they have a different value for every user. For instance, the name of a student.

3. *Local role property*. Only accessible in the instance of a Unit of Learning and it has a different value for every role. For instance, two different roles, meaning two different groups, with a different approach to a problem.

4. *Global personal properties*. Defined in the Unit of Learning, and set-up and viewed in every run of this Unit of Learning for the owner of the property. Each user has different values. For instance, personal information of a student in a school.

5. *Global properties*. A constant value, set-up in one instance of a Unit of Learning and viewed in every instance by all the people who have access to it. For instance, a numeric threshold in an evaluation.

2.2   Global elements

Global elements are included in external XML or XHTML files to read or to write the property values that are defined in a learning design. These files must be of type *imsldcontent* to prepare for appropriate processing in the IMS LD engine. Global elements are used basically to address two things: information layers and properties. If we use information DIV layers, some information can be prepared and conditionally shown or hidden. If we use properties, once a property is correctly declared in the manifest file, it can be shown (*view-property*) and it can also be given a value (*set-property*). For instance, the request of a name, or even the request of several fields in a form, collected in a group of properties. In order to set a property, a specific user interface control or form is generated depending on the type of property (integer, text, file, etc.).

2.3 Monitoring service

A monitoring service provides the possibility to track the progress of users or groups of users and of the properties related to them. This service can be set-up to define which role can access the information. For instance, the teacher role monitors a student role, allowing for a tracking of the different properties related to the student role, such as grades, remarks and completion of activities.

2.4 Conditions

Conditions in IMS LD have an *if-then-else* structure. We can use this structure to chain a series of conditions and create a more complex rule. Conditions in IMS LD are largely used to adapt learning flows, contents and other aspects of personalized learning, as we will explain later on. The rules are defined at design-time (when the UoL is modeled) and they are evaluated at run-time (when the UoL is executed), leading to content which is adapted dynamically.

2.5 Calculations

Calculations are basic arithmetic in IMS LD. Inside the learning design section of a manifest we can sum, subtract, multiply and divide numbers and values of properties to store the final result in another property. Later, this property can be seen using the global element *view-property* in a XML external file, already described.

3. MAIN TYPES OF ADAPTATION AND RELATED REPRESENTATION WITH IMS LD

The literature describes eight types of adaptation, divided into three groups (Burgos et al., 2006). The first group a) points to learning flow, content and interface (Baeza-Yates and Ribeiro-Nieto, 1999; Brusilovsky and Miller, 2001; Chin, 2001; Brusilovsky and Paylo, 2003; Ahmad et al., 2004; De Bra et al., 2004); the second group b) is based on interactive problem solving support, adaptive information filtering and adaptive user grouping (Baeza-Yates and Ribeiro-Nieto, 1999; Brusilovsky and Paylo, 2003); the third group c) consists of adaptive evaluation and changes on-the-fly (Merceron and Yacef, 2003; Van Rosmalen and Boticario, 2005). The groups b) and c) could be considered as subgroups of a), as they make use of the types in a) to define and feed themselves. Hereafter, we will focus our research on the first group of adaptation (learning flow, content and interface based), explaining what these approaches consist of and how to represent them in IMS LD.

3.1   Adaptation based on the learning flow

The modification of the learning flow as the Unit of Learning is being executed is one of the most often used types of adaptation. Taking the flow as a base, the Unit of Learning provides different activities, resources and services, depending on these four inputs during execution (user's behavior and performance, user's decision, teacher and set of rules). The activity structure in an IMS LD UoL is defined using plays, acts, activity structures, learning activities, support activities and environments. We can also use the property of *visibility* to hide and show these elements and to adapt the learning flow. In these cases the property works as a flag, switching on and off the elements referred to We now show five scenarios and their related implementations of learning-flow based adaptation focused on the several possible inputs. The pseudo XML code shown is an abstraction of the IMS LD original source, concentrating on the key elements of the specification needed for a more self-understandable explanation; all the examples can be found at (LN4LD, 2005).

3.1.1   The set of rules modifies the learning flow taking the user's behavior as an input

Scenario: One activity is shown the very first time that a user logs into the Unit of Learning, and it remains hidden from the second time onwards. User and the set of rules are the inputs involved.

Implementation: We create a personal local property (*Prop-Firsttime*) (type Boolean) and it is initialized to 0. When the user logs-in the first time the property is set to 1. A condition shows a specific activity (*LA-FirstActivity*) only when this flag property is 0:

```
<locpers-property identifier="Prop-Firsttime ">
  <title>PropFirsttime</title>
  <datatype datatype="boolean"/>
  <initial-value>0</initial-value>
</locpers-property>
```

```
<if>
  <is>
    <property-ref ref="Prop-Firsttime"/>
    <property-value>0</property-value>
  </is>
</if>
<then>
  <show>
    <activity-structure-ref ref=LA-FirstActivity"/>
  </show>
  <change-property-value>
    <property-ref ref="Prop-Firsttime "/>
    <property-value>1</property-value>
  </change-property-value>
</then>
<else>
  <hide>
    <activity-structure-ref ref=LA-FirstActivity"/>
  </hide>
</else>
```

3.1.2   The set of rules adapts the learning flow based on the user's performance

Scenario: The behavior of a user is a possible input. Also, the performance and the cognitive load of the user during an activity could adapt the learning flow. This example, *GeoQuiz3*, provides a general quiz on Geography with five questions and multiple answers. The user gets a score, an average and an accuracy measure. The subsequent activity to be studied by the student depends on these results, and it is taken from four possible activities, including the repetition of the task if a certain threshold is not reached. Therefore, user and engine are the inputs involved.

Implementation: This example guides the learning flow of the student based on his performance and on a set of pre-defined rules. Also, the pre-defined algorithm interlaces properties, activities and conditions to get the final result. First, a set of properties is arranged:

```
<locpers-property identifier="Value1">
  <datatype datatype="integer"/>
  <initial-value>0</initial-value>
</locpers-property>
<locpers-property identifier="Question1">
  <datatype datatype="string"/>
  <initial-value>Select</initial-value>
  <restriction type="enumeration">Select</restriction>
  <restriction type="enumeration">Malasia</restriction>
  <restriction type="enumeration">The Moon</restriction>
  <restriction type="enumeration">Canada</restriction>
</locpers-property>
```

Second, every question is included in an external XML file, using the global element *set-property*. In this case, HTML code and IMS LD code are combined:

```
<html>
  <td>Where is the Mare Tranquilitatis?</td>
  <td><p>
    <set-property ref="Question1" property-of="self" view="value"/>
  </p></td>
</html>
```

And third, the conditions are established in the learning design to check the results and to define the adaptive feedback and the next activity to be undertaken. For instance, by changing the completion value of a question, as follows:

```
<if>
  <is>
    <property-ref ref="Question1"/>
    <property-value>The Moon</property-value>
  </is>
</if>
<then>
  <change-property-value>
    <property-ref ref="Value1"/>
    <property-value>1</property-value>
  </change-property-value>
</then>
```

3.1.3   The user himself modifies the learning flow based on his personal decision

Scenario: In *Learning to Listen to Jazz* the user can choose the learning itinerary out of two possible paths: Historic and Thematic. The user can swap between both at three different points in the learning flow. The activities already done in one path remain in the same state when the user moves to the alternative path. Therefore, they are the same activities but with two different ways of study. In this case, the adaptation comes from the user, based on a pre-design of the course by the author/tutor.

Implementation: Both paths are predefined and are shown and hidden depending on the value of the Boolean property *SelectionOfRoute* that the user can change on request:

```
<if>
  <no-value>
    <property-ref ref="SelectionOfRoute"/>
  </no-value>
</if>
<then>
  <hide>
    <activity-structure-ref ref="AS-Thematic"/>
    <activity-structure-ref ref="AS-Historic"/>
  </hide>
</then>
<else>
<if>
  <is>
```

```
          <property-ref ref="SelectionOfRoute"/>
          <property-value>Thematic</property-value>
        </is>
    </if>
    <then>
        <show>
          <activity-structure-ref ref="AS-Thematic"/>
        </show>
        <hide>
          <activity-structure-ref ref="AS-Historic"/>
        </hide>
    </then>
```

3.1.4   The teacher modifies the learning flow of the user

Scenario: The teacher monitors the performance of a user or of a group of users and he decides which activities should be shown and hidden and in which order. The adaptation comes from the teacher, taking into consideration several other inputs from the user or group of users.

Implementation: Two things are needed. The first one is a monitoring service *S-Performance* defined in an environment in the learnign design that allows for the observation of every user. The second one is the definition of a set of flag properties (personal or role properties). These properties show and hide activities, structures and environments to the end-user/s, e.g. *FlagForActivity1*. The definition is made in the *imsmanifest.xml* file; the actual view and set-up is made in an external XML file using global elements (*view-property* and *set-property*):

```
<environment identifier="E-Performance">
   <title>You can watch the performance of every user</title>
   <service identifier="S-Performance">
      <monitor>
        <role-ref ref="Tutor"/>
        <title>Tracking personal performance</title>
        <item identifierref="R-Performance"/>
      </monitor>
   </service>
</environment>
```

```
<set-property ref="FlagForActivity1" property-of="supported"/>

<view-property ref="StudentPerformance" property-of="supported"/>
```

3.1.5   Integrated approach

A last scenario is based on the integrated decision of several of the previous scenarios agreed by consensus. More than one input (user, teacher, set of rules) are taken at the same time and the final decision leans on one of them. For example, a teacher can take the suggestion of a learner, his behavior, his performance, the recommendation of a set of rules and make the final decision. Alternatively, the engine takes the role of the teacher when making the final decision. Or even the student takes the suggestions of the teacher and of the engine and decides what to carry out next.

3.2   Adaptation based on the content

In the previous section, we saw that a learning flow is mainly focused on the sequence of the activities in a Unit of Learning. However, content based adaptation is focused on the information of every activity, and on the activity itself. There are two main approaches for content based adaptation: Flag properties and content of properties.

3.2.1   Flag properties

This approach is focused on the use of flag properties that switch on and off a certain information layer (such as a DIV layer in XHTML).

Scenario: A student follows a questionnaire. The right answer to every sequenced question is the key to read the next question (example *GeoQuiz1*). Depending on the answer, some support information is shown.

Implementation: The actual definition of the layers (*Answer1_Wrong* and *Answer1_Right*) and the information inside them is defined in external XML file/s. These files are linked to the *imsmanifest* and identified as resources of type *imsldcontent*; they also have the layers to be shown and hidden and they use global elements:

```
<html>
    <h1>Question 1/5</h1>
    <p>Where is the Eiffel Tower?
    <blockquote><b>A</b> Paris</blockquote>
    <blockquote><b>B</b> Brussels</blockquote>
    </p>
    <p>Your answer is:
        <set-property ref="Answer1" property-of="self"/></p>
    <div class="Answer1_Wrong">
      <p>Choose another answer.
        '<view-property ref="Answer1" />` is not right</p>
    </div>
    <div class="Answer1_Right">
      <p>Congratulations! It's the right answer</p>
      <img src="eiffel.jpg"></img>
    </div>
</html>
```

The definition of the method is in the *imsmanifest.xml* file. The definition and initialization of the flag properties and the learning activities are also done in this file, as well as the management of the visibility of the DIV layers described in the external files. When *QuestionTrue1* turns to 1 the first activity *question1* is finished:

```
<locpers-property identifier="QuestionTrue1">
  <datatype datatype="boolean"/>
  <initial-value>0</initial-value>
</locpers-property>
```

```
<learning-activity identifier="question1">
    <title>Question 1</title>
    <activity-description>
      <item identifierref="res-question1"/>
    </activity-description>
    <complete-activity>
      <when-property-value-is-set>
        <property-ref ref="QuestionTrue1"/>
        <property-value>1</property-value>
      </when-property-value-is-set>
    </complete-activity>
</learning-activity>
```

```
<if>
  <is>
    <property-ref ref="Answer1"/>
    <property-value>A</property-value>
  </is>
</if>
<then>
  <hide>
    <class class="Answer1_Wrong" />
  </hide>
  <show>
    <class class="Answer1_Right"/>
  </show>
  <change-property-value>
    <property-ref ref="QuestionTrue1"/>
    <property-value>1</property-value>
  </change-property-value>
</then>
```

3.2.2 Content of properties

The second approach to adaptation allows for the modification of the content of a property that has been pre-defined inside an activity. In this case, the property of visibility remains always on, but the content of the field changes. We need two steps, therefore. One is at design-time - making the definition and configuration of the property, done in the learning design of the *imsmanifest* file. The second step, at run-time, involves changing the content of the property, made in an external XML file. We use the global elements *set-property* and *view-property* to configure and see the content of the field/property. In the example *GeoQuiz3* used above, the property with the adaptive feedback (*prop-feedback*) is shown after the completion of the form:

```
<td><p>Your   adaptive   feedback   is:   <view-property   ref="prop-
feedback" property-of="self" view="value"/></p></td>
```

Depending on the final score, the content of the property (*prop-feedback*) is different, though:

```
<if>
  <and>
    <greater-than>
      <property-ref ref="score"/>
      <property-value>49</property-value>
    </greater-than>
    <less-than>
      <property-ref ref="score"/>
      <property-value>76</property-value>
    </less-than>
  </and>
</if>
<then>
  <change-property-value>
    <property-ref ref="prop-feedback"/>
    <property-value>Well done! Your score is promising. You are in
Level 2</property-value>
  </change-property-value>
</then>
```

Another possible scenario is set-up when a teacher changes the content of some fields dynamically while executing the Unit of Learning. In *Quo Builder2* the student can see the questions and possible answers in a questionnaire as long as the teacher defines them. The teacher can also design the basic configuration of the form: the general welcome messages, the adaptive feedback and the scoring system. At the end, it becomes an interactive and dynamic evaluation test, modified at run-time.

3.3   Adaptation based on the interface

Interface based adaptation is quite different to content based adaptation. Content adaptation is based on the information inside an activity that is shown and handled. Interface adaptation is based on options, navigation and visualization facilities. In (Burgos et al., 2006) the authors state that interface adaptation is not possible with today's tools for IMS LD, such as CopperCore Player (Vogten and Martens, 2005), Reload LD Player (Bolton, 2004) and Sled (OUUK, 2005), or the editors CopperAuthor (Van der Vegt, 2005) and Reload LD Editor (Bolton, 2004). As long as the adaptation of the interface is based on the tool and not on the Unit of Learning that is interpreted by the player, this is still true. Today's players do not yet provide facilities to change the size or the position of the navigation panels, or even open and close the working areas in the player. Either, these tools cannot change the style sheets related to a HTML file, part of the content, and any of the linked features, as font-size, font-type or background color, for instance. Although the CopperCore engine provides the appropriate infrastructure, no player uses it so far.

Nevertheless, some kind of adaptive interface is possible, using DIV layers and environments.

Scenario: The options and the look and feel of an interface are adapted on the user's request.

Implementation: Regarding activities, several DIV layers or learning activities can be set-up with a different visualization for the same content. For instance, linking the same file to different CSS style sheets. First, we define the different activities:

```
<learning-activity identifier="Activity1InterfaceA">
   <title>Question 1</title>
   <activity-description>
      <item identifierref="firstlessonInterfaceA"/>
   </activity-description>
</learning-activity>

<learning-activity identifier="Activity1InterfaceB">
   <title>Question 1</title>
   <activity-description>
      <item identifierref="firstlessonInterfaceB"/>
   </activity-description>
</learning-activity>
```

Later, we link the CSS style sheets with the same file lesson1.html, resulting in two different resource identifiers:

```
<resource     identifier="firstlessonInterfaceA"     type="webcontent"
href="lesson1.html">
   <file href="lesson1.html" />
   <file href="stylesheetA.css" />
</resource>

<resource     identifier="firstlessonInterfaceB"     type="webcontent"
href="lesson1.html">
   <file href="lesson1.html" />
   <file href="stylesheetB.css" />
</resource>
```

And finally, we show and hide the activity linked to the related resource:

```
<if>
   <is>
      <property-ref ref="InterfaceToChoose"/>
      <property-value>A</property-value>
   </is>
</if>
<then>
   <show>
      <activity-structure-ref ref="firstlessonInterfaceA"/>
   </show>
   <hide>
      <activity-structure-ref ref="firstlessonInterfaceB"/>
   </hide>
</then>
```

Another possibility could be to adapt not only the look and feel of a DIV layer, but also its content and the options of interaction inside it, resulting in a block of information and interaction.

Last one additional set-up is to define different environments with several contents and services and link them to different activities or activity structures. They will be shown/hidden together with the related activity. This approach can be managed following any of the methods aforementioned. Furthermore, we could count different services, contents and options in every environment that are depending on the learning tree. To some extent, this means a *de facto* sub-division on the screen and a different adapted interface. So, one activity linked to one environment, and both are shown or hidden, resulting in a final personalized interface:

```
<show>
   <environment-ref ref="ENVfirstlessonInterfaceA"/>
</show>
<hide>
   <environment-ref ref="ENVfirstlessonInterfaceB"/>
</hide>
```

4.   CONCLUSION

In this chapter we have shown three main types of adaptation with some typical scenarios and their related implementations, based on the learning flow, the content and the interface. Also, we have stated the four different inputs involved in the adaptation process: a) the user, based on his behavior and his performance; b) the user, based on his personal decision; c) the personal decision of the teacher; and d) the set of rules in an engine, pre-defined by a learning designer. To implement these scenarios in IMS LD we use the basic structure that Level A provides and the core elements of Level B: properties, global elements, monitoring service, conditions and calculations.

We conclude that it is possible to represent strategies for adaptation taken from all these inputs and types, in IMS LD. Whether we talk about adaptivity or about adaptability, the issue of personalized learning can be modeled with the specification, using different approaches in order to support learners build better competences and skills.

ACKNOWLEDGEMENTS

This chapter is partially supported by the European Projects ProLearn (Pro-Learn, 2006) and TENCompetence (TENCompetence, 2005).

REFERENCES

ADL, 2000, Sharable Object Reference Model, SCORM (May 9th, 2006); http://www.adlnet.org/index.cfm?fuseaction=Scormabt.

Ahmad, A., Basir, O. and Hassanein, K., 2004, *Adaptive user interfaces for intelligent e-Learning: issues and trends*, The Fourth International Conference on Electronic Business, ICEB2004, Beijing.

Baeza-Yates, R. and Ribeiro-Nieto, B., 1999, *Modern Information Retrieval*, Addison-Wesley, Boston, MA, USA.

Bell, B. and Kozlowski, S., 2002, Adaptive guidance: Enhancing self-regulation, knowledge, and performance in technology-based training, *Personnel Psychology,* **55**(2): 267-306.

Bolton, 2004, Reload Project (April 16th, 2006); www.reload.ac.uk.

Brusilovsky, P. and Miller, P., 2001, Course Delivery Systems for the Virtual University, in: *Access to Knowledge: New Information Technologies and the Emergence of the Virtual University*, Tschang F.T. and T. Della Senta, ed., Elsevier Science and International Association of Universities, Amsterdam: pp. 167-206.

Brusilovsky, P. and Paylo, C., 2003, Adaptive and Intelligent Web-based Educational Systems, *International Journal of Artificial Intelligence in Education,* **13**: 156-169.

Burgos, D., Tattersall, C. and Koper, R., 2006, *Representing adaptive eLearning strategies in IMS Learning Design*, International Workshop in Learning Networks for Lifelong Competence Development, TENCompetence Conference, Sofia, Bulgaria.

Cristea, A., 2005, Authoring of Adaptive Hypermedia, *Educational Technology & Society,* **8**(3): 6-8.

Chen, S. Y. and Magoulas, G. D., 2005, *Adaptable and Adaptive Hypermedia Systems*, IRM Press, Hershey, PA.

Chin, D., 2001, Empirical Evaluation of User Models and User-Adapted Systems., *User Modeling and User-Adapted Interaction,* **11**: 181-194.

De Bra, P., Aroyo, L. and Cristea, A., 2004, Adaptive Web-based Educational Hypermedia, in: *Web Dynamics, Adaptive to Change in Content, Size, Topology and Use*, M. Levene and A. Poulovassilis, ed., Springer: pp. 387-410.

De Bra, P., Stash, N. and Smits, D., 2005, *Creating Adaptive Web-Based Applications*, 10th International Conference on User Modeling, Edinburgh, Scotland.

Dougiamas, M., 2003, Moodle (May 10th, 2006); http://moodle.org.

IMSCP, 2001, IMS Content Packaging (May 10th, 2006); www.imsglobal.org.

IMSLD, 2003, IMS Learning Design (February 27th); http://www.imsglobal.org/learningdesign/index.cfm.

IMSQTI, 2000, IMS Question and Test Interoperability (May 10th, 2006); www.imsglobal.org.

IMSSS, 2003, IMS Simple Sequencing [www.imsglobal.org] (May 10th, 2006); www.imsglobal.org.

Klann, M., 2003, *The EUD-Net's Roadmap to End-User Development*, Workshop on End User Development at ACM CHI 2003 Conference, Fort Lauderdale, USA.

Koper, R. and Burgos, D., 2005, Developing advanced units of learning using IMS Learning Design level B, *International Journal on Advanced Technology for Learning,* **2**(3).

LN4LD, 2005, Units of Learning developed by several authors at Learning Network for Learning Design of The Open University of The Netherlands (March 6th); http://moodle.learningnetworks.org/course/view.php?id=20 and http://dspace.ou.nl.

Merceron, A. and Yacef, K., 2003, *A Web-based tutoring tool with mining facilities to improve learning and teaching*, AI-Ed'2003, IOS Press.

Mödritscher, F., García, V. and Gütl, C., 2004, *The Past, the Present and the Future of adaptive E-Learning. An Approach within the Scope of the Research Project AdeLE*, ICL, Villach, Austria.

OUUK, 2005, Sled player (April 13th, 2006); http://sled.open.ac.uk.

Park, O. and Lee, J., 2003, Adaptive Instructional Systems, *Educational Technology Research and Development*, **25**: 651-684.

Pro-Learn, 2006, Pro-Learn Project (July 31st, 2006);

Snow, R., 1980, Aptitude, learner control and adaptive instruction, *Educational Pshychologist*, **15**(13): 151-158.

Tattersall, C., Vogten, H., Brouns, F., Koper, R., van Rosmalen, P., Sloep, P. and van Bruggen, J., 2005, How to create flexible runtime delivery of distance learning courses, *Educational Technology & Society*, **8**(3): 226-236.

TENCompetence, 2005, TENCompetence Project (July 31st, 2006); www.tencompetence.org.

Tennyson, R. D., 1980, Instructional control strategies and content structure as design vairables in concept acquisition using computer-based instruction., *Journal of Educational Psychology*, **72**: 525-532.

Tennyson, R. D., 1981, Use of adaptive information for advisement in learning concepts and rules using computer assisted instruction, *American Educational Research Journal*, **18**: 425-438.

Van der Vegt, W., 2005, CopperAuthor (April 13th 2006); www.copperauthor.org.

Van Rosmalen, P. and Boticario, J., 2005, Using Learning Design to support design- and runtime adaptation, in: *Learning Design: A Handbook on Modeling and Delivering Networked Education and Training*, R. Koper and C. Tattersall, ed., Springer Verlag, Heidelberg, Germany.

Van Rosmalen, P., Vogten, H., Van Es, R., Van, P., H., Poelmans, P. and Koper, R., 2006, Authoring a full life cycle model in standards-based, adaptive e-learning, *Educational Technology & Society*, **9**(1): 72-83.

Vogten, H. and Martens, H., 2005, CopperCore 3.0 (April 13th 2006); www.coppercore.org.

Wasson, B., 1997, Advanced educational technologies: The learning environment, *Computers in Human Behavior*, **13**(4): 571-594.

Chapter 5

SCHOOLSENSES@INTERNET
CHILDREN AS MULTISENSORY GEOGRAPHIC INFORMATION CREATORS

Maria José Marcelino[1]; Cristina Azevedo Gomes[2]; Maria João Silva[3]; Cristina Gouveia[4]; Alexandra Fonseca[5]; Bruno Pestana[2]; Carlos Brigas[6]

[1]Departamento de Engenharia Informática, Universidade de Coimbra - Polo II, 3030-290 Coimbra, Portugal; [2]Escola Superior de Educação, Instituto Politécnico de Viseu, R. Maximiano Aragão, 3504-501 Viseu, Portugal; [3]Escola Superior de Educação, Instituto Politécnico do Porto, R. Dr. Roberto Frias, 4200-465 Porto, Portugal; [4]Ydreams, Madan Parque, Quinta da Torre, 2829-516 Caparica, Portugal; [5]Centro para a Exploração e Gestão de Informação Geográfica, Instituto Geográfico Português, R. Artilharia Um, 107, 1099-052 Lisboa, Portugal; [6]Escola Superior de Educação, Instituto Politécnico da Guarda, Av. Dr. Francisco Sá Carneiro, 6301 - 559 Guarda, Portugal

Abstract: The SchoolSenses@Internet project aims at improving the quality of primary education learning using ICT. The project envisages achieving this aim by supporting the collaborative creation of geo-referenced multisensory information by school children. Results from the work with teachers and children while using Google Earth and the first project Website design are presented.

Key words: Multisensory information; Geographic information; Simulation; Elementary Education.

1.   INTRODUCTION

The SchoolSenses@Internet project elected the creation of geo-referenced multisensory Web contents by primary school children as a strategy to improve the quality of primary education learning. Geo-referenced multisensory information is the integration of information acquired by the different human senses in the context of "embodied" and geographically situated experiences (Silva et al., 2005). It is the kind of information that supports our behavior in the world. It is the result of giving attention to the different sensory representations that integrate our thoughts (Damasio, 2003).

B. Fernández-Manjón et al. (eds.), Computers and Education: E-learning, From Theory to Practice, 57–66.

In order to promote educational success, multisensory communication can be used as a bridge to concrete experiences, to different learning and expression styles, to complexity and real learning (Paztor et al., w. d.). In addition, geographic navigation is an ingredient of success in what concerns the exploration of Websites by children (Gilutz and Nielsen, 2002).

The specific aims of the SchoolSenses@Internet project are:

- To create a multisensory Web mapping of local and global contexts;
- To built an identitary Website to share experiences and projects, to establish relations, to mobilize the actors in this community;
- To develop new interfaces and tools to support the use and the creation of multisensory geographic information, empowering different learning styles;
- To develop new modeling and simulation tools specific to primary education;
- To develop hybrid methodologies to deal with learning evaluation that arises from a socio-constructivist use of ICT.

This chapter is structured as follows: in section 2 a survey of some paradigmatic projects and products dealing with the production of geographic information by children, geo-referenced collaboration using Google Earth (Google Earth, 2005), multisensory approaches and simulation for primary education is done; in section 3 the fieldwork done with children and teachers in the project as well as the implications for project design are presented; in section 4 the project Website main features are described; finally, in section 5, the conclusion and future work plans are presented.

2.   RELATED WORK

2.1   Children as creators of geographic information

We find currently several projects, at national or international level, where children act as creators of geographic information. Among them are Internet@EB1 (Internet@EB1, 2005), HyConExplorer (Bouvin et al., 2005) and "A New Sense of Place?" (Williams et al., 2005).

Internet@EB1 is a Portuguese project that supported almost every Portuguese public elementary school in the development of a Web Page, with the active participation of children. Central topics within these WebPages are schools' community and environment. So, a huge quantity of geographic information has been created and is available in more than 7000 school sites.

HyConExplorer is a geospatial hypermedia system that allows children to "browse with their feet" (to access information about the place they are moving through), to "annotate the world" (linking a photo to a given location can be used as a form of "digital graphiti") and to "overview of a glance" (children are allowed to retrospectively trace their journey and knowledge building both spatially, temporally and conceptually (Bouvin et al., 2005)). HyConExplorer was used with children aged 11-14. This work, in a different way from SchoolSenses@Internet, did not address the creation of multisensory information and its educational value.

"A New Sense of Place?" is a project that invited children, aged 9 and 10, to create "soundscapes" in the outdoor environment, using mobile and wireless technology. Using a handheld soundscape edit tool the children could see their outdoor gps location and mark it as a preferred sound 'spot' in a soundscape. The created soundscapes could be experienced in the field with headphones. This project merged digital with field multisensory information and allowed children to explore, imagine and implement *audio augmented* experiences, through spatial and sensory awareness activities.

2.2 Geo-referenced collaborative projects using Google Earth

The development of multisensory geo-referenced collaborative applications for educational contexts requires the ability to integrate data from multiple senses – images, sounds, smells, tastes and haptics – and link it to a place on Earth. Furthermore it requires the inclusion of collaborative tools that allow enabling different users to contribute with their knowledge to a common pool, communicate and share information and track the flow of information that takes place in such a community.

The emergence of Web 2.0 enables the creation of new types of applications, more dynamic and interactive, and above all facilitating the underlying social networking that has been growing with Internet. Google Earth (GE) is one example of such applications. Through GE it is possible to interact with geo-referenced contents – from satellite images, maps, photos and graphs – in an engaging way (Norman, 2006). This way, GE has successfully conquered a new type of audience on geographic exploration.

However, GE does not currently integrate neither data from senses other than vision or collaborative tools. Nevertheless this has not excluded its use to support the development of collaborative projects, like the Antweb project (Antweb project, 2006) where users can plot the ants known to AntWeb on a 3D interactive globe of satellite images.

At present, most collaborative projects that use GE explore it mainly to share data collected by multiple users. To support collaborative processes and share GE files, users benefit from tools such as forums (e.g. the GE Community), Flickr groups (Flickr, 2006), blogs or wikis. An example of this approach is the Chimpanzee GeoBlog (Goodal, 2006) where posts are published on GE files. On the other hand, technological developments such as the upcoming of Geographically Encoded Objects for Really Simple Syndication (GeoRSS) may allow leapfrogging this domain by making available an easy-to-use geotagging language. The wide use of such type of tools may enable the creation of services that aggregate information based on location, facilitate geo-referenced data search and also enable users to follow information changes based on location.

The integration of multimedia data on GE has still a long way to go. GE currently integrates photos, graphs and 3D models. The version 4 of GE has expanded such capabilities and integrates textures of buildings and other 3D terrain features. The integration of sounds may be a good extension to add richness to data exploration and enable eye-impaired people to navigate through the globe. The integration of other sensory data is more difficult to achieve in a desktop environment. However, alternative ways, that do not demand specific hardware, may be created as showed in the next subsection.

2.3   A multisensory collaborative project

Senses@Watch is a Portuguese research project ended in 2005. This project involved some of the authors of this paper and was developed to support the use of sensory data collected within environmental public participation tasks, including environmental complaints (Gouveia et al., 2004). These complaints were geo-referenced and used the metaphor of postcards: citizens created their messages with photos, sounds, graphics and text to describe a situated environmental problem. The short textual descriptions were used to translate sensory data into environmental quality information (Silva et al., 2003).

The structure of those multisensory messages was designed to be compatible with the MMS of mobile phones. Using the clipart metaphor, a database of multisensory messages was also developed to support the creation of meaningful messages. This clipart is Web-based, but it has been thought to be accessed by multimedia mobile phones and interactive TV (Silva et al., 2003).

2.4   Simulation for primary school children

There are two main ways of using educational simulation in Internet. One is in sites that include closed simulations, with which the learner can play (change some simulation values and run it essentially). Another is using simulation and modeling authoring-tools that allow model or simulation building (and use) for Web contents without programming.

We find many examples, for diverse educational areas, of the first type, but few are for elementary education. One example is the Kent National Grid for Learning Website (Kent NGfl, 2005). The major problem with these products is that they become exhausted when used for a while.

Although second type applications are scarce, two successful cases, specifically developed for children, are AgentSheets (AgentSheets, 2005) and Stagecast (Stagecast, 2005). Though not being Web tools, a simulation can be created and saved after as a Web Page. In AgentSheets a model is represented by a grid of agents with user programmed behaviors. Many models can be built easily, but others not, as a fair knowledge of programming is necessary. Stagecast follows a similar approach, but the programming is easier.

3. EXPLORING GOOGLE EARTH TO CREATE GEO-REFERENCED MULTISENSORY INFORMATION

The SchoolSenses@Internet project was planned to be a collaborative system with customized Web mapping services, to allow navigation (pan, zooms, etc.) and input of geo-referenced data by users. However, with the emergence of GE and its rapidly growing adherence, the more motivating and usable geographic tool for children and teachers that appeared in the last years, we decided to start by exploring this tool. In a small, but impressive article, Norman states about the experience of interacting with GE:

> "Although it is indeed useful and fun to examine the entire world in exquisite photographic detail, a good deal of the pleasure comes from the smooth movement as one flies around the world, soaring up in the air to travel large distances, then swooping down at the destination points. It's emotionally engaging" (Norman, 2006).

3.1 Working with children and teachers

In order to support the design of the SchoolSenses@Internet site three workshops were developed to explore the ease of use of GE by teachers and children. These workshops also allowed the assessment of GE's affordances to be the main geographic element of the Website collaborative tasks.

Two of these workshops involved only teachers and were planned to find how useful they considered the creation of geo-referenced multisensory information in elementary schools and how they judged the usability and utility of GE in this context. The first involved 7 teachers, of several levels, and the second workshop 20 elementary school teachers. The participants were invited to explore GE as a tool to create geo-referenced multisensory messages. They showed involvement and enjoyment during such exploration. All teachers found local and distant familiar places, with little or no navigation help. Furthermore, elementary school teachers were unanimous in saying that GE is a very useful resource for educational activities with children. In the first workshop the suggested theme was "Portuguese forest fires". Teachers easily got pictures from Internet to compose their messages, but found it difficult to discover sounds. Sounds, as well as odors and other sensations, were typically textually described. Yet, the messages were not produced with GE. In the second workshop, on the contrary, it was suggested the use of GE to create multisensory messages with the theme of "Water in the Portuguese landscape". This time a few sound libraries were also provided. As a consequence, teachers spent more time planning the content of their messages than struggling with the lack of available media resources as in the first one. The end result was the production of integrated messages including diverse kinds of photos (satellite, aerial, etc.), sounds and small texts.

The last workshop took an exploratory form with 6 elementary school children - 3 boys and 3 girls, with ages 8-10, working in pairs. They were invited to explore GE to find a particular river, town, and their own school and to trace an itinerary from the school to the nearest football stadium. All enjoyed the experience and were able to find the required geographic elements as well as others distant familiar places (such as Madagascar). They showed some difficulties due to the lack of experience with scales and the forms that geographic elements take when viewed from the sky, but they also showed the ability to easily learn new strategies to overcome them. Children were also invited to design games to run with GE and to present them to the class. Games included rallies and races with cars, boats and planes all around the world. To build and change the urbanized space or to play sports on the streets were also common projected activities.

3.2   Implications for design

The workshops confirmed that the use of GE to explore geographic information is an engaging and meaningful task both for teachers and children. The interface and the information available in GE involved every child and adult, inviting them to cross and fly over the entire planet. It was observed that GE allowed teachers and children to easily integrate geographic information in their natural discourse about everyday events, like exploring their daily itineraries or the exotic sceneries of movies.

During the workshops, teachers developed meaningful environmental multimedia multisensory messages to overlay GE geographic information. The unavailability of sounds, odors and icons, as well as the unavailability of a customized edition tool, were confirmed as key factors to the creation of multisensory messages.

Following these observations, it was decided to continue to explore GE to create geo-referenced multisensory information in elementary schools. It was also decided to support the creation of multisensory messages with a multisensory editor that should include cliparts of sounds, odors and icons.

4. THE SCHOOLSENSES@INTERNET WEBSITE

4.1 Overview

From the above fieldwork it was decided to adopt the interface metaphor of GE as the project Website central metaphor. Also the lessons learned in the Senses@Watch project, namely the concept of multisensory messages as well as the clipart and message metaphors, influenced the Website design that includes:

- Access to a GE window;
- Information about the participating schools and the challenges already launched and running;
- A multimedia multisensory message editor with multisensory cliparts;
- A modeling and simulation tool with multisensory objects;
- A viewer of the geo-referenced multisensory messages created and edited by the schools' community.

The multimedia multisensory message editor is currently being developed using a participatory design methodology with the children. Multisensory cliparts are also being developed and can be accessed from this editor to help create and edit the multisensory messages.

Some messages can result from the use of models or simulations. For that, modeling and simulation tools are provided to enable children to create their own models or simulations. These tools are structured around themes or collections of objects. Object attributes and model/simulation parameters can depend on geographical location, meaning that we can reach different results in different zones. These results can combine images, sounds, animations, that can evocate information related to odors, temperature sensations, etc.

Figure 5-1. Project Website. The message shown was produced by the teachers in one of the workshops and associates text and image to represent the idea of a cold landscape.

In the context of this Website, schools' main activities are:

- Creating and editing multisensory messages in the multimedia multisensory message editor or in the modeling and simulation tools and linking them to GE placemarks.
- Sending multisensory messages as geo-referenced MMS using smart phones with GPS.
- Viewing multisensory messages. Searching and viewing are structured in layers similar to GE layers. These layers can be content centered, e.g. "Water in the landscape", sensory centered, e.g. a specific "sound" or "odor", or with a focus on communication, e.g. schools interactions.

Collaboration and negotiation among schools are made mainly through message (re)editions. Messages and their several editions can be visualized as a net using a metaphor that blends the blog and Flickr metaphors. Figure 1 shows a screenshot of the project Website with a message produced by the teachers in one of the workshops and linked to a GE placemark. This is a first approach that we are working on with teachers and children.

4.2   Website structure

All the activity in the Website is kept in a database that supports the whole project. Figure 2 represents the data flow from the creation of a school message, using a computer or a mobile device, to a GE placemark. This

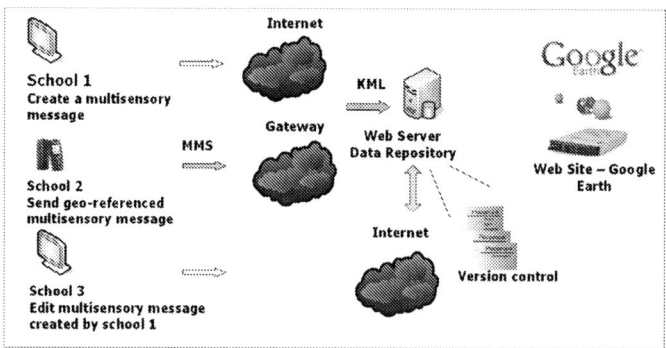

Figure 5-2. Project information flow.

database integrates information about the participants' schools, the multisensory clipart objects, and the activities taking place in the Website as responses to the challenges launched. Each message or re-edited message is associated with a school, a challenge, geographic co-ordinates, date and time, subject, sounds, odors, etc. The database also includes information about interactions and all the information needed to support the search using the layer metaphor and the evaluation of the complex learning processes that are taking place in this environment.

5.   CONCLUSION

We have described SchoolSenses@Internet, a project that was designed to support the collaborative creation of geo-referenced multisensory information in the context of elementary Portuguese schools. The project Website uses GE to support the collaborative creation of geo-referenced multisensory messages and the sharing of those messages. Messages can be constructed and edited with a multimedia multisensory message editor or sent as MMS using smart phones with GPS. Integration of a multisensory modeling and simulation tool in the site will also allow children and teachers to enhance the learning value of the used information. Children interactions and information flows will be tracked to assess learning activities that will take place in the scope of this project.

In the meantime, the participatory design of activities and interfaces with children and teachers, as well as the collaborative development of knowledge and the experiences supported by the project Website, will continue. We hope that they will promote what is more important for us, the quality of primary education learning through the use of ICT.

ACKNOWLEDGEMENTS

The authors would like to acknowledge Professor Dias de Figueiredo for all the ideas and support he offered to SchoolSenses@Internet project, as well as University of Porto, Engineering Faculty and Professor Correia Lopes that supervises a MSc thesis in collaboration with this project.

The authors thank all the children and teachers that participated in the workshops.

This research was partially funded by POSC/EIA/56954/2004.

REFERENCES

AgentSheets (May 19, 2005); http://www.agentsheets.com/.

Antweb project (January 15, 2006); http://www.antweb.org/google_earth.jsp.

Bouvin, N. O., Brodersen, C., Hansen, F. A., Iversen, O. S., and Nørregaard, P., 2005, Tools of contextualization: Extending the classroom to the field, in: *Proceedings of the 2005 conference on Interaction design and children*, ACM Press, Boulder, pp. 24-31.

Damasio, A., 2003, *Ao Encontro de Spinoza*, Europa América, Lisboa.

Flickr (March 23, 2006); http://flickr.com/.

Gilutz, S., and Nielsen, J., 2002, *Usability Websites for Children: 70 Design Guidelines*; (March 17, 2005) http://www.Nngroup.com/reports/kids.

Goodal, J., 2006, Chimpanzee GeoBlog (March 27, 2006); http://gombechimpanzee. blogspot.com.

Google Earth (June 5, 2005); http://earth.google.com/.

Gouveia, C., Fonseca, A., Câmara, A., and Ferreira, F., 2004, Promoting the use of environmental data collected by concerned citizens through information and communication technologies, *Journal of Environmental Management* **71**, pp. 135-154.

Internet@EB1 (May 20, 2005); www.acompanhamento-eb1.rcts.pt/.

Kent NGfl (May 30, 2005); http://www.kented.org.uk/ngfl/index.htm.

Norman, D. A., 2006, Emotionally centered design, *Interactions*. **53**, pp. 71.

Paztor, A., Hale-Haniff, M., and Valle, D., w. d., Coming to our senses: Reconnecting mathematics understanding to sensory experience (February 15, 2005); www.cs.fiu.edu/ scspage/professor/ Pasztor/education/revised4.pdf.

Silva, M. J., Gomes, M. C., and Marcelino, M. J., 2005, Geo-referenced multisensory information: A productive concept for elementary school, in: *Proceedings of the VIII IASTED International Conference on Computers and Advanced Technology in Education*, V. Uskov, ed., Acta Press, Oranjestad, pp. 405-410.

Silva, M. J., Hipolito, J., and Gouveia, C., 2003, Messages for environmental collaborative monitoring: The development of a multisensory clipart, in: *Proceedings of Ninth IFIP International Conference on Human-Computer Interaction - INTERACT'03*, M. Rauterberg, M. Menozzi, J. Wesson, eds., IOS Press, Zurich, pp. 896-899.

Stagecast (June 5, 2005); http://www.stagecast.com/index.html/.

Williams, M., Jones, O., Fleuriot, C., and Wood, L., 2005, Children and emerging wireless technologies: Investigating the potential for spatial practice, in: *Proceedings of the SIGCHI conference on Human factors in computing systems*, ACM Press, Portland, pp. 819-828.

Chapter 6

DESIGN AND DEVELOPMENT OF DIGITAL EDUCATIONAL CONTENT
Institutional proposals and actions

Manuel Gértrudix Barrio, María del Carmen Gálvez de la Cuesta, Sergio Álvarez García, Antonio Galisteo del Valle
National Centre for Education Information and Communication (Spanish Ministry of Education and Science)

Abstract: Digital educational content is a key element in the successful application of Information and Communications Technologies into the area of education. For years, the Spanish education authorities have been very active in both in the design and development of materials and the establishment of standards and specifications. In this chapter we present all these advances: the strategic plans and the operative actions, the main lines of the programs "Internet in the School" and "Internet in the Classroom" for the development of digital educational contents, and the standards application.

Key words: Education, Information and Communication Technologies, Digital Educational Content, Digital object, Standardisation, Metadata.

1.   CONTEXT

In the last decade, European institutions have released a variety of documents and communications regarding Information and Communication Technologies (ICT) in the area of education, focussing on the need to promote the creation, diffusion and evaluation of quality multimedia materials.

Almost all declarations and strategic plans have insisted on the need to exploit the potential of ICT in the development of pedagogical methodologies. This potential should lead to a learning environment based on autonomy, flexibility and the interrelation of different areas of knowledge. ICT can and must contribute decisively to the historic

67

B. Fernández-Manjón et al. (eds.), Computers and Education: E-learning, From Theory to Practice, 67–76.

opportunity for change in European educational models. For this purpose, it is necessary to encourage and promote the creation and development of digital educational content, offering quality educational materials while contributing to the development of an emerging industry which can compete on a global level.

It is imperative to reinforce all those initiatives that favour research and development in effective education and training models. While digital educational material is still in its early stages of development (similar to the beginnings of other media such as film, television or radio), it is fundamental to explore all avenues for the creation of these products and establish a standardised evaluation model permitting the identification and sharing of "best practices" in education.

In this new learning environment, it is necessary to have a variety of content and services which respond to the educational and training needs of the general public. From this perspective, quality, reliability, utility and "recognition" are the most valued characteristics. The establishment of quality criteria, effective systems of cataloguing and indexing permitting agile "knowledge management" and academic or professional "recognition" criteria for content and levels will all be necessary in order to guide education-training processes within the new European educational environment promised by ICT.

2.   STRATEGIC PLANS AND ACTIONS

The Spanish educational authorities have been active in the development of general action plans, recognising the importance of promoting the use of new technologies in education and the acquisition of skills to take maximum advantage of the opportunities offered by ICT languages and systems. This is a response to the strategy of the eEurope initiative (eLearning Action Plan) outlined during the European Council in Lisbon of March 2000.

Both the "Internet in School" plan (2002-2005) and the current "Internet in the Classroom" program (2005-2008) are based on an ambitious series of actions aimed at creating an educational environment where these resources, services and applications are implemented in a natural, integrated and efficient manner. These plans have been conceived to promote strategies that encourage the effective incorporation of digital resources.

In this scenario, the education community requires an agile and simple access to quality digital education materials which can be used and adapted to diverse teaching needs and circumstances. To meet this need, various initiatives are underway to promote the creation, diffusion and cataloguing of quality multimedia materials providing a wide range of digital content for all non-university education levels.

In addition to these broad programs, the various Spanish education administrations are carrying out a series of initiatives to promote research and develop in this area. These actions include a number of competitions for the development of educational materials, the establishment of multimedia content development programs under the auspices of the Ministry of Science and Education (MSE) and the Autonomous Communities (AC), as well as European projects such as the Minerva Program.

3. INTERNET IN SCHOOL: ON-LINE EDUCATIONAL RESOURCES CNICE

The Spanish education authorities offer a wide range of digital educational content, including a significant collection of materials provided to the public by the National Centre for Educational Information and Communication (CNICE in Spanish) of the Ministry of Science and Education. Since the 1990's, and particularly since the year 2000, this Centre has been active in supporting education and training processes within the classroom (CNICE, 2006). With these actions, the CNICE is addressing the growing demand for content, with the progressive incorporation of tools, services and technological infrastructures from different sectors of society and applying them to distinct educational and training contexts.

The economic resources and strategies deployed for the "Internet in School" plan (2002-2005) have provided a significant incentive for innovation in methodological materials and the production of educational content. The role of teachers as the ultimate and optimum specialists in creating strategies for developing ambitious didactic materials is combined with the experience of professionals specialised in the production, programming and development of multimedia material. This will ensure the efficient application of resources and the latest languages to meet educational goals: the concepts 'interactivity' and 'multimedia' are therefore fully realised, providing greater effectiveness and value in their application and integration into educational and learning processes.

Initially organised, presented and published in an aggregate form – generally in blocks and thematic modules – around an area and educational level, these projects provide specific access and work areas for three basic profiles of potential users: students, teachers and families or the general public. The concept of the "eBook" has been surpassed, and the methodological models and production are experiencing constant and dynamic growth. This is in parallel to the increasing availability and flexibility in the creation, organisation, presentation and publication of software and content.

At the same time, the "Internet in School" plan represents an area for collaboration between distinct Spanish authorities bringing significant benefits. These benefits include the development of digital educational content, the optimisation of actions, methodological and productive innovation, an increase and greater diffusion of the existing materials and their adaptation to the distinct social and cultural contexts where they are applied.

4.   INTERNET IN SCHOOL: DIGITAL EDUCATIONAL CONTENT MSE-AC

The first fruit of the collaboration among Spanish education administrations, under the auspices of the "Internet in School" plan, is the ceding of materials developed by the CNICE to the Autonomous Communities for distribution, modification or translation into co-official languages according to local conditions and requirements. (Technical Committee for Information and Communication Technologies MSE-AC, 2003).

This provides a snapshot of the common and public availability of digital content for the non-university education in Spain. It illustrates the emphasis placed on materials for GCSE, A-level and Professional Training courses, and focussing on objectives for the immediate production of materials in Kindergarten, Primary Education, Foreign languages and other areas of a transversal nature such as Special Needs and Social Integration and Communication.

In order to produce new materials, a collaborative system with three areas has been established: decision making, administration/management and production. This last area is where the most interesting phenomena occur, with the start-up of 14 work groups, each consisting of members with different profiles (teachers, professionals and companies). The teams are organised into three areas (Content, Graphic and Audio-visual production and Technical Development) co-ordinated by an expert in education and ICT and collaborating on-line.

The resulting content reflects the notable development of strategies, languages, resources and production tools. These materials respond to the those needs which cannot be met by other classroom resources and take advantage of the possibilities of interactivity as well as the languages and expressive resources of multimedia. These have been specifically developed with close attention to diversity and accessibility to persons suffering from disabilities. Technologically, these applications are concerned with accessibility and are open, flexible, easily modified, adaptable and translatable. Structurally, the content is modular according to content and learning objectives. Beyond its educational utility, this content also provides valuable experience in development avenues and strategies for a future that is becoming increasingly present.

5. DEVELOPMENT ACTIONS: CONTENT IN COLLABORATION WITH THE "INTERNET IN THE CLASSROOM" PLAN

The "Internet in the Classroom" plan (2005-2008) arose as a continuation of the "Internet in School" plan, as an expansion of established objectives to promote the creation, diffusion and use of digital educational content. Under the auspices of the Ministry of Science and Education, the Ministry of Industry, Tourism and Commerce and Red.es (the Public Business Entity), it proposes a wide range of actions to be carried out in collaboration with the Autonomous Communities.

The prior experience with the "Internet in School" plan created a forum for consultation between various education authorities and demonstrated the need to produce quality content which is useful, accessible, modular, inter-operable and reusable in order to optimise production (by and for all parties involved). The aim is to complement the general educational content currently available, share experiences, knowledge and solutions, provide an impulse to innovation, ensure the presence of experts in each area and generate a production system defined by professionalism and high technical standards.

Based on these principles, a development process was set up for digital educational content characterised by institutional collaboration, giving priority to the experience of the user. The learning model is based on Core Learning Goals, as part of a structure of eLearning Objectives, designed to meeting specific education targets. The development is based on standardised processes to ensure the content conforms to the characteristics mentioned above (inter-operability, accessibility, etc). The Learning Goals are defined through "Modular Hierarchy" where each module is self-contained and independent, meeting its own specific goals. This structure is divided into Intermediate, Intermediate Integrated, Learning Goals, Teaching Sequences, Training Programs and Educational Resources.

In this line, and with the experience gained from the "Internet in School" plan, various expert working groups have been created to focus on the development of Learning Objectives and Teaching Sequences, carrying out a needs analysis within each area of activity. For this purpose, collaborative working tools have been designed to ensure effective communication between experts and those responsible for the technical aspects of the content.

Areas and stages are defined annually for which digital educational content is created. The entire process is defined according to multi-annual actions based on the following priorities:

1.- Kindergarten Education
2.- Primary Education
3.- Special Needs
4.- Transversals:
4.1.- Environmental Education
4.2.- Health Education
4.2.- Civic Values Education
5.- Languages
6.- GCSE
7.- A-level

Once the needs analysis phase is complete, each team of experts proceeds in the creation of "Teaching Files" for established Teaching Sequences and Learning Objectives. Through these, pedagogical information is structured, establishing the principles for the development and production of multimedia materials.

Taking these files as a base, the Autonomous Communities and Red.es, with the coordination of the Ministry of Science and Education, will create content through a variety of formulae and in collaboration with different agents from the private and public sectors.

The legal framework for the development of this content is defined by Creative Commons licenses, which, under the premise of "distributed digital communication", have a "some rights reserved" structure of intellectual property rights.

The quality of this content will be optimum, given that the process is subject to continuous assessment by experts in each area as well as experts in new technologies from the different educational administrations.

When production is complete, accessibility assured, in accordance with applicable legislation, and with the collaboration with institutions related to disabled learners, the final product will be translated into the various co-official languages of Spain and standard international English.

Annually, and throughout the execution of the plan, the digital content will be stored using an 18-module digital platform distributed and made available in integrated packs according to Goals and Metadata. In this way, and through a system of data search and retrieval, the Education Community can access a wide spectrum of quality digital educational content which is accessible, modular, useable, recyclable and constantly expanding.

6. DEVELOPMENT ACTIONS: STANDARDS APPLICATION

In conjunction with these projects and linked to the actions mentioned above, various initiatives are being carried out for the development and application of standards for Learning Objectives. These actions are a response to those needs which may arise as objectives are achieved. These objectives are: multimedia, interactivity, accessibility, flexibility, modularity, adaptability, reusability, interoperability and portability.

In this way, a series of sequential projects for analysis, research and development are initiated:

- Firstly, the standardisation of management processes related to administration, search engines, visualisation and recovery of learning modules (*technical and didactic interoperability*)

- Secondly, the standardisation of management processes related to the combination, packaging and transfer of these modules (*technical and didactic portability*)

6.1 Standardisation by indexing of standard metadata

The work at this level, which is the most advanced at the moment, is being carried out by the Ministry of Science and Education, the Ministry of Industry, Tourism and Commerce (thorough Red.es) and the Autonomous Communities. The project falls within the area of the SC36-Educational Information Technologies program of the Spanish Agency for Standards and Certification (AENOR in Spanish). To date, it has been agreed that both the organisation and the classification of the educational objectives should comply with a structure of *Modular Hierarchy* (based on aggregate models). This means that aggregate modules define and organise the structure and function of learning goals based on three variables: *structure, function* and *curricular coverage*.

With the finalisation of the previous phases, a standardisation initiative adapted to the needs of the project has been selected: this is the *Learning Object Metadata (LOM) of the Learning Technology Standars Committee (LTSC-IEEE)*. From here, a consensus has been reached on the design and creation of specific application profiles (LOM-ES) which address and meet the needs of institutional programs and the target education community. The following is a description of the changes with regard to the original standard.

6.2   Profile description of application LOM-ES v.1.0

▪   Category 1. General: Element 1.4. Description: information is added related to the technical and expressive characteristics of intermediate and intermediate integrated objectives. Element 1.8. aggregation level: these are given a more specific definition without altering the original standard.

▪   Category 4. Technical: Element 4.4.1.2 Name: the vocabulary of names of operating systems and navigators is expanded.

▪   Category 5. Educational Use: Element 5.2. Type of Educational Resource. A new vocabulary is developed which incorporates level 1 aggregation typologies (intermediate and integrated intermediate) and levels 2-4 typologies from active learning methods. Element 5.5. Audience. New expanded vocabulary which groups its values according to the following variables: educational agent, management agent and group. Element 5.6. Context. New expanded vocabulary which groups its values according to the following variables: location, attendance and modality. Element 5.10. Description. Information is added related to the educational design of the ODE. Element 5.12. Cognitive Process. New element imported from the profile of the French application LOM-FR but with a new and expanded vocabulary which incorporates cognitive processes from active learning methods.

▪   Category 6. Rights: in Element 6.2. Intellectual property rights. New vocabulary expanded with open licenses from the GNU and Creative Commons initiatives. In Element 6.4. Access. New element providing information about existing access restrictions.

▪   Category 9. Classification: Purpose of classification "Education Level". New taxonomy source which includes the levels of the Spanish education community. Purpose of classification "Competence". New taxonomy source with classifies basic competencies within three factors: general-personal, academic and social-working in teams (LOE, 2005; CCE, 2005; CAI, 2001 and Birembaum, 1995). Purpose of classification "Accessibility". New taxonomy source which includes the classification corresponding to the objective with regards to accessibility criteria. Purpose of classification "Discipline". New taxonomy source based on the European thesaurus *European Treasury Browser (European schoolnet-ETB)* and the *LRE thesaurus (European Resource Exchange)*.

In conclusion, and in relation to this standardised level, it can be said that generally, the metadata associated with eLearning objectives allows greater efficiency in management processes and the administration of information and knowledge (design, production, cataloguing, publication, recovery, use, transference, etc.). Furthermore, the knowledge of this information is closely related with performance, motivation and satisfaction of those who use and work with these types of educational materials (Alonso, 1999).

All of this reflects the importance the education authorities attach to standardisation processes for the development of digital educational content.

7. CONCLUSIONS

The realisation of the Knowledge based Society and the effective integration of Information and Communications Technologies in Education is based on multiple factors. Among these are the general consensus which exists about the need to have an ample catalogue of quality digital educational content available on-line.

Given the response to this need, for years the Spanish education authorities have been making a significant effort to expand the offer of this content. The "Internet in School" and "Internet in the Classroom" plans (Plan Avanza) are clear examples of the success of these efforts. Thanks to these plans, there is now a significant amount of eLearning modules at the disposal of the Education Community for all levels and areas of pre-university education with projects underway to expand this supply.

In parallel, aware of the importance of facilitating recovery systems for users, as well as guaranteeing aspects of interoperability or portability, actions have been taken oriented towards the adoption and adaptation to the context of Spanish education the international standards and specification which have proved most effective.

In the immediate future, the development of digital educational contents coordinated for different administrations, the putting at the disposal of a federated system of nodes, and the advances as for standardization are extraordinary challenges that chase the aim to promote the effective and habitual use of Information and Communication Technology in the classroom.

8. DOCUMENTARY SOURCES

Alonso, J. y López, G. (1999) Efectos motivacionales de las actividades docentes en función de las motivaciones de los alumnos. En *El aprendizaje estratégico.* (pp. 35-57). J.I. Pozo y C. Monereo (Eds.). Madrid: Santillana (Col. Aula XXI).

Birenbaum, M. (1995). *Alternatives in assessment of achievements, learning processes, and prior knowledge.* M. Birenbaum and F. Dochy (Eds.). Boston: Kluwer Academic Publishers.

CAI. Centro de Aprendizaje e Instrucción (2001). *Proyecto Educ@Sup* [online summary]. Universidad Autónoma de Madrid. Available at: http://www.uam.es/servicios/apoyodocencia/ cai/lineasinves.htm [June 21, 2006].

CNICE. Centro Nacional de Información y Comunicación Educativa (2006). *Recursos educativos en línea* [on line]. Ministerio de Educación y Ciencia. Available at: http://www.cnice.mec.es/sobre_cnice/recursos_educativos_en_linea/ [June 21, 2006].

CCE. Comisión de las Comunidades Europeas (2005, 10 de noviembre). Recomendación parlamento europeo y consejo sobre competencias generales para el aprendizaje permanente. *EUR-Lex* [online], Brussels. 10.11.2005. COM(2005)548 final. 2005/0221(COD). Available at: http://eur-ex.europa.eu/LexUriServ/LexUriServ.do?uri= CELEX:52005PC0548:ES:HTML [June 21, 2006].

Comité Técnico de Tecnologías de la Información y la Comunicación MEC-CCAA (2003). *Documento marco para el diseño y elaboración de Recursos Educativos Multimedia MEC-CCAA..* Unpublished working document.

European Treasury Browser (European schoolnet-ETB), [online]. Brussels. European Commission. Available at: http://www.eun.org/eun.org2/eun/en/etb/sub_area.cfm?sa=440 [June 21, 2006].

LOE. Proyecto Ley Orgánica de Educación (December 26, 2005). In *Boletín Oficial de las Cortes Generales* (BOCG Nº 43-13) [online]. Available at: http://www.mec.es/mecd/ gabipren/documentos/loe_congreso.pdf [June 21, 2006].

LRE thesaurus (European Resource Exchange), [online data base]. Brussels. DG Enterprise (European Commission) and CEN/ISSS Workshop on Learning Technologies. Available at: http://cenisss.eun.org/kms/sites/cenisss/index.cfm [June 21, 2006].

Chapter 7

APPLYING SEMANTIC TECHNIQUES TO INTEGRATE ELECTRONIC COURSE CATALOGUES

Juan M. Santos, Martín Llamas and Luis Anido
E.T.S.E.T., Campus Universitario S/N, E-36310, Vigo (Pontevedra), Spain

Abstract: Today's technology enhanced learning landscape is characterized by a high and growing number of heterogeneous educational service providers in the international arena. This fact, intrinsically positive, raises the need of appropriate searching mechanisms that allows particular users and organizations to locate the most suitable courses for their requirements. The existence of specialized e-learning brokers or intermediaries which gather and integrate the existing educational offers (Electronic Course Catalogues) can alleviate this situation. This chapter presents the basis of an innovative brokerage system in the e-learning domain.

Key words: E-learning Brokerage; Semantic Techniques; Ontologies; Logic Rules.

1. INTRODUCTION

Currently there exists several high-quality popular search engines (like Google or Yahoo!) that provide users with results based on Information Retrieval theories; however they do not offer the appropriate support for particular contexts like e-learning. Thus, the institutions that deliver on-line courses usually promote their educational services mainly by means of the publication of electronic catalogues that are accessible through the institution's own web pages. A potential student makes use of these catalogues in order to obtain detailed information on the different courses offered and, in the case of finding some suitable, to carry out the corresponding enrolment request. To locate alternative courses to the one found is usually a complex task since the user has to manually repeat the search operation in all the institutions that he/she knows.

B. Fernández-Manjón et al. (eds.), Computers and Education: E-learning, From Theory to Practice, 77–87.

The educational services intermediation systems (or Brokers) are entities that makes it easier, on the one hand, to the different academic institutions, the publication and dissemination of electronic catalogues of offered courses and other educational resources in a common repository, and, on the other hand, to the users and potential students, the searching, comparison and location of educational resources suitable to their needs and preferences.

Brokers can collect the descriptions of the courses through standardized mechanisms as those defined in IMS-DRI (Riley and McKell, 2003) or CORDRA (Rehak et al., 2005), as well as the referring contextual information in which they are given (data about the institution, delivering tools, dates for enrolment/delivery, etc.), from affiliated academic institutions to provide high level services to people or institutions looking for appropriate online courses. The institutions, or Educational Services Providers (ESPs), can register in a Broker providing, among other data, the profile of the institution and the mechanism to access the repositories with the catalogues of the products they offer.

We are working on the development of an architecture for an innovative brokerage system in the e-learning domain which, bringing together the last standards and recommendations defined in the Learning Technologies Standardization Process and making use of the new techniques related to the emerging Semantic Web, improves the searching and location processes. The proposed architecture extends the previous works of the authors in the field (Anido et al., 2002, 2003) with semantic and inference practices.

The Business Model and the Functional Architecture of our approach is briefly discussed in Santos (2004). This chapter is mainly focused on the supporting ontology that is required, introducing several sub-ontologies about, for instance, courses and learning objects, on-line service providers, content providers, learners, etc. This ontology, named ELEARNING-ONT, provides the semantics required to let computers automatically deal with personalized intermediation in the e-learning domain.

The organization of the chapter is as follows: Section 2 describes ELEARNING-ONT, an integrative ontology for the e-learning brokerage field, Section 3 outlines the conceptual framework of the semantic brokerage architecture, Section 4 deals with the identification of logic rules required for preprocessing collected data in order to obtain significant information and, finally, Section 5 concludes and summarizes the chapter.

2.   SUPPORTING ONTOLOGY

An ontology (Chandrasekaran el al., 1999) defines the terms used to describe and represent an area of knowledge (like medicine, tool manufacturing, automobile repair, financial management, etc.), including computer-usable definitions of basic concepts in the domain and the relation amongst them. For the construction of a semantic Broker, we need the definition of a specific ontology that includes all the relevant terms required to describe all the involved entities (courses, providers, clients, e-learning platforms, etc.) and their particularities. ELEARNING-ONT is a set of interconnected OWL (McGuinness and van Harmelen, 2004) ontologies that facilitate the automatic management of the data collected and the development of intermediation services in the e-learning domain.

2.1 Development methodology

In order to identify the most suitable terms to be included in a domain OWL ontology for educational brokerage, we defined a systematic methodology. This methodology is based on the guidelines proposed by Noy and McGuinness (2000), and the recommendations described in the Unified Software Development Process (Jacobson et al, 1999).

The first stage of the development process involves the literature review and documentation of the most basic functional requirements from the client's point of view. Starting from a set of core requirements, we successively redefine the most basic "Course Search in Broker" use cases in order to capture new and different query possibilities. For each stage we apply the steps proposed by Noy and McGuinness:

1. Identification of the aim and the scope of the ontology.
2. Consider to reuse existing vocabularies (in our case, we make use of the elements defined on the data models identified by the learning technologies standardization process).
3. Enumerating the most important terms in ontology.
4. Defining the classes and their hierarchy.
5. Defining the properties of the classes.
6. Defining the features of the properties.
7. Creating instances.

In this way, the development of the ontology is an iterative process, centred on the architecture and driven by use cases, where each stage refines the previous one. As the use cases mature and are refined and specified in more detail, more of the ontology terms are discovered. In turn, this can lead to new use cases. Therefore, both the ontology and the use cases mature together.

2.2   ELEARNING-ONT description

Due to the great quantity of identified terms, the ontology is organized in a range of namespaces (or sub-ontologies). There exists a basic namespace, where fundamental concepts such as "Educational Resource", "Course" or "Educational Services Provider" are defined (c.f. Fig. 7-1). A series of sub-ontologies include the properties, with their corresponding vocabularies, that can be used to describe in detail the instances of the most basic classes:

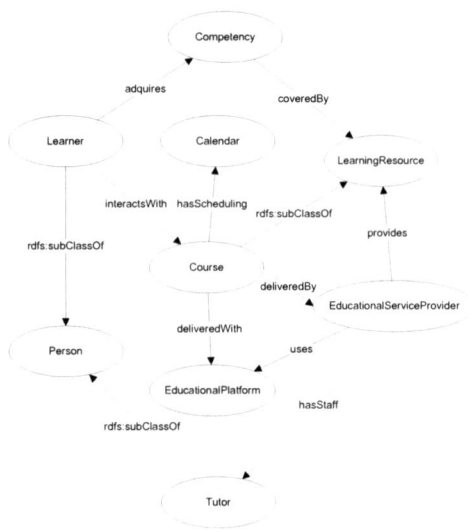

Figure 7-1. Partial view of the base ontology

- *Users Ontology:* This sub-ontology (Fig. 7-2) includes the properties and classes related directly to the characterization of the users of the brokerage system. The terms identified in this namespace have been mainly extracted from the Learning Information Package (Norton and Treviranus, 2001) and Accessibility data models (Norton and Treviranus, 2003), developed by the IMS Consortium. The first of these models identifies the necessary elements to describe the characteristics of a student, whereas the second one extends the previous model with elements that allow us to specify certain user preferences. The existence of the user's ontology allows to accomplish the searches adapted to the user needs and preferences in order to obtain more relevant results.
- *Courses and Educational Resources Ontology:* Metadata is one of the most prolific fields in the Learning Technologies Standardisation Process. Currently, the Learning Object Metadata model (Hodgins and Duval, 2002), developed jointly by several of the institutions involved in this process, is already an official standard of the IEEE. This standard,

and in particular its RDF binding, developed by Nilsson et al. (2003), has been used as the basis for the sub-ontology of ELEARNING-ONT that includes the classes and properties needed to characterize academic courses (Fig. 7-3).

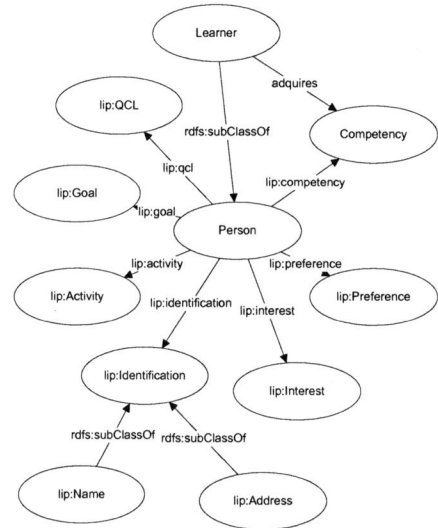

Figure 7-2. Partial view of the Users Ontology

Figure 7-3. Partial view of the Courses Ontology

- *Educational Service Providers Ontology:* Online courses are offered to students throughout e-learning platforms. An e-learning platform is a Web application that includes Internet tools and services into an enclosed space specifically configured and organized to provide learning in a convenient and satisfactory way. Many educational platform surveys have been used to elaborate the sub-ontology that allows the characterization of these applications and the terms considered to be more convenient have been taken from them. The experience of the authors related with the construction of e-learning platforms has been essential in this field. Mostly, the terms in this sub-ontology allow defining the available tools in a platform (Fig. 7-4*)*.

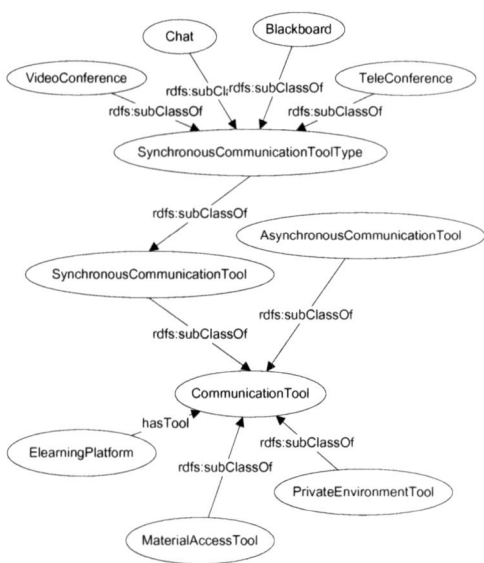

Figure 7-4. Partial view of communication tools ontology

- *Educational Platforms Ontology:* This sub-ontology gathers some terms that allow making descriptions about educational services providers. These are entities or organizations that deliver online courses throughout a particular e-learning platform. Due to the lack of standardized conceptual models in the e-learning domain related to this topic, we have taken from the e-commerce domain common schemes used that allow to describe enterprises. Particularly, our sub-ontology is based on the Enterprise Ontology (Uschold et al., 1998), developed by the Artificial Intelligence Applications Institute from the University of Edinburgh.
- *Other Ontologies and Taxonomies:* Besides the mentioned sub-ontologies, some other vocabularies and taxonomies have been used. Among them we can mention a subset of the Universal Decimal

Classification scheme, to use it as vocabulary for several of the properties defined in ELEARNIG-ONT. The DAML-Time ontology has also been imported to represent temporal concepts (for example, course calendars). Several other data models are currently under study, like ontologies that allow us to describe user's devices.

3.   BROKERAGE ARCHITECTURE

Fig. 7-5 shows the functional elements of a scalable and adaptable Semantic E-learning Brokerage architecture. The proposed architecture extends the previous works of the authors in the field of semantic and inference practices. It makes use of particular ontologies (described in the previous section) and inference rules that can be refined without structural changes in the infrastructure as new statements are identified. The most important elements in the architecture are briefly described herebelow:

- *Knowledge Base:* This is the basic and core element of the brokerage system. All the information collected and inferred by the Broker is available here, both from the ESP and from the different types of clients. It is a repository where Ontologies, Inference Rules, Educational Resources and Course Descriptions, Service Provider Profiles, User Profiles and E-learning Platform Descriptions are stored.
- *Search Engine:* It is the software component that provides an API with methods for querying the Knowledge Base. Although there are many ontology query languages, currently RDQL (Seaborne, 2004) is the most used until a recommended language is issued by the W3C.
- *Inference Engine:* This component is responsible for inferring new facts from a set of previous facts taking into account additional information defined by a particular ontology and in a set of inference rules.
- *Data Collector:* It is the component that semi-automatically gathers information from the affiliated ESPs using standardized protocols (IMS-DRI, CORDRA).
- *Services:* Different services are offered by the described infrastructure. Some of them are Anonymous Searches, Personalized Searches, Notification Service, Course Annotation, Relevance Estimation Service, Taxonomy Management and Supporting Services.
- *Access Interfaces:* Different interfaces are provided to the clients in order to support different devices (PCs, PALMs, Pocket PCs, WAP devices, etc.). Likewise, Fig. 7-5 shows an access entry point for software agents. This interface consists of a set of Web Services conforming IMS-DRI.

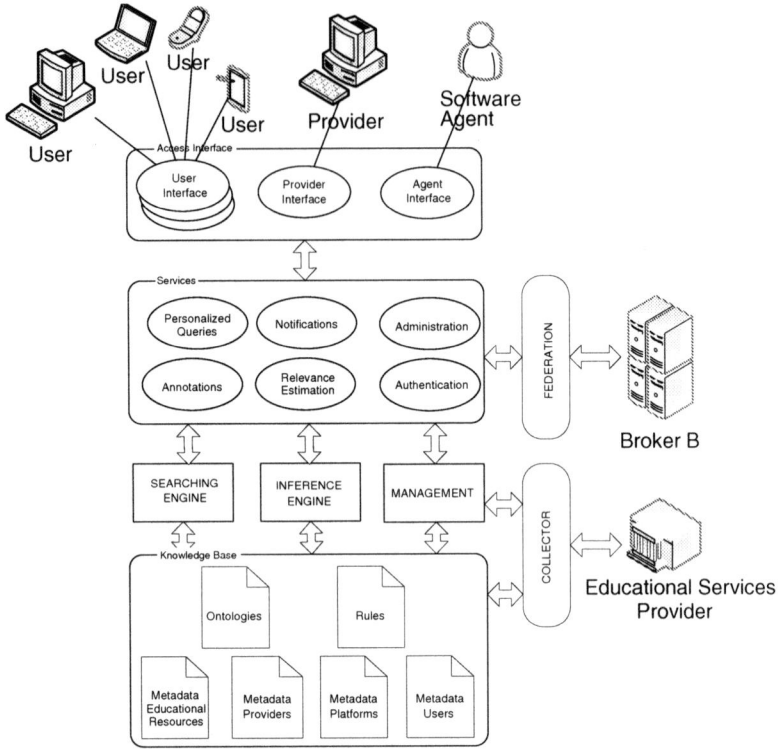

Figure 7-5. Conceptual Brokerage Architecture

4.   DATA PROCESSING AND ENHANCEMENT

The data manually provided by the ESPs managers and the data automatically harvested by the Broker collector must accomplish a process of adaptation of the metadata registries obtained to the canonical format of the Broker. It must be transformed into OWL statements –or facts– that use the terms and properties defined in ELEARNING-ONT. Because the present version of IMS-DRI and CORDRA are oriented to the storage and interchange of XML-LOM descriptions, a set of transformation rules, defined on XSLT, aimed at this task, is available in the knowledge base.

The ontology-based kernel of the broker is a Knowledge Information System where facts (that describe registered courses, e-learning platforms, educational institutions and users) are stored. Logic rules can be used by an inference engine for processing and enriching the stored information and for drawing semantic conclusions. We define two basic groups of rules:

- *Semantic augmentation rules:* These rules allow making explicit knowledge that is hidden or implicit in the knowledge base. For example, the following rule (that checks the "Learning Resource Type" properties of all the elements "E" of a course "C" in order to find an element of type "simulation"):

$$element(C,E), \ learningResourceType(E,"simulation") \\ \rightarrow \ interactivityType(C,"active")$$

can be used to identify courses that are active or with a high degree of interactivity. These other two rules allow establishing a normalized "Level" property to a course and a user respectively:

$$courseContext(C,"high \ school") \rightarrow courseLevel(C,"10") \\ userStudies(U,"high \ school") \rightarrow courseLevel(C,"10")$$

- *Matching rules:* These rules allow inferring new knowledge by matching the preferences and characteristics of a particular user with the properties of the registered courses and their particular context. This set of rules is established in order to facilitate the searching processes. For example, the following rule (that checks the particular level "X" of a course "C" with the particular level of a user "U"):

$$courseLevel(C,X), \ userLevel(U,X) \ \rightarrow \ levelFitting(C,U)$$

can be used to identify those courses that are "Level Appropriate" for a particular user.

A proper set of such explicit rules, expressed in a rule markup language, semantically complements the knowledge base of the broker. This enriched knowledge base can be queried through ontology query languages, like RDQL, to obtain relevant results for the user, providing meaningful advantages compared to traditional searching tools when we are looking for the most appropriate courses for our needs and preferences.

5. CONCLUSIONS

The application of the Semantic Web techniques in the e-learning area is being considered by multiple researchers as a valuable alternative for the improvement of several *add-on* services (e.g. in our case brokerage and location of educational objects, adaptive learning). This chapter deals with the foundation of an e-learning brokerage system that extends previous works of the authors in this field with semantic and inference practices. We have presented the basis of ELEARNING-ONT, a set of ontologies that includes the definition of the concepts, and their inter-relations, necessary to develop brokerage services in the e-learning domain. It's an innovative proposal based on data models coming from the e-learning standardization process, allowing in this way the treatment of information which is compatible with the current trend of data and services shared between heterogeneous systems. The pre-processing of the instances of this ontology by means of suitable inference rules allows the optimization of the intermediation results in a search and location context.

ACKNOWLEDGMENTS

We want to thank MEC for their partial support to this work under grant "Metodologías, Arquitecturas y Lenguajes para la creación de servicios adaptativos para E-Learning - MetaLearn" (TIN2004-08367-C02-01). We also want to thank the DG EAC for their support through the LIFE project.

REFERENCES

Anido L., Fernández M.J., Caeiro M., Santos J.M., Rodríguez J., and Llamas M., 2002, Educational metadata and brokerage for learning resources, in: *Computers and Education*, **38**(4): 351-374.

Anido L., Rodríguez J., Caeiro M., and Santos J.M., 2003, High-level brokerage services for the e-learning domain, in: *Computer Standards & Interfaces*, **25**(4): 303-327.

Chandrasekaran B., Josephson J.R., and Benjamins V.R., 1999, What are ontologies and why do we need them, in: *IEEE Intelligent Systems*, **14**:20-26.

Hodgins W., and Duval E., 2002, *Learning Object Metadata Standard*. IEEE 1484.12.1-2002.

Jacobson I., Booch G., and Rumbaugh J., 1999, *The Unified Software Development Process*, Addison-Wesley, 1999.

McGuinness, D.L., and van Harmelen, F., 2004, *OWL Web Ontology Language Overview*. W3C Recommendation.

Nilsson M., Palmér M., and Brase J., 2003, The LOM RDF binding: principles and implementation, in: *Proc. of the 3rd Annual ARIADNE Conference*, Leuven, Belgium.

Norton M., and Treviranus J., 2001, *IMS Learner Information Package Information Model Specification*. IMS Technical Report.

Norton M., and Treviranus J., 2003, *IMS Learner Information Package Accessibility for LIP Information Model*. IMS Technical Report.

Noy N.F., and McGuinness D.L., 2000, *Ontology Development 101: A Guide to Creating Your First Ontology*. Standford-Protégé Project Report.

Riley K., and McKell M., 2003, *IMS Digital Repositories Interoperability - Core Functions information model*. IMS Technical Report.

Rehak, D.R., Dodds, P., and Lannom, L., 2005, A model and infrastructure for federated learning content repositories, in: *Proc. of the WWW'05 Workshop on Interoperability of Web-Based Educational Systems*, Chiba, Japan.

Santos J.M., Anido L., and Llamas, M., 2004, Hacia un sistema de intermediación semántico en el campo del e-learning, in: *Proc of 6º Simposio Internacional de Informática Educativa*, Cáceres, Spain.

Seaborne A., 2004, *RDQL - A Query Language for RDF*, W3C Member Submission.

Uschold M., King M., Moralee S., and Zorgios Y., 1998, The enterprise ontology, in: *The Knowledge Engineering Review*, **13**(1):31-89.

Chapter 8

TELE-EDUCATION OF THE INSTRUCTION DYNAMIC SCHEDULING USING A WEB SIMULATOR

Miguel A. Vega-Rodríguez, Juan A. Gómez-Pulido, Juan M. Sánchez-Pérez, J. Carlos Burgueño-Suárez and José M. Granado-Criado
Dept. Informática, Univ. Extremadura, Escuela Politécnica, Campus Universitario s/n, 10071 Cáceres, Spain, mavega@unex.es, Fax: +34-927-257-202, http://arco.unex.es

Abstract: Communication and information technologies have become a fundamental tool in education, due to their great advantages: any place and moment, saving of costs, interactivity, etc. For these reasons, we believe it is important to dedicate efforts in the development of educational proposals and prototypes via Internet. In this chapter a multimedia simulator is presented, based on Internet, which has been developed and it is applying for the teaching of Instruction Dynamic Scheduling (IDS). At present, IDS is studied in all subject about Computer Architecture because it is a fundamental aspect inside the pipelined processors, and any current computer has a pipelined processor. The platform we present here is named PDIWeb, and it has been developed thanks to a grant for Projects of Educational Innovation at the University of Extremadura (Spain). This chapter presents a general description of this web simulator, as well as the methods and tools used for its implementation. The chapter also includes the results obtained after the platform use and the realization of anonymous surveys by the students. In conclusion, it is an educational innovation that allows improving the teaching in Computer Architecture.

Key words: Internet; Multimedia; Simulator; Computer Uses in Education; Computer Architecture.

1. INTRODUCTION

Internet is already, at present, a very important educational resource, since it allows overcoming the place and time limitations, reducing costs. Also, it should not be forgotten the effect that the interactive software has in the

89

B. Fernández-Manjón et al. (eds.), Computers and Education: E-learning, From Theory to Practice, 89–98.

learning process. Therefore, we believe very important to dedicate efforts in the development of proposals and teaching prototypes through Internet. In this line, and from 1998, our research group has worked on diverse projects, as EDONET (Sánchez et al., 2000), TEDA (Vega et al., 2002a) or SD2I (Vega et al., 2002b).

At present, we are focused on the project PDIWeb. This project arises from the application of our research to our teaching. The global objective is the development of a system for the teaching through Internet of part of the subject Computer Architecture and Engineering (CAE). CAE is an annual compulsory subject of 90 hours that is given in fourth course of Computer Engineering (see (Vega et al., 2006b) for a more detailed description of CAE), at the University of Extremadura (UEX). In particular, this system is focused on the lessons given during the first quarter and dedicated to instruction dynamic scheduling, fundamental aspect inside the instruction pipelining.

The project PDIWeb began after obtaining a grant for Projects of Educational Innovation, being supported by the Vice-Chancellor's Office of Educational Innovation and New Technologies, and the Institute of Education Sciences (both at the University of Extremadura, Spain).

The rest of the chapter is organized as follows: next section explains the methods and tools we have followed for the implementation of our platform. In section 3 we give an overview of the platform, indicating its fundamental characteristics. Then, in section 4, we detail our experiences in the use of PDIWeb and the opinion of the students. Finally, the conclusions of this work are presented.

2.   METHODS AND TOOLS

For the development and maintenance of PDIWeb we have a server that supports the educational system through Internet. The server, under Windows 2003 Server and with Internet Information Server (IIS), offers web page publication and administration services (WWW), file transfer (FTP), Gopher, electronic mail (e-mail), mail distribution lists compatible with *Majordomo*, etc.

For the implementation of PDIWeb we have used, mainly, the programming language PHP 4.1 (McCarty, 2001), (The PHP Group, 2006). PHP 4.1 is executed in web servers and it allows creating HTML pages in a dynamic way. Furthermore, it is a similar language to ASP (Active Server Pages) of Microsoft, but more potent, quick, free (of charge), multiplatform and open to improvements and extensions permanently. Due to this, PHP is prevailing over other programming languages as alternative for the development of computer applications in Internet.

For some specific functions, it has been necessary to include scripts coded in JavaScript (Goodman and Morrison, 2004), a language designed so that the applications support the remote execution. HTML code fragments also exist (Morrison, 2002), since, after all, the simulator is formed by a set of web pages. In spite of this, 80% of the code is implemented in PHP.

The editing of all this code in PHP, JavaScript and HTML has been performed by means of the tool Macromedia Dreamweaver MX (Lowery, 2003), a powerful application for the creation and maintenance of websites. Furthermore, Macromedia Fireworks MX (Cohen, 2004) has also been used for the graphic design of diverse web elements: images, animations, flash texts, etc.

3. PDIWEB CHARACTERISTICS

PDIWeb (Vega et al., 2006a) is a web simulator, based on the architecture of a pipelined MIPS processor with instruction set of 64 bits, which simulates the instruction dynamic scheduling using two different techniques: one centralized by means of the *Scoreboard method*, and another distributed according to the *Tomasulo algorithm* (Hennessy and Patterson, 2003).

The simulator does not require any installation in the PC by the student, since it is executed through Internet in a remote server. Therefore, in order to execute the simulator, a student only needs a PC with access to Internet and a browser that can visualize web pages designed with HTML frames (Morrison, 2002) and multimedia elements of flash type. In short, the simulator has been tested with success in the last versions of Internet Explorer and Netscape.

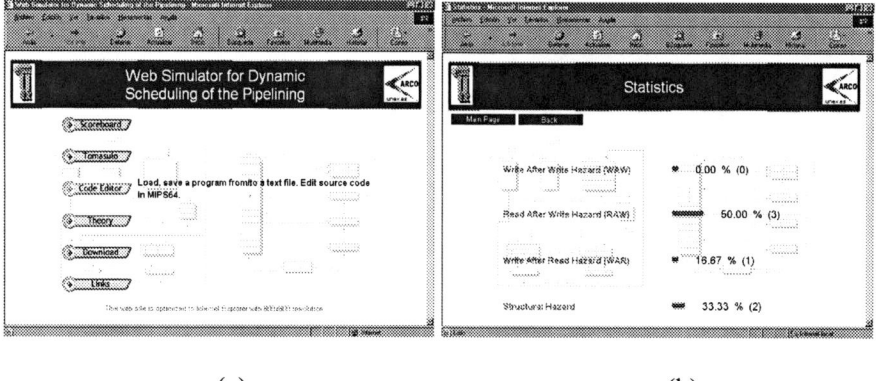

(a)   (b)

Figure 8-1. (a) Main page. (b) Web page with the statistics about hazards after a simulation

Figure 8-1(a) shows the main page of the simulator. This web page contains the main menu of the platform. The student can see a help text moving the mouse over each option. The following subsections describe the PDIWeb interface briefly.

3.1   Scoreboard

Figure 8-2 presents the web page for the Scoreboard method. This web page contains a menu, followed by the options that control the simulation progress: *Partial Cycle*, *Current Cycle*, *Previous* and *Next*. *Partial Cycle* allows the use of breakpoints or complete simulations (without stops). The rest of the page is occupied by the tables used by the Scoreboard method: Instruction Status, Register Result Status, Functional Unit Status, and Stage Status.

By means of the menu options the student can: go back to the main page (option *Main Page*, figure 8-1(a)), start a simulation (option *Go Simulation!!!*), go to the code editor (option *Code Editor*, subsection 3.3) in order to change the program to simulate, print a simulation (option *Print Simulation*, figure 8-3(a)), configure the functional units in the processor (option *F.U. Configuration*, figure 8-3(b)), and show the statistics about hazards (in graphic, percentual and numerical format) for the current simulation (option *Statistics*, figure 8-1(b)).

When the student prints a simulation the report includes: the tables of the Scoreboard with the current simulation results, the current simulation cycle, the hazards, and the configuration of the functional units. Figure 8-3(a) shows an example, with the HTML page generated by the simulator before the student prints it.

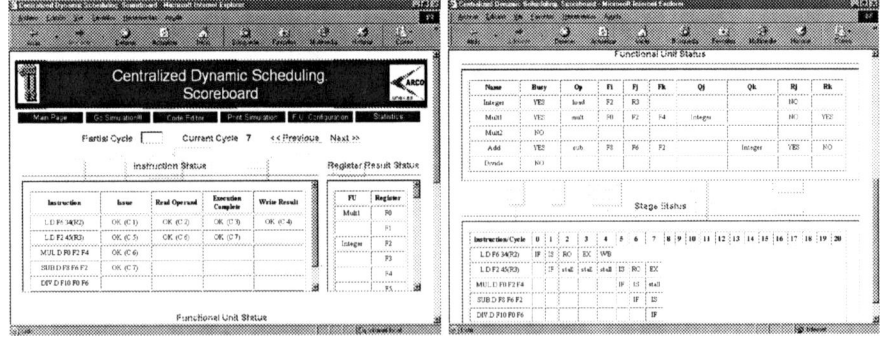

Figure 8-2. Web page for the Scoreboard method: from top to bottom

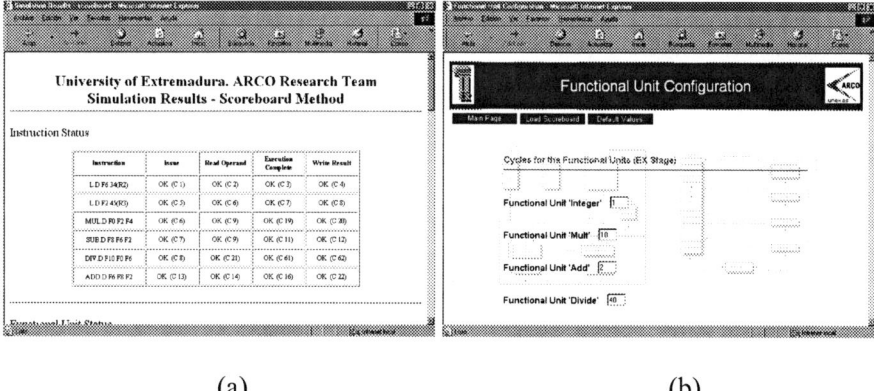

(a)   (b)

Figure 8-3. (a) Printing the results of a simulation. (b) Configuring the functional units

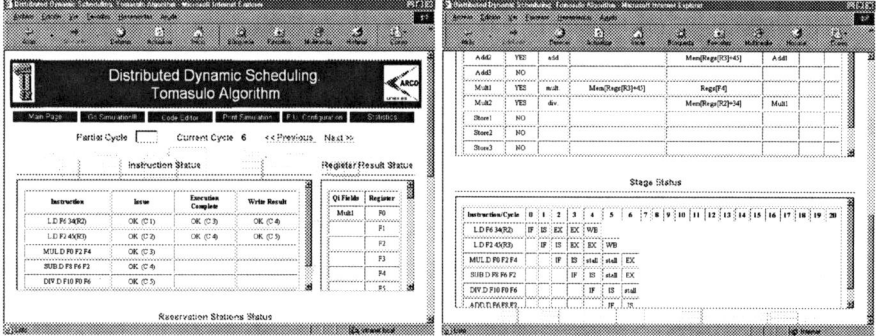

Figure 8-4. Web page for the Tomasulo algorithm: from top to bottom

Figure 8-3(b) displays the web page for configuring the functional units of the processor. The page has a different appearance depending on whether the Scoreboard method or the Tomasulo algorithm is being used. Note that, in this web page, the user can set default values for all the configurations (option *Default Values*).

3.2 Tomasulo

Figure 8-4 shows the web page for the Tomasulo algorithm. As you can observe, the top of the page is occupied by a menu with the possible operations. These options are very similar to those explained for the Scoreboard method in the previous subsection. The options that control the simulation progress are below this menu: *Partial Cycle, Current Cycle, Previous* and *Next*; whose functionality is identical to the one explained for the Scoreboard method previously.

The rest of the web page is occupied by the tables used by the Tomasulo algorithm: Instruction Status, Register Result Status, Reservation Stations Status, and Stage Status.

3.3   Code Editor

Figure 8-5(a) presents the code editor, where the student can indicate the program to simulate. In the central area, there is a text editing window (where the user will introduce the code, the instructions, of the program to simulate) and information about the instruction subset of MIPS64 that the simulator accepts. At the top, there is a menu with the different editor functions:

- *Main Page*. Link to the main page (figure 8-1(a)) of the web platform.
- *Load Scoreboard*. It loads the code edited in the simulator, performing the simulation by means of the Scoreboard method. The code should be validated before selecting this option, otherwise an error message will appear.
- *Load Tomasulo*. It loads the code edited in the simulator, performing the simulation following the Tomasulo algorithm. Before loading the code, this should be validated.
- *Check Code*. It performs a verification of the code written in the text editing window. At the top of the web page a table will be shown with the results of this validation, indicating the possible errors in each instruction.
- *Reset Code*. It deletes the code that has been written in the text editing window.
- *Example Code*. It displays at the top of the page several examples of programs written in a correct way for the simulator.
- *Open Code File*. It allows the user to open a disk file to load the code stored in it. After selecting this option a window will appear, allowing the user to examine the hard disk (and other devices of massive storage) in order to set the path of the file to open. The file to open should be of text type (*.txt).
- *Save Code File*. It allows the student to save the edited code in a disk file. When choosing this option, the student will be able to examine the hard disk (and other storage devices) to set the path of the file to save. The file to save should be of text type (*.txt).

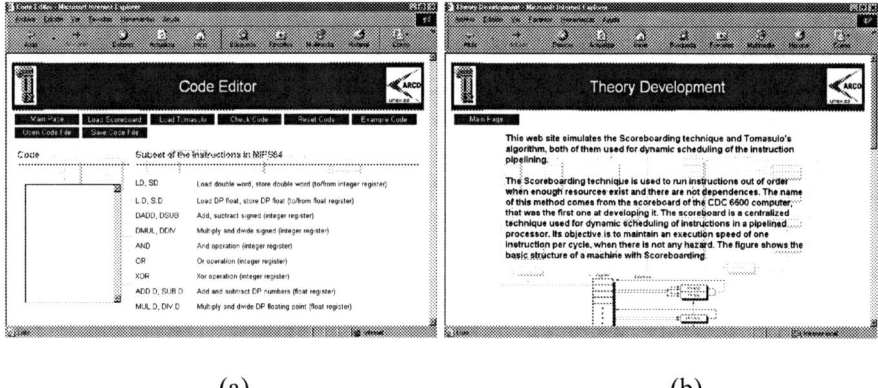

(a)   (b)

Figure 8-5. (a) Code editor. (b) Page with the theory within the web platform

3.4 Other Options

The Theory web page includes an introduction to the theoretical foundations of the Scoreboard method and the Tomasulo algorithm, as well as the instruction dynamic scheduling in pipelined processors (see figure 8-5(b)).

In the Downloads page the student can download didactic material related to the simulator. At present, for example, it is possible to download a local application that simulates the Scoreboard method. This local application is an application for Windows, with an user-friendly and full graphic interface. This application has been developed in Delphi, using object-oriented programming. The page presents a brief description of each application that can be downloaded, explaining its main characteristics, showing images of that application, and including its technical specifications (name of the installation file, size, language, etc.).

Finally, the Links web page includes a list of links to websites that, due to their contents, have some relation with PDIWeb.

4. STUDENTS OPINION

After the system construction (the results can be observed in (Vega et al., 2006a)), the platform has been evaluated by the students. That is, once it has been concluded, we have asked the students to test the developed platform. In this way, the defects and virtues of the system, in comparison to the traditional teaching method, can be detected. This evaluation has been carried out by means of the system use by the students in a massive way, and the realization of surveys to them.

Furthermore, the experience allowed checking the correct system operation, as well as the acceptance degree by the student body. A total of 50 students tested the system and answered to an anonymous survey. All of them attend to the subject CAE. Students had enough knowledge about instruction dynamic scheduling and experience on the conventional teaching of this subject, so they were able to evaluate the PDIWeb platform for comparing it with the traditional classes (professor explanations). We did not give any explanation about the platform use to the students. The student age ranged from 21 to 29 years. Due to space reasons we only detail the most significant results of the survey.

As for the evaluation to the PDIWeb platform contents (*How do you value, in general, the contents of the PDIWeb platform? Very good, Good, Average, Bad, Very bad*), the 95.8% of the students believes that the contents are good or very good. The other 4.2% thinks that the contents are average.

The results about the platform pedagogical utility (*Value the pedagogical utility of the PDIWeb platform. Very good, Good, Average, Deficient, Very Deficient*) also are encouraging. Again, around the 90% of the students (concretely, the 89.6%) thinks that the pedagogical utility is good or very good. It must be observed that, from the pedagogical point of view, none of the students evaluates the platform negatively (the other 10.4% thinks that the pedagogical utility is average).

Regarding the utility degree given by the students to the platform for its use within the subject CAE (*Do you consider that the application of PDIWeb is useful within the subject? Very useful, Useful, Moderately useful, Little useful, Not useful*), again the 90% is exceeded, since the 93.8% considers that the platform is useful or very useful for this subject (the other 6.2% considers that the platform is only moderately useful).

We also asked for the decision of adopting the platform in other subjects about Computer Architecture (*Would you advise the use of PDIWeb in other subjects about Computer Architecture? Yes, No*). In this occasion, the 95.8% of the students, after evaluating the PDIWeb system, says that it should be used in other subjects about Computer Architecture. This question corroborates, and even it improves, the results obtained in the previous question where the platform was described by more than 93% of the students as useful.

Now, we focus on the results obtained when students are asked about if they would advise the implementation of this type of applications for other subjects (*Would you advise the implementation of applications of this kind for other subjects? Yes, No*). In this case, the answer is almost unanimous, the 97.9% supports this type of initiatives, and they see the development of educational contents (theory, exercises, etc.) through Internet as a need in order to improve the teaching quality of the subjects, independently of their topic.

Another question of interest is the following: *After having examined PDIWeb, what would your recommendation be for learning instruction dynamic scheduling? Only professor explanations, Prof. explanations + PDIWeb, Only PDIWeb.* The 97.9% thinks that the best alternative is to hold the conventional classes (professor's explanations) using the platform as didactic reinforcement. These results indicate that students evaluate positively the presence of the professor in the class. In conclusion, they think that the personal contact is important.

Not only the results obtained in the previous questions are good, but also the later comments of the students in a free-answer question were notably positive and encouraging in order to continue with this line.

5. CONCLUSIONS

In this chapter we have presented the PDIWeb system, which has been developed and it is applying for the teaching via Internet of instruction dynamic scheduling, topic given in the subject Computer Architecture and Engineering (CAE), in fourth course of Computer Engineering, at UEX. As it can be seen (section 4), the results of the survey about PDIWeb are very good, and they are exportable to other subjects.

As for the simulator advantages, it is important to highlight that, previously, this part of the subject was explained by means of problems in class. The carrying out of the problems on the blackboard limited the versatility and quantity of the problems. The development of this simulator allows the student to continue practicing the learned concepts at his/her own home, and at his/her own learning pace. Also, the quantity of practical exercises to carry out is only limited by the quantity of tests that the student wants to perform with the simulator. In fact, the simulators are the best way of understanding many of the practical concepts related with the design of processors, in which a great quantity of elements interact, making difficult the carrying out of problems. In conclusion, the simulator strengthens the concepts introduced in class, it gives the students a better appreciation of the internal work of a processor, and it motivates the students to carry out more practical exercises, redounding to an improvement of the teaching.

Finally, it is important to indicate that PDIWeb is not only applicable in the subject CAE at UEX, but also in other many subjects about Computer Architecture that are given at most of Universities, and in which the concepts about instruction dynamic scheduling are explained. In particular, it is possible to access to the simulator through the URL (Vega et al., 2006a).

ACKNOWLEDGMENTS

This work has been supported by *Vicerrectorado de Innovación Educativa y Nuevas Tecnologías* and *Instituto de Ciencias de la Educación* (University of Extremadura), under the frame of Projects of Educational Innovation.

REFERENCES

Cohen, S., 2004, *Macromedia Fireworks MX 2004 for Windows and Macintosh: Visual QuickStart Guide*, Peachpit Press.
Goodman, D., Morrison, M., 2004, *JavaScript Bible*, 5th edition, John Wiley & Sons.
Hennessy, J.L., Patterson, D.A., 2003, *Computer Architecture: A Quantitative Appproach*, 3rd edition, Morgan Kaufmann.
Lowery, J.W., 2003, *Dreamweaver MX 2004 Bible*, John Wiley & Sons.
McCarty, W., 2001, *PHP 4: A Beginner's Guide*, McGraw-Hill.
Morrison, M., 2002, *Faster Smarter HTML & XML*, Microsoft Press.
Sánchez, J.C., Sánchez, J.M., Gómez, J.A., September 2000, EDONET: Sistema Piloto para la Docencia a través de Internet, *VIII Congreso de Innovación Educativa en Enseñanzas Técnicas / I International Congress in Quality and in Technical Education Innovation*, Donostia-San Sebastián, Spain, vol. 2, pp. 25-33 (in Spanish).
The PHP Group, 2006, website for PHP (December 1, 2006); http://www.php.net.
Vega, M.A., Nieto, I., Sánchez, J.M., Chávez, F., Gómez, J.A., November 2002a, System of Tele-Education for People with Hearing Disability, *International Conference on Information and Communication Technologies in Education, ICTE'2002*, Badajoz, Spain, vol. 3, pp. 1261-1266.
Vega, M.A., Sánchez, J.M., Rubio, M., Gómez, J.A., November 2002b, Application of Information and Communication Technologies to the Teaching of Digital Systems, *Informatics Education 2002, VI Latin-American Congress on Computers & Education, IE'2002*, Vigo, Spain, pp. 1-6.
Vega, M.A., Burgueño, J.C., Sánchez, J.M., Gómez, J.A., 2006a, website for the PDIWeb Simulator (December 1, 2006); http://arco.unex.es/pdiweb.
Vega, M.A., Sánchez, J.M., Ballesteros, J., 2006b, website for the Subject CAE (December 1, 2006); http://arco.unex.es/mavega/AIC.htm (in Spanish).

Chapter 9

UNIVERSALIZING CHASQUI REPOSITORIES WITH A FLEXIBLE IMPORTATION / EXPORTATION SYSTEM

José Luis Sierra, Alfredo Fernández-Valmayor

Facultad de Informática. Universidad Complutense de Madrid

Abstract: Chasqui defines an architecture for repositories of learning objects in specialized domains that has been refined during the virtualization of two academic museums at Complutense University of Madrid (Spain). Learning objects in Chasqui follow the *virtual object* model, a specific model that has arisen and evolved during the two virtualization experiences cited. In this paper we describe how the Chasqui architecture can be extended with a flexible importation / exportation system that lets Chasqui repositories store learning material developed with other application profiles as virtual objects. This system makes the practical interoperability between Chasqui repositories and other third-party e-learning platforms and authoring tools possible. We also illustrate this feature with several case-studies.

Key words: Domain-Specific Learning Objects, Repositories, Interoperability, Virtual Objects, Domain-specific Descriptive Markup Languages, IMS Content Packaging, IMS Learning Design.

1. INTRODUCTION

The dissemination of cultural heritage is a key application area for information and communication technologies (Adison, 2000; Gladney, 2006; Walczak et al., 2006). By digitalizing the materials contained in the museums and other sorts of cultural and research archives, and by giving access to these digitalized materials by means of usable (frequently web-based) user interfaces, it is possible to make an invaluable cultural patrimony, which would otherwise be relegated to the elite, accessible to the general public. This is especially true for the academic museums and archives that can be found in many academic and research centers.

B. Fernández-Manjón et al. (eds.), Computers and Education: E-learning, From Theory to Practice, 99–110.
© 2007 *Springer*.

We have realized this fact during the virtualization of two academic museums at Complutense University of Madrid (Spain): the *Antonio Ballesteros* Museum of Archeology and Ethnology, located at the Department of American History II, and the *José García Santesmases Museum* of the History of Computing, located at the Computer Science School (Navarro et al., 2005). In addition, we have realized the benefits of structuring the digitalized materials as reusable learning objects (Polsani, 2003; Wiley, 2000) in order to enhance the educational value of these materials. As described in (Sierra et al., 2006c) the adoption of the learning object paradigm enables many interesting educational experiences based on the resulting repositories, facilitates problem-based learning strategies (Hmelo-Silver, 2004) and encourages the active involvement of learners in the production of new knowledge by assembling simpler learning objects to yield more complex ones. This fact is leading us to apply similar approaches to more abstract learning domains, like the domain of *language processors* and the domain of *computational linguistics*.

As result of the aforementioned virtualization experiences we have formulated an architecture for the production and maintenance of repositories of learning objects called *Chasqui*[1] (Navarro et al., 2005; Sierra et al. 2006c). As described in (Sierra et al., 2006c), the use of a specific model of learning object is one of the main features of the architecture. Learning objects in *Chasqui* are called *virtual objects*, and in their more basic form they strongly resemble the real objects and dossiers present in the virtualized museums and archives. This model has greatly improved the usability and the acceptance of the resulting applications by the final users who populate, update and consult the repositories (researchers, teachers, and students experts in the domain, but not necessarily experts in computer science). Nevertheless, the use of a specific model of learning object hinders interoperability between *Chasqui* repositories and other e-learning systems (e.g. authoring tools, players and other e-learning platforms). In this paper we describe how these drawbacks can be overcome by adding a flexible importation and exportation system on top of the Chasqui architecture.

The structure of the paper is as follows. In section 2 we summarize the main details of the *Chasqui* repositories. In section 3 we describe the envisioned importation / exportation system. Section 4 exemplifies its applicability in several scenarios. Finally, section 5 gives the conclusions and some lines of future work.

---

[1] *Chasqui* is *Messenger* in *Quechua*, the language spoken in the Inca Empire.

2.   CHASQUI REPOSITORIES

In this section we survey the main features of the *Chasqui* repositories: the virtual object model (point 2.1) and the *Chasqui* architecture (point 2.2).

2.1   Virtual Objects

A virtual object (VO) structures the information that represents, or is closely related to, one specific object (physical or conceptual). This information includes a set of attribute-value pairs with *data* about the object that are considered relevant to its scientific study (e.g. *word length* and *bus bandwidth* of a computer). It also includes another set of attribute-value pairs containing the *metadata* of the object, which represent features useful for the description and classification of the object from a pedagogical point of view (e.g. the *author* of the virtual object, its *version number* and its *classification* in one or several taxonomies). Metadata are taken from the IEEE LTSC Learning Object Metadata (LOM) (IEEE, 2002). Finally, it includes the set of *resources:* digital files that result from the virtualization process, together with another set of attribute-value pairs describing these resources and their relation to the object.

Resources are further categorized into three different types. *Own resources* are a set of multimedia archives (e.g. a set of photographs of a computer or a video illustrating its operation). *Foreign* resources are references to resources owned by other VOs (e.g. the documents related to the research and design processes of a type of computer will be owned by a conceptual VO but referenced by all the VO describing computers of that type). Finally, *VO resources* are references to other VOs (e.g. VOs for the different components of a computer). Foreign and VO resources allows for the representation of *ad hoc* networks of VOs, where VO resources are used for constructing more complex VOs by aggregating simpler ones, and foreign resources establish other basic relationships between VOs. Besides, VOs can be classified in several taxonomies, by using the LOM classification element in the metadata. These taxonomies are not necessarily pre-established, but can be dynamically generated as more and more VOs are added to the repositories.

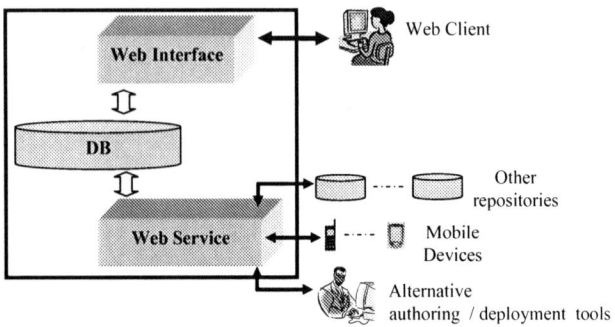

Fig. 1. *Chasqui* architecture.

2.2   The Chasqui Architecture

The architecture for *Chasqui* repositories is outlined in Fig. 1. According to this architecture, the repository is supported by a relational database. The architecture also includes a domain-specific web-based authoring and deployment tool, which is employed by users to populate, update and browse the repository. Finally, it also adds a web service interface (Cerami, 2002).

The web service interface is very valuable for facilitating the connection with third-party systems (e.g. other *Chasqui* repositories, mobile devices providing alternative ways of accessing the repository, or other authoring and deployment tools). The next section also details how this interface can be used to feature the *Chasqui* repository with sophisticated importation and exportation capabilities, therefore increasing the interoperability spectrum.

3.   ADDING A FLEXIBLE IMPORTATION / EXPORTATION SYSTEM TO CHASQUI REPOSITORIES

Chasqui already incorporates some basic importation and exportation facilities of VOs encoded in accordance with the IMS Content Packaging specification (IMS CP) (IMS, 2004), which are accessible by using both the web interface and the web service. Data are encoded in a XML file that follows a specific XML-based markup language, and which is included as a resource of the resulting package. In Fig. 2a we show an example of such a file for a VO in the *José García Santesmases Museum* (original tags are in Spanish; we have translated them to English). Metadata are included in the global metadata section of the IMS manifest. In this manifest, resources are listed in the resource part, and they are organized in a single organization as a sequence of items. In Fig. 2b we show an example corresponding to the VO mentioned before. When packed to be exported, VO's foreign resources are converted into resources owned by the object. Finally, all the VOs connected to the one packaged are included as subfolders in the package, and VO resources are encoded by referring to the corresponding IMS manifests. Therefore, and despite of the fact that IMS CP is being used as an interchange format, the encoding conventions followed in *Chasqui*, which are a consequence of the specific nature of the VO model, only allow for direct interoperability with *Chasqui*-aware systems, as well as direct exportation to generic IMS CP tools, e.g. IMS packagers like Reload editor (Reload, 2006). More complex importation and exportation processes require the use of the appropriate *mappings*, which must translate between the VO model and other

(a)

```
<attributes>
  <attribute>
    <name>Nombre</name>
    <value>Analizador
           diferencial analógico</value>
  </attribute>
  <attribute>
    <name>Conservación</name>
    <value>Buena</value>
  </attribute>
  ...
  <attribute>
    <name>Alto</name>
    <value>180</value>
    <unit>cm</unit>
  </attribute>
  ...
  <attribute>
    <name>Generación</name>
    <value>Primera (válvulas
           de vacío)</value>
  </attribute>
</attributes>
```

(b)

```
<manifest ...
          identifier="VO01">
  <metadata>
    <lom:classification>
      <lom:taxonpath>
        <lom:taxon>
          <lom:entry>
            <lom:langstring>
              Catálogo de Piezas
            </lom:langstring>
          </lom:entry>
        <lom:taxon>
          <lom:entry>
            <lom:langstring>
              Computador Analógico
            </lom:langstring>

       <!-- continue -->
```

```
<!-- cont. of the manifest -->

            </lom:entry>
          </lom:taxon>
        </lom:taxon>
      </lom:taxonpath>
    </lom:classification>
    ... <!--other metadata -->
  </metadata>
  <organizations>
    <organization identifier="default">
      <item identifier="r1"/>
      <item identifier="r2">
        <title>Explicación del analizador
               diferencial electrónico
        </title>
      </item>
      <item identifier="r3">
        <title>Biografía de José
               García Santesmases
        </title>
      </item>
    </organization>
  </organizations>
  <resources>
    <resource identifier="r1"
              type="image/jpg">
      <file href="MIGS-0001-p1.jpg"/>
    </resource>
    <resource identifier="r2"
              type="application/pdf">
      <file href="pieza1recurso2.pdf"/>
    </resource>
    <resource identifier="r3"
              type="application/pdf">
      <file href="pieza1recurso3.html"/>
    </resource>
    <resource identifier="r4"
              type="text/xml">
      <file href="datos.xml"/>
    </resource>
  </resources>
</manifest>
```

Fig. 2. (a) Example of XML document with the data of a VO; (b) Fragment of the IMS manifest for this VO.

leaning objects models. In this section we propose an extension of the VO model that facilitates this incorporation (point 3.1), we identify the operational support required (point 3.2), and we depict how the resulting importation / exportation system can be plugged into the architecture by using the web service interface (point 3.3).

3.1   Evolution of the Virtual Object Model

As recognized in (Sierra et al., 2006c), adding new features to *Chasqui* usually implies an evolution of the VO model. This is also true when adding new flexible importation and exportation capabilities. For this purpose, two new features are required:

- *Composite resources.* Composite resources are sets of digital files that make up an inseparable entity. They will usually be hidden to final users. Notice that composite resources can be directly represented as IMS CP resources, since they directly support grouping a main file with a set of secondary files. Nevertheless, the aim of these resources in the VO model is completely different and it responds to an evolution of the model to satisfy a pragmatic need.
- *View resources.* Resources generated to facilitate browsing the content of composite resources as well as other housekeeping processes. These resources can not be edited, updated or deleted, in order to keep them consistent with the corresponding composite resources.

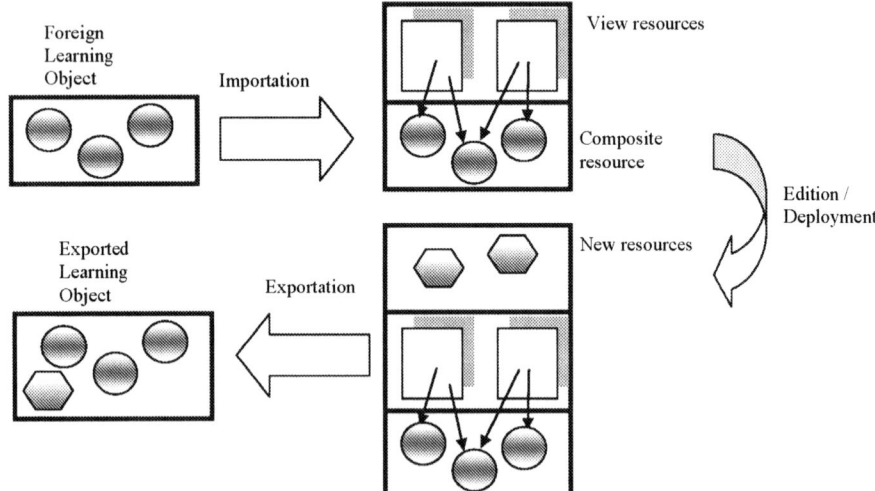

Fig. 3.Typical lifecycle of a foreign learning object inside a *Chasqui* repository.

Notice that these two extensions are very valuable in addressing the entire cycle of a foreign learning object inside a *Chasqui* repository. Indeed, when the object is imported, it will be stored as a composite resource in the resulting VO, and a suitable set of view resources will be produced. These resources will usually refer to the material comprising the imported object (e.g. if they are HTML pages, they will use the standard reference mechanisms of HTML for doing so). Users will be able to manipulate the resulting VO in the *Chasqui* repository by adding and maintaining new resources, as well as by updating the data and the metadata, although the composite and the view resources will remain unchanged. Finally, the object will be exportable, and the exportation process will be enabled by the original learning object and the new added resources (Fig. 3). Importation and exportation themselves will be instrumented using importation and exportation mappings, as described in the next point.

3.2 Importation and Exportation Mappings

The interoperability between *Chasqui* and another system dealing with a different application profile *P* is ruled with two different kinds of mappings:

- *Importation mappings*, which translate learning objects in *P* into VOs. This is usually comprised of an interpretation of the source learning objects as VOs composed of data, metatada and view resources. Besides, the original object will be stored as a composite resource.
- *Exportation mappings* translating VOs into *P* learning objects. In order to do so, the VO model needs to be represented in *P* terms. For this purpose the information stored in the composite resource, as well as in the updated data, metadata and the other normal (non view) resources of the VOs, can be used.

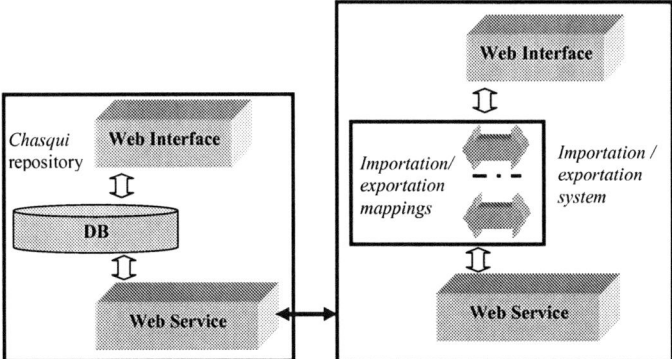

Fig. 4. Plugging the importation / exportation system into the *Chasqui* architecture

The implementation of importation / exportation mappings configures a flexible importation / exportation system that can enrich a *Chasqui* repository. Notice that it is possible to have several importation and exportation mappings to interoperate with the same application profile, each one supporting different interpretations. In this case, the user is in charge of choosing the appropriate mappings. The next section details how this system can be plugged into the overall architecture.

3.3   Evolution of the Chasqui Architecture

The *Chasqui* architecture can easily incorporate the importation / exportation system in a minimally invasive way, as depicted in Fig. 4:

- The internal organization of the repository only needs to be adapted to support composite and view resources. This extension can be accommodated in the current architecture in a straightforward way.
- Importation and exportation mappings are located in a different tier. They are made accessible with a new web application used to manage importation and exportation, as well as with a new web service interface, which acts as a common façade to the importation / exportation facilities. Besides, they are connected with the repository using the basic web service interface already available in the original architecture.

4.   CASE STUDIES

This section outlines some examples that show how the importation / exportation system enhances *Chasqui* interoperability and contributes to the universalization of the *Chasqui* repositories. In point 4.1 we address the incorporation of further specialized VOs with some of their resources structured in terms of domain-specific descriptive markup languages. Point 4.2 outlines how to add support for the basic IMS CP specification. Point 4.3 addresses the support of IMS Learning Design (IMS LD) (IMS, 2003; Koper and Olivier, 2004).

4.1   Incorporating Domain-Specific Descriptive Markup Languages

XML-based domain-specific descriptive markup languages have been shown to be very valuable mechanisms in enhancing the production of VOs with document-oriented resources (Sierra et al., 2006a). Domain experts can indeed design their own markup languages, and they can use these languages to structure the documents. Then the marked documents are processed to produce presentations, which are included as resources in the VOs produced. With the inclusion of the importation / exportation system this situation, which until now has been manually managed using offline transformation support (e.g. an XSLT transformation tool), can be tackled in a general and systematic way.

Strictly speaking, the introduction of a specific markup language to structure a piece of information can be conceived as a specialization of the VO model to meet the needs of a particular expert or group of experts. This specialization comprises a set of document grammars (XML DTDs or Schemas), which can be used to author the values of the resources of the VOs. Besides, a set of transformations can be included to produce presentations of suitable XML documents. The specialized model is supported with suitable importation and exportation mappings:

- A typical importation mapping applies the transformations on the XML-structured resources to produce suitable (e.g. HTML based) presentations as view resources. Besides, the original XML documents, together with the document grammars and transformations, are stored in a composite resource. This importation behavior can be further specialized with other, more specific mappings, e.g. dealing with situations requiring more sophisticated transformation capabilities by using, for instance, advanced processing frameworks for domain-specific markup languages as that described in (Sierra et al., 2005).
- Typical exportation mappings recover the original XML documents from the corresponding composite resources. Besides, there are mappings that either preserve or ignore the newly added resources, as well as the updated data and metadata.

Notice that these mechanisms allow the editing of the corresponding XML documents by using a third-party tool like the described in (Kim, 2003), without needing to incorporate specific XML editing support into the basic authoring tool of the repository.

4.2   Supporting Generic IMS Content

Generic IMS packages can be readily incorporated into *Chasqui* as follows:

- A typical importation mapping generates a view resource with a DHTML page from the manifest's organizations, which can be used as a default user interface for browsing the resulting VO. The mapping also generates a default data file, as well as extracts the metadata from the global metadata of the package's manifest. The contents of the package itself are preserved in the corresponding composite resource. Other, more sophisticated mappings also try to extract and encode a VO from the package on the basis of the encoding conventions described in section 3.

- A typical and simple exportation mapping limits itself to recovering the original packages. Other mappings also add the new resources, as well as the data file as an additional resource, and consider the modifications performed on the metadata.

This mechanism is specially suited to enriching VOs with other IMS CP features (e.g. richer organizations and more localized metadata). These features can be authored by using external tools (e.g. Reload), and they can be exploited in third-party platforms.

4.3   Supporting IMS LD Units of Learning

IMS LD can be considered, to some extend, a specialization of IMS CP with a richer markup language for representing instructional designs. That way, the importation / exportation of IMS LD units of learning in *Chasqui* follows the same strategy as the importation / exportation of more generic IMS packages. In this case, the learning design itself is used to generate a more complete user interface for the VO as a DHTML page. Indeed, we envision a complementary web application / service that could be used to better simulate the *execution* of such units of learning.

As with IMS CP, the importation / exportation mechanisms allow the authoring of richer VOs. Now VOs will contain complex instructional designs encoded in IMS LD, they will be authored by using authoring tools oriented to IMS LD, e.g. Reload LD (Reload, 2006), and they will be deployed from *Chasqui* repositories to IMS LD-oriented players –e.g. CopperCore (Copercore, 2006). Still, they will preserve their specific nature as VOs able to be used in the context of the *Chasqui* system.

5.   CONCLUSIONS AND FUTURE WORK

In this paper we have described how to extend *Chasqui* repositories with a flexible importation / exportation system that allows them to interoperate with different third-party platforms and tools dealing with different application profiles. On one hand, it lets *Chasqui* users take advantage of such external facilities to produce and maintain the VOs integrated in the system. On the other hand, it also lets them enrich VOs with additional features that can be exploited in the appropriate third-party platforms. Finally, such third-party systems can take advantage of the valuable material stored in the *Chasqui* repositories.

We have also carried out some preliminary experiments with the importation / exportation system. Currently we are starting a project oriented to implementing it using robust web-based technologies, and to integrating it in the two *Chasqui* repositories for the archeology and the computing museums. In this project we are also planning to deploy the material collected on a great variety of devices (e.g. mobile devices and interactive TV). In the near future we want to refine the architecture as a basic support for producing collections of reusable learning objects from pre-existing research and teaching material, and for integrating this material in the virtual campus at the Complutense University. We are also planning to further use the main principles behind our document-oriented paradigm for the production and maintenance of content-intensive applications (Sierra et al., 2006b) in order to maintain the exportation / importation system, as well as the rest of the *Chasqui* architecture.

6. ACKNOWLEDGEMENTS

This work has been partially supported by the Spanish Council of Education and Science (Projects TIN2004-08367-C02-02 and TIN2005-08788-C04-01).

7. REFERENCES

Adisson, A. C., 2000, Emerging Trends in Virtual Heritage. IEEE Multimedia 7(2), pp. 22-25.

Cerami, E. , 2002, Web Services Essentials. O'Reilly.

Coppercore Project, 2006, http://www.coppercore.org

Gladney, H. M., 2006, Principles for Digital Preservation. Communications of the ACM 49(2), pp. 111-116.

Hmelo-Silver, C., 2004, Problem-based learning: What and how do students learn? Educational Psychology Review, 16, pp. 235-266.

IEEE, 2002, Standard for Learning Object Metadata. IEEE Standard 1484.12.1-2002.

IMS, 2004, IMS Content Packaging Information Model Version 1.1.4 Final Specification. Retrieved June 8, 2006, from, http://www.imsglobal.org/content/packaging.

IMS, 2003, *IMS Learning Design 1.0*. Retrieved June 8, 2006, from, http://www.imsglobal.org/learningdesign.

Kim, L. , 2003, The Official XMLSPY Handbook. Wiley Publishing.

Koper, R. and Olivier, B., 2004, Representing the Learning Design of Units of Learning, Educational Technology & Society, 7(3), pp. 97-111.

Navarro, A., Sierra, J. L., Fernández-Valmayor, A., Hernanz, H., 2005, From Chasqui to Chasqui II: an Evolution in the Conceptualization of Virtual Objects. Journal of Universal Computer Science 11(9). pp. 1518-1529.

Polsani, P.,2003, Use and Abuse of Reusable Learning Objects. Journal of Digital Information, 3(4).

Reload Project, 2006, website: http://www.reaload.ac.uk/

Sierra, J. L., Fernández-Valmayor, A, and Guinea, M., 2006a, Exploiting Author-Designed Domain-Specific Descriptive Markup Languages in the Production of Learning Content.

6th IEEE International Conference on Advanced Learning Technologies, ICALT 2006. July 5-7, Kerkrade, The Netherlands.

Sierra, J. L; Fernández-Valmayor, A; Fernández-Manjón, B., 2006b, A Document-Oriented Paradigm for the Construction of Content-Intensive Applications. The Computer Journal 49(5). pp. 562-584.

Sierra, J.L; Fernández-Valmayor, A; Guinea, M; Hernanz, H., 2006c, From Research Resources to Virtual Objects: Process model and Virtualization Experiences. Journal of Educational Technology & Society 9(3). pp. 56-68.

Sierra, J.L; Navarro, A; Fernández-Manjón, B; Fernández-Valmayor, A., 2005, Incremental Definition and Operationalization of Domain-Specific Markup Languages in ADDS. ACM SIGPLAN Notices, 40(12), pp. 28-37.

Walczak, K., Cellary, W., and White, M., 2006, Virtual Museum Exhibitions. IEEE Computer 39(3), pp. 93-95.

Wiley, D. A., 2000, Connecting learning objects to instructional design theory: A definition, a metaphor, and a taxonomy. In D. A. Wiley (Ed.), The Instructional Use of Learning Objects: *Online Version*. Retrieved May 23, 2006, from the World Wide Web: http://reusability.org/read/chapters/wiley.doc.

Chapter 10

AN APPROACH FOR MODELLING INTERACTIVE AND COLLABORATIVE ASPECTS IN CSCL SYSTEMS

Ana Isabel Molina[1], Miguel Ángel Redondo[2] and Manuel Ortega[3]

Department of Technologies and Information Systems. School of Computer Science. University of Castilla – La Mancha Paseo de la Universidad 4, 13071 Ciudad Real (Spain). {[1]AnaIsabel.Molina, [2]Miguel.Redondo, [3]Manuel.Ortega}@uclm.es

Abstract: In the last years the production of systems supporting learning and work in-group has been high. Besides, the User Interface is acquiring greater attention, since it can be decisive in order to determine if an application is accepted or rejected by users. We propose a design and development process of the presentation layer in groupware systems. This methodological approach is based on the use of several models to represent the collaborative and interactive aspects of such systems. In this paper we present the application of this proposal to a collaborative e-learning system, called Domosim-TPC.

Key words: CSCL, Interaction modelling, Groupware design.

1. INTRODUCTION

The development of Computer Supported Collaborative Work (CSCW) and Computer Supported Cooperative Learning (CSCL) systems is not a trivial task due to the multidisciplinarity of such systems. Problems generated in this kind of applications come from mainly three areas: the social nature of these systems, problems in the field of distributed systems and problems in relationship with Software Engineering. Modelling that support cooperative behaviours or workspaces for shared information are becoming requirements to take into account when developing these systems. Additionally, most CSCL systems can be considered as CSCW systems used in educational scenarios. However,

111

B. Fernández-Manjón et al. (eds.), Computers and Education: E-learning, From Theory to Practice, 111–122.

we think it is important to consider, from the initial stages of their development, some issues such as the roles involved in the learning activity and the way in which the students work in group. Also, the User Interface is acquiring greater attention, since it can be so decisive to determine if an application is accepted or rejected by the users.

Studying the existing alternatives for modelling cooperative tasks (Paternò, Santoro et al. 1998; Hourizi, Johnson et al. 2002; England and D. 2003; Gea, Gutierrez et al. 2003; Johnson 2003; van Welie and van der Veer 2003; Lim 2004) we have noticed certain lack in modelling the collaborative aspects, particularly, proposals that combine group work aspects and interactive aspects in related applications. These problems confirm and justify the lack of a methodological framework supported by a coherent set of notations for modelling and designing interactive and collaborative CSCL tools. We have defined a methodological approach (Molina, Redondo et al. 2006), based on the use of a notation called CIAN (*Collaborative Interactive Applications Notation*). Using CIAN we can model collaborative and cooperative task in a differentiated way. Considering the definition given by Dillenbourg (Dillenbourg, Baker et al. 1995), the distinction between these kinds of tasks is translated in two important aspects: the *division of tasks* (in individual tasks in the case of cooperation) and the manipulated *objects* (that are shared in case of collaboration).

In this paper we present this methodological approach. In section 2, a brief presentation of its stages is shown. Section 3 explains an example of its application, and the notations used in each stage. Finally, the conclusions obtained are explained.

2.   METHODOLOGICAL FRAMEWORK

In this section we present the stages in our methodological approach, named *CIAM* (*Collaborative Interactive Applications Methodology*). Our proposal implies adopting different viewpoints for creating conceptual models of this kind of systems. The first stages undertake a group-centered modelling, going on in subsequent stages to a process-centered modelling (cooperative, collaborative or coordination process), approaching, as we go deeper into the abstraction level, a more user-centered modelling, in which interactive tasks are modelled, that is, the dialog between an individual user and the application. Two first modelling approaches describe the context (Beyer and Holtzblatt 1998) in which the interactive model is created, and serve as starting point for the last one. In this way, collaborative aspects (groups, process) and interactive (individual) modelling problems are tackled jointly. These framework acts as a guide for designers to create conceptual specifications of the main aspects that define the User Interface (UI) of CSCW and CSCL systems. Specified information in each stage serve as a basis for modelling in the following stage. This information is extended, related or specified in a more detailed way in the next stage in the process. The stages in this proposal are: (1) Sociogram Development, (2) Responsabilites Modelling, (3) Inter-Action Modelling, (4) Work in-group Task Modelling and (5) Interaction Modelling. In the following section and by means of an example, we will describe the notation proposed for creating the models in each stage of our methodological approach.

3. APPLYING CIAM FOR MODELLING COLLABORATIVE TASKS IN DOMOSIM-TPC

In this section a complete example of the application of this method for the development of the user interface in collaborative and interactive applications is presented. For each of the stages previously presented, we will show the models obtained and we will explain elements that compose the notation proposed for creating each one. Domosim-TPC is a comprehensive environment for learning/teaching of design techniques of domotic installations (for the comprehensive automation of housing and buildings) that supports the realization of collaborative activities in group and at a distance, distributed simulation of the performed design, analysing the process followed by the group, evaluation of the solution proposed and relations between process and solution. Details about this environment can be found in (Redondo and Bravo 2006). In (Molina, Redondo et al. 2006) we presented an evolution of this system towards PDA (*Personal Data Assistant*) support. In this paper we pointed out the difficulties found for modelling several aspects of this system using existing modelling approaches. The CIAN notation solves these limitations. The modelling process of the Domosim-TPC system goes through the stages shown in the previous section which are described in the following subsections.

3.1   Sociogram

In this stage, the organization structure is modeled, as well as the relationship between its members. The members of the organization are in one of those categories: *roles, actors, software agents*; and related associations, forming *groups* of persons with homogeneous responsibilities or *work teams*, consisting of several roles. Elements in those diagrams might be interconnected by means of three kinds of basic relationships (*inheritance, performance* and *association*). Figure 1 shows the structure of the organization described in the Domosim-TPC system.

In the example we have the following roles: *Teacher, Student, Observer* and *System* (that adds expert knowledge to the learning process). We identify some specialized students called *Planner* and *Designer* that take part in the two main tasks in the environment. The inheritance relationships can be enriched with the definition of *conditions*. For example, we show that a *Student* can be specialized in the *Designer* role in the context of the *"Design"* Task. The *Planner* role has several subroles (*Plan Designer, Critic* or *Specialist*). A *Planner* can play any of them depending on the *"Task Allocation"* chosen for the activity.

Once the *inheritance* (generalization/specialization) *relationships* among roles established, the *actor-role acting relationship* is added for the main roles in the diagram. This kind of relationship can be labelled when we want to express the cardinality (minimum and maximum) in the cases in which the specification establishes restrictions on the matter. The diagram can also show the relationships among roles that can, at a certain moment, work together. These relationships are expressed by means of *association relationships*. In figure 1 we can see that the *Student* role and the *Teacher* role are associated, creating work group. This indicates that there are tasks in which both with their respective responsibilities take part.

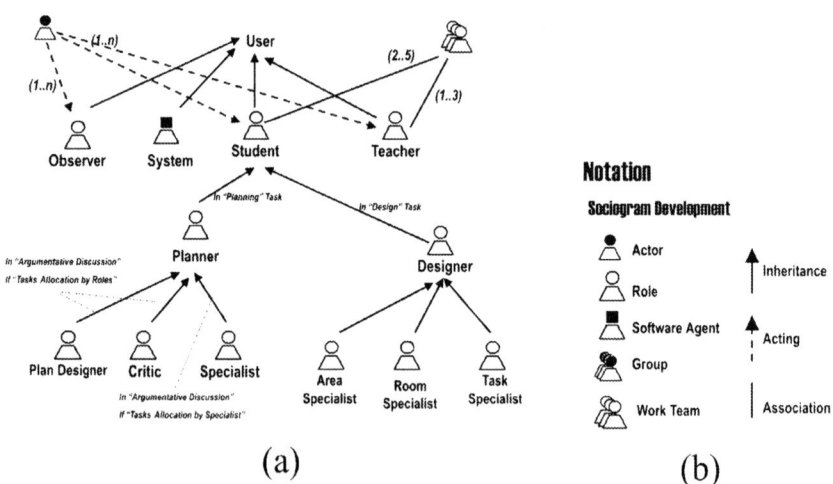

(a)   (b)

Figure 1. Sociogram that represents the organization in Domosim-TPC system (a). Notation symbols for describing the Sociogram (b)

3.2 Responsibilities Modelling and Inter-Action Modelling

The two following stages can be approached indistinctly in any order, since the information contributed in the models generated in each is supplemented with the information that is specified in the other, with a mutual feedback, with modifications and refinements. They even have to be revised in a cyclical way. In the *Inter-Action Modelling* stage (that shows the interaction/collaboration that takes place among the group members), creating the so-called *participation table* is of great help (see figure 2.a). Using this specification technique, of textual nature, allows the designer to have an initial idea about the division of the work at the highest level in abstraction. This table is composed of as many lines as tasks of greater level of abstraction identified by the designer and of as many columns as roles identified in the previous stage. A cell (T_i, R_i) will be marked when the role R_i is implied in the accomplishment of the task T_i, being possible that several roles take part in the same task (group work tasks); a certain role can take park throughout the whole process in several tasks, as well. Once the appropriate cell marked, the last column is filled. This allows classifying the tasks identified in three categories, making use of a different icon for each type. These categories are shown in figure 2.b.

Tasks \ Roles	Student	Teacher	System	Type
Configure Experiences		X		⚛
Individual Planning	X		X	⚛
Argumentative Discussion	X	X	X	⚛
Visualize Results	X			⚛
Design	X	X		⚛
Parameterization	X	X		⚛
Cases and Simulation Hypothesis Definition	X	X		⚛
Simulation	X	X		⚛

Tasks types	Icons
Individual Tasks	⚛
Cooperative Tasks	⚛
Collaborative Tasks	⚛

(a)   (b)

Figure 2. Participation table elaborated from the example statement (a). Types of tasks handled by notations used in the methodology stages (b)

Once the participation table has been constructed, we will centre on the *Responsabilities Model* definition. Information expressed by means of the previous techniques serves as base for the definition of the responsibilities model associated to each one of the roles of the system. Taking a reading by columns (by roles) of the previous table, we complete the tasks that each role has to carry out, adding those that are of individual nature and are not wrapped in the group work processes of the organization. This way, we can create a listing of responsibilities for each role detected, indicating for each their nature (individual task, task carried out collaboratively or cooperatively). For each task the objects manipulated are specified, including the *access modifiers* to these objects (R, Reading; W, Writing; C, Creation; and any combination of the previous ones). Also, for each task the *pre-requirements* are defined in order to allow a satisfactory execution,. The pre-requirements make reference to the tasks that should have been completed before the current task, and the object/s in data model must be previously created by some role in the system.

This way, we can establish *execution temporal dependencies* (order) among the main processes, as well as the *data dependencies*. Figure 3 shows the *responsibilities model* for the *Teacher* role.

Once the main tasks that characterize the group work and the responsibilities for each role have been defined, we will create the *inter-action model*. This model allows specifying the complete operation of the group process that can be cooperative, collaborative or mixed. This model use a diagram of states that allows relating all the information defined by means of the two previous techniques. This diagram is represented by

Responsability	Task Type	Objects in Domain Model	Pre-requirements	
			Task	Data
Configure Experiences	👤⬜	C: Activities	*INI*	
Argumentative Discussion	👤⬜👤	R/W: Individual Plan C/R/W: Discussion Tree C/R/W: Group Plan	Individual Planning	Individual Plan
Design	👤⬜👤	R/W: Group Plan C/R/W: Detailed Design	Argumentative Discussion	Goup Plan
Parameterization	👤⬜👤	R/W: Detailed Design	Design	Detailed Design
Cases and Simulation Hypothesis Definition	👤⬜👤	R: Detailed Design C: Cases C: Hypothesis	Design	Detailed Design
Simulation	👤⬜👤	R/W: Detailed Design R: Cases R: Hypothesis	Cases and Simulation Hypothesis Definition	Detailed Design

Figure 3. Responsibilities Model of *Teacher* role

means of a graph whose nodes are the states and the arcs are their transitions among states. Each state of the diagram (see figure 4) is represented by means of a node in form of a rounded rectangle that contains three parts with the following information: (1) The top of the state includes the *task name* (on the right) and its type (on the left). To indicate the type we use the icons shown in the Figure 2.b. (2) At the bottom on the right the roles involved in the execution of this task are enumerated. (3) At the bottom on the left the objects manipulated by the task are shown, preceded by *access modifiers* (*R*, *W* and/or *C*) at task level. The specification of the access modifiers at role level will be made in later stages of the methodology in which a lower abstraction level is used.

The transitions of the graph allow indicating the dependencies that can exist among the tasks. These can be of the following types: *Temporal Dependencies, Data dependencies, Notification dependencies, Completion dependencies, Period dependencies* and *Execution Dependencies*. These dependencies are expressed using CTT (Paternò 2004) operators and another that we have introduced.

Figures 4 and 5 show the inter-action model associated to the system taken as example. In this example we use an additional symbol to express *Abstract Task* (figure 4.a), that is, group work tasks that can be decomposed into others in a lower level of abstraction and of different kinds. Collaborative and Cooperative tasks must specify the roles involved in its execution, whereas in the individual tasks only a role must appear. For all the tasks the objects manipulated and their access modifiers are indicated. For each task we can specify the so-called *Domain Independent Support Tool* (figure 4.b). These are the supporting tool that implement well-known patterns or interaction protocols. Between

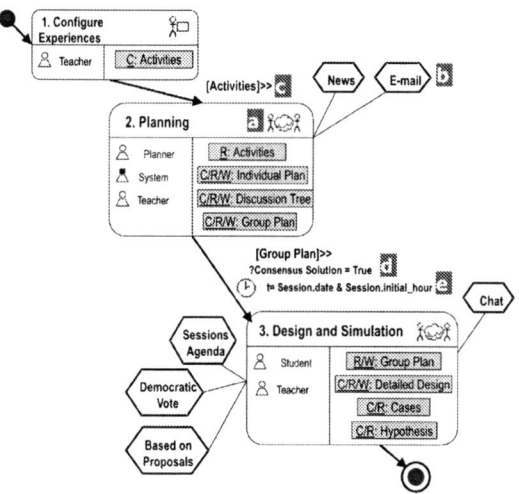

Figure 4. High Level Inter-action model of the system Domosim-TPC

the tasks *Configure Experiences* and *Planning* we can see temporal and data dependencies (figure 4.c), indicating that the data *Activities* are transferred and the relation between these tasks is sequential (>>). Between task *Planning* and *Design and Simulation*, there is a period dependence (figure 4.e) and a condition that must be checked (figure 4.d).

3.3   Work in-group Tasks Modelling Stage

In this stage the level of detail is increased. For example, it is important to highlight the necessity to model in a differentiated way the cooperative tasks from the collaborative ones. The outstanding information in each one varies.

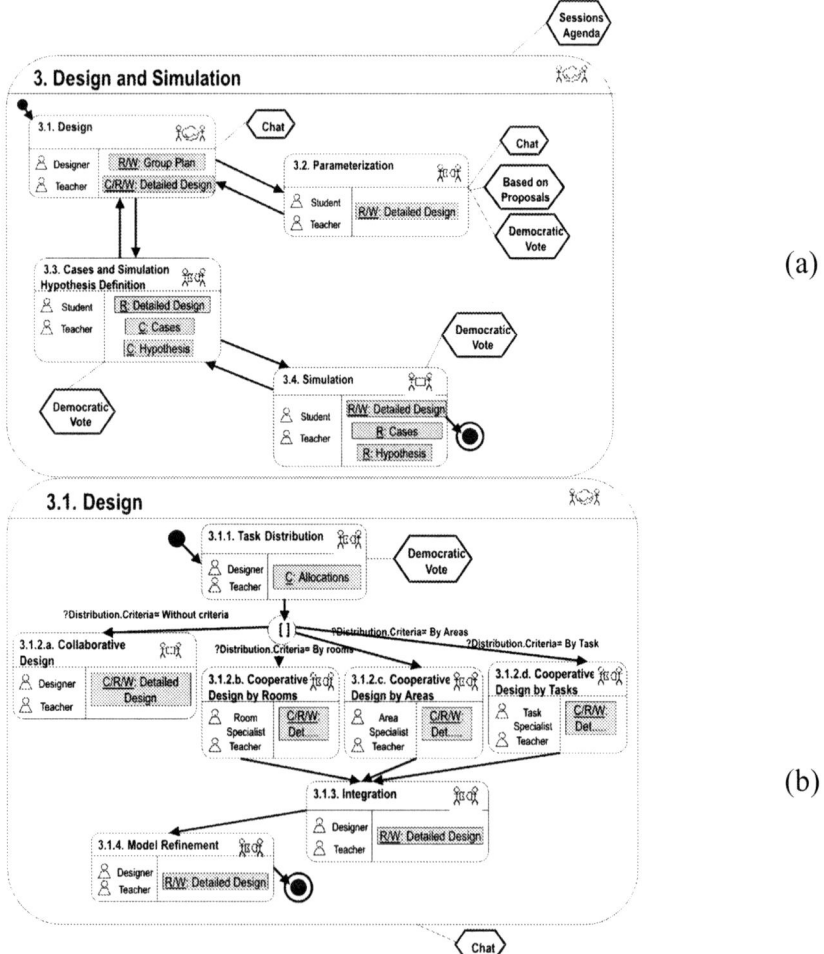

Figure 5. Detailed inter-action model for *Design and Simulation* Task (a). Low level specification for *Design* Task (b)

The **cooperative tasks** modelling uses the called *Responsibilities Decomposition Graph*. The notation used for cooperative task modelling is similar to the one used in the stage of creation of the *inter-action model*. This way, we maintain coherence in the notations. The elements that compose this graph are states (nodes) connected by means of directed arcs showing the work flow. Arcs can be labelled to express dependencies (notification, period, etc) as we have pointed in previous sections. The nodes of the graph represent individual tasks in which a single role is involved.

Modelling **collaborative tasks** implies to know the roles involved in its execution and the shared objects of the data model that are manipulated. The specification of this kind of tasks is based on the definition of the *shared context* (this is, the set of objects that are visible to the users and the actions that can be performed). Figure 7 shows the appearance of the specification of the *Collaborative Design* task. The area on the left shows the roles involved, the objects manipulated and the access mode to those objects (reading and/or writing). The right area shows the objects of the data model that constitute the shared context. For specifying the shared context we use UML notation. Once the objects that make up the *shared context* have been decided, it is necessary to fragment this information in three different parts (figure 6): objects and/or attributes manipulated in the *collaborative visualization area*, the ones which appear in the *individual visualization area* and the ones that make up the *exclusive edition segment* (a subset in the data model that is accessed in an exclusive way for only one application user at a time).

Another aspect that is defined when we specify a collaborative task is the way in which its finalization is agreed. We can identify three possible situations: (a) Finalization by *individual responsibility*. When one of the

Icon	Definition
⧞⊕⧞	Area of the shared context for collaborative visualization
⧞⊕	Area of the shared context for individual visualization
⧞⬚	Segment of the shared context for access of exclusive modification

Figure 6. Icons for representing visualization features and exclusive access to the shared context.

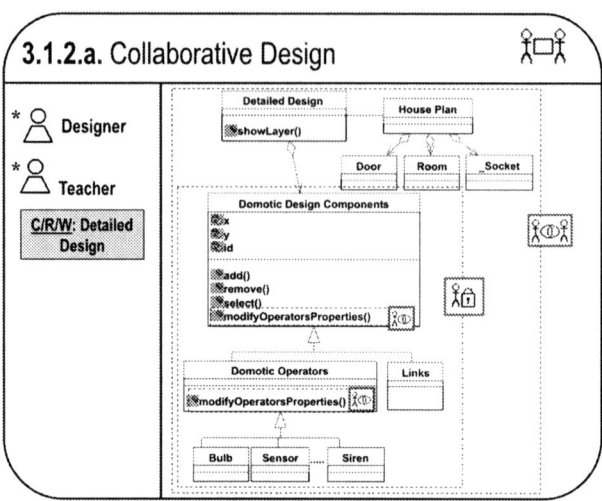

Figure 7. Model of the *Collaborative Design* task

roles must order the finalization of the collaborative task. (b) Finalization by *shared responsibility*. This is, when several roles in combination decide the termination of the task. In these cases the policies of decision-making can vary (democratic agreement, etc). (c) *Supervised* finalization. In this case the system determines when the task must finalize. Each of these circumstances is represented graphically by means of an asterisk (*) by the role icons. In this case, there is a shared responsibility (all the roles involved are marked with asterisk).

3.4   Interaction Modelling

In the last stage the interactive aspects of the application are modeled. An *interaction model* for each individual task detected in the diverse stages of the gradual refinement process is created. An *interactive tasks decomposition tree* in CTT (Paternò, Mancini et al. 1997; Paternò 2004) is developed. As for the collaborative tasks, the interactive model is directly derived from the shared context definition. Our methodological approach includes the way of obtaining this model from the shared context modelling. This method obtains the CTT interaction tree from the data and operations specification. The division of the shared context made in the previous stage is used for organizing the user interface in *workspaces*. The interaction model obtained and the application of *interaction patterns* allow us to obtain the final UI (Molina, Redondo et al. 2006).

4. CONCLUSIONS

Reviewing the approaches that deal with modelling and development of user interfaces supporting collaborative tasks, we have detected that there is no proposal linking both interactive and collaborative characteristics. In this paper we have introduced a methodological approach for solving this lack. This framework acts as a guide for designers to create conceptual specifications (models) of the main aspects that define the presentation layer in CSCW and CSCL systems. We have defined a notation called CIAN, which allows expressing collaborative tasks and cooperative tasks separately. CIAN gives more complete support and greater semantics than the rest of proposals that deal with the design of the presentation layer in groupware systems. We have applied our methodological approach CIAM for modelling an e-learning collaborative system called Domosim-TPC. A prototype of the system resulting from applying this modelling process is presented in (Molina, Redondo et al. 2006b). This environment is designed from the beginning and from the modelling stage as a system to support CSCL activities. This system has a user interface quite suitable for learning activities since it has been modeled with this aim.

ACKNOWLEDGMENTS

This work has been partially supported by the Junta de Comunidades de Castilla – La Mancha in the GAMTest (PCI-05-005) project and the Ministry of Science and Technology in TIN2005-08945-C06-04 project.

REFERENCES

Beyer, H. and K. Holtzblatt (1998). Contextual Design: Defining Customer-Centered Systems. San Francisco, Morgan Kaufmann Publishers.

Dillenbourg, P., M. Baker, et al. (1995). The Evolution of Research on Collaborative Learning. London.

England, D. and M. D. (2003). Modelling Multiple and Collaborative Tasks in XUAN. Whorshop in HCI2003, England.

Gea, M., F. L. Gutierrez, et al. (2003). Modelling collaborative environment. 10th International Conference on Human-Computer Interaction, Creta, Grecia.

Hourizi, R., P. Johnson, et al. (2002). Modelling Collaborative Work in UML. 21th European Conference on Human Decision Making and Control, Glasgow.

Johnson, P., J. May, et al. (2003). "Introduction to multiple and collaborative tasks." ACM Transactions on Computer-Human Interaction 10(4): 277-280.

Lim, Y.-k. (2004). Multiple aspect based task analysis (MABTA) for user requirements gathering in highly-contextualized interactive system design. 3rd annual conference on Task models and diagrams (TAMODIA 2004), Prague, Czech Republic, ACM International Conference Proceeding Series.

Molina, A. I., M. A. Redondo, et al. (2006a). A conceptual and methodological framework for modelling interactive groupware applications. 12th International Workshop on Groupware (CRIWG 2006), Valladolid. Spain, Springer-Verlag (LNCS).

Molina, A. I., M. A. Redondo, et al. (2006b). "A System to Support Asynchronous Collaborative Learning Tasks Using PDAs." Journal of Universal Computer Science (JUCS) 11(9): 1543 - 1554.

Molina, A. I., M. A. Redondo , et al. (2006c). Using Patterns in Reengineering Processes for Mobile Learning User Interfaces. The 6th IEEE International Conference on Advanced Learning Technologies (ICALT 2006), Kerkrade, The Netherlands, IEEE Computer Society Press.

Paternò, F. (2004). ConcurTaskTrees: An Engineered Notation for Task Models. The Handbook Of Task Analysis For HCI. D. Diaper and N. A. Stanton. LEA, Mahwah, NJ.,: 483-501.

Paternò, F., C. Mancini, et al. (1997). ConcurTaskTree: A diagrammatic notation for specifying task models. IFIP TC 13 International Conference on Human-Computer Interaction Interact'97, Sydney, Kluwer Academic Publishers.

Paternò, F., C. Santoro, et al. (1998). Formal model for cooperative tasks: Concepts and an application for en-route air traffic control. 5th Int. Workshop on Design, Specification, and Verification of Intractive Systems DSV-IS '98, Abingdon, Springer-Verlag.

Redondo, M. A. and C. Bravo (2006). "DomoSim-TPC: Collaborative Problem Solving to Support the Learning of Domotical Design." Computer Applications in Engineering Education. . Ed. John Wiley & Sons, vol. 4, Nº1: 9-19.

van Welie, M. and G. C. van der Veer (2003). Groupware Task Analysis. Handbook Of Cognitive Task Design. E. Hollnagel. LEA., NJ: 447-476.

Chapter 11

SKC: MEASURING THE USERS INTERACTION INTENSITY

Jaime Moreno Llorena[1] and Xavier Alamán Roldán[2]
Dpto. de Ingeniería Informática, EPS, Universidad Autónoma de Madrid, 28049 Madrid, Spain; [1] *Jaime.Moreno@uam.es and* [2] *Xavier.Alaman@uam.es*

Abstract: Semantic KnowCat (SKC) is a groupware system for knowledge management in the Web, by means of semantic information and users interaction without supervision. SKC tries to organise the knowledge contained in the system paying attention to its use. In order to resolve the lack of information about users activity on client side, typical of the Web client/server architecture, SKC has a Client Monitor in charge of taking data on users activity and dealing with the analysis of the user activity register. This analysis results in new information that makes knowledge classification easier, reducing the need for user explicit opinions.

Key words: Knowledge Management; Computer-Supported Cooperative Work; CSCW; Human-Computer Interaction; HCI; Data Mining; Semantic Web.

1.   INTRODUCTION

Semantic KnowCat (SKC) (Moreno, 2003; Moreno and Alamán 2005) is a Web groupware system for knowledge management, which enables the collaborative creation of knowledge among students and tutors. This process is based on semantic information and on user interactions, without the need for explicit supervision (Alamán and Cobos, 1999). SKC tries to classify knowledge, which is incrementally accumulated in the system in the form of documents, by paying attention to its use by a virtual community of users. In order to resolve the lack of information about users activity on client side, which is typical of client/server systems such as a Web service, SKC incorporates a Client Monitor (CM) that is in charge of taking data on the

B. Fernández-Manjón et al. (eds.), Computers and Education: E-learning, From Theory to Practice, 123–132.

users activity (Fenstermacher and Ginsburg, 2002; Hilbert and Redmiles, 2000). Furthermore, the CM analyzes this activity (Srivastava et al., 2000), in order to deduce new information that makes knowledge classification easier, reducing the need for users explicit opinions. The result of this analysis is the "Interaction Intensity Degree" (IID), which could be considered as an indicator of the user interest in each of the system documents and therefore could be used as a ranking index. We have performed two experiments that show that this IID ranking, in an e-learning context, obtains results that are quite similar to these obtained by means of expressing opinions explicitly. Both experiments have been carried out using a KnowCat system (KC) (Alamán and Cobos, 1999) with a prototype of SKC´s Client Monitor added to it. KC includes a knowledge ranking mechanism ("knowledge catalyzing"), which indexes documents by order of relevancy based on users access and explicit votes to the documents. This mechanism has been validated previously (Cobos, 2003) and has been used now for checking the new ranking procedure based on IID that is described in this paper. A high level of correlation between IID and "knowledge catalyzing" rankings has been observed, as a result of both experiments. These outcomes suggest that it is possible to approximate a good indexation of relevant documents in the context of KC use, without the need of explicit expression of the opinions regarding these documents.

2.   OUR CLIENT MONITOR PROPOSAL

Client Monitor (CM) of the Semantic KnowCat (SKC) system has been conceived with the purpose of obtaining information about the user activity on the system's client side, information to be used for knowledge indexing. CM only monitors the users activity when they interact with the system Web interface on Explorer and Mozilla browser.

   CM carries out a low-level users activity monitoring, paying attention to certain events that are considered activity indicators, such as the application change of focus, window scrolling, keyboard pulsations and mouse movements and clicks. While the activity on the client side interface is maintained, the monitor registers the number of occurrences of each one of these events, but it stops monitoring when the activity disappears or moves to other application beyond SKC control. From time to time, if there has been activity in the last interval, CM notifies to the server the registered data and resets the occurrence counters. On the server, the monitor takes note of the data sent, and analyzes them when such action is requested.

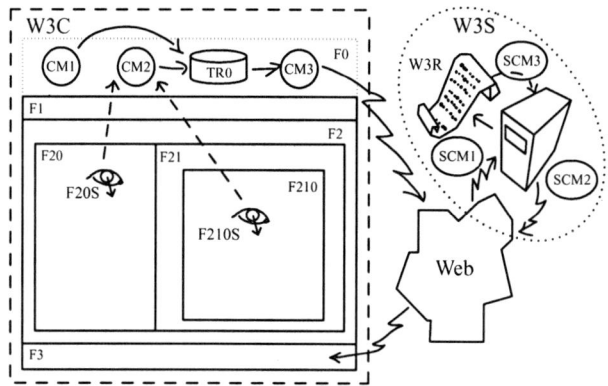

Figure 11-1. CM on client (W3C) and server (W3S) side

CM establishes client side sessions, which consist in continuous sequences of activity without interruptions (in fact, where the eventual interruptions are shorter than an established time span, specified in the system configuration). This approach is similar to server sessions that are used in some Web applications, but considering the activity on the client side, not on the server. The monitor consists of two well differentiated parts, one embedded on the client side interface of the system, and the other on the system's server side, the latter distributed between the system's administration application and the Web server that supports the system.

2.1 CM on the client side

On the client side the module consists of a client application (W3C in Figure 11-1) that works on a Web navigator (Explorer or Mozilla). This application uses an interface based on frames (F0, F1 in Figure 11-1) built in such a way that the base frame code is loaded when an interaction session begins and it is not loaded again while the session continues. This approach endows with memory the application and provides the necessary logic of monitoring for its whole interface.

In particular, the base frame loads a JavaScript library that includes variables and functions (TR0, CM1, CM2… in Figure 11-1). These variables allow to count events and to maintain the monitoring process. The functions take charge of all the necessary tasks for the monitoring: identifying the user and the interaction session on the client side in a univocal way; establishing sensors (F20S and F210S in Figure 11-1) in frames and windows; implementing monitoring cycles; registering locally the events produced during these cycles; and informing the server about the registered activity at the end of each cycle.

On the areas established by the base frame, the different frames -which will be changing and constitute the system interface on the client side- are loaded. Every time that one of these frames changes, the necessary sensors are initialized and the appropriate state is established to continue the monitoring from the previous state.

Five events are considered: mouse movements and clicks, scrollbar movements, focus changes between the interface elements, and keyboard clicks. The occurrences of each are counted in an independent variable, every occasion that the sensors detect their appearance.

Monitoring cycles establish the moments to inform the server about what has occurred on the client side during the last period. Timers are used to control the information sent by means of resetting a special frame of the interface. This frame also shows the environment activity in this way. However, notifications do not take place if there is no activity during the monitoring cycle. Monitoring cycle duration is configurable and should be chosen to inform the server frequently, without disturbing the user by overloading the system and the communication line. In fact, the data sent and the corresponding server answers are very light. However, communication proactivity is not a typical behaviour of Web applications, and may displease users.

In this way, the application objective and behaviour can make the system suspicious of violating the user privacy, although in its implementation the established restrictions about this issue on navigators and on the programming language have been respected.

The possibility of maintaining a memory on the client side is the basis of monitoring. Without this it would not be possible to follow the process, count the events and regulate the information sent to the server. The proposed implementation approach is not the only possible, for example "cookies" could be utilized to keep data, and other programming languages could be used to implement the client side functionality. However, the use of JavaScript with frames covers all the problem requirements, using common elements generally accepted in commercial Web applications.

2.2   CM on the server side

On the server side (W3S in Figure 11-1) three basic monitoring functions are carried out: attending the activity reports of the monitoring cycles on the client side, registering the corresponding activity and providing support for the analysis of the stored data.

The activity information of the monitoring cycles is received by means of CGI calls (call to Common Gateway Interface) on the Web server (SCM1 in Figure 11-1). The CGI program simply responds by re-directing the call to the Web address in charge of composing the appropriate response (SCM2 in Figure 11-1), which corresponds to a special frame on the client side interface. Although the aforementioned CGI has seemingly not done anything, in fact some lines are appended to the Web server access log file (W3R in Figure 11-1) with the information received through the URL (Uniform Resource Locator) that invokes it.

The election of the Web server access log file as a repository of the activity observed on the client side is not accidental. In this file is where the system activity observed on the server side is usually registered. In this way, the activity observed on the client side is stored as a complement of the conventional activity registered on the server. This circumstance facilitates the combined processing of both sources of information and the application of conventional processing technologies for this kind of files. For example, see (Srivastava et al., 2000) for a more detailed discussion of Web usage mining techniques.

In practice, the new client side activity register lines (CARs) are inserted between the usual Web server activity register lines (SARs). Both kinds of registers collect part of the same kind of data, as for example the address IP, the register time or the URL that originated the annotation with all its parameters. In the CARs case, the parameters of this URL include all the event counters, the client-side session univocal identificator and the time references used on this side.

Between the first CAR of any client session and the last one registered in such session on the Web server log file, most of the SARs corresponding to this client session are included. It would be very interesting to determine which are these corresponding SARs, because it would allow relating the activity on the client side with the contents served by the system, which is the final objective of this whole mechanism.

In order to carry out this task we came across some difficulties. On one hand, the CARs are registered at the end of each monitoring cycle, that is to say that such CAR refers to the SARs that precede it in the Web server log file. This has several inconveniences derived from the necessity of considering previous register lines when the file is analyzed sequentially in apparent chronological order. On the other hand, both kinds of registers, CARs and SARs, share information that is not always enough to associate them in an unequivocal way. For example, two serial registers of the same time and IP address can belong to two different user machines connected to the net through the same PROXY (intermediary server between a workstation user and the Internet).

Sometimes these problems can be solved making the analysis programs a little more complex. Other times, they can be worked out considering concrete applications characteristics, such as the case of applications that maintain server sessions (monitoring the continuous sequences of clients interaction) or the use of some type of identification included in all their URLs. Finally, there are times where, simply, the question can be obviated by allowing a little incidence of some (possible) linking mistakes between registers at the beginning or at the end of client sessions (or concurrent users connected through the same PROXY).

All these questions are handled in the last function, analysis, and MC deals with them on the server side (SMC3 in Figure 11-1). Contrary to the other two functions -attending and registering activity reports (that are carried out as part of the service)- the analysis function is executed under demand at particular times; usually during Web server log file processing.

In order to carry out the aforementioned analysis, the weight assigned to each event considered in MC (mouse, scrollbar, focus and key events) should not be the same, since some of these events are very frequent and could be accidental, such as mouse movements, and others are uncommon and almost always voluntary, such as scrollbar movements or mouse and keyboard clicks.

In our approach, events weights have been assigned in an empiric way, checking the proportion of the events on different activities with documents through the system. In particular, three activity levels have been considered for each cycle: high (10), when the registered events are scrollbar movements, mouse or key clicks, or more than thirty mouse movements; middle (5), when focus has been obtained more times than lost or when between fifteen and thirty mouse movement events have taken place, but there are not any events occurrences of other types; and low (0), in all other cases.

In order to establish the interaction target elements on the client side, it is necessary to analyze the system interface structure. In this particular case, the pages (or the CGI invoked from each frame) determine what kind of elements are interaction targets. With this idea, a classification of Web pages and CGIs that show information of each kind of element has been established. Also, the incompatibility of pages and CGIs that share the same frames has been determined, since they cannot simultaneously coexist on the interface.

During the Web log file analysis, the elements of each category that should account the activity on the system are established progressively. These elements are replaced by other excluding elements, that appear on the activity register. The particular elements, such as a specific document, are identified by the identification that their URLs include.

The Web server log file analysis requires three steps: firstly, the log file is divided in client session log files classified by days; secondly, the client session files obtained are processed to eliminate null register lines and to establish periodic activity intervals; lastly, the refined client session log files are processed to evaluate the activity time slots for sessions, and to evaluate the activity of nodes, topics, documents and users in according to the slots in which these appear.

The result of this analysis process is the "Interaction Intensity Degree" (IID), which is a value that qualifies each of the system documents and other elements that are part of the SKC system (topics, authors and nodes). IID could be considered as an indicator of the users interest in each these documents -and in the rest of system elements- and therefore could be used as a ranking index of the corresponding categories. In this paper two experiments are reported where IID is used essentially for documents indexing.

3.   EXPERIMENTS

In order to test the validity of the approach -and the viability of its implementation-, we have developed a SKC MC prototype that has been incorporated in a KnowCat system (KC) to prove it in two real educational experiences carried out in the Higher Polytechnic School of the Universidad Autonoma de Madrid (UAM) during the 2004-2005 course. In both cases, various academic activities have been carried out using the system, trying to cause different interaction patterns with the knowledge incorporated in the system. All the students were aware that their activity on the client side was being monitored, however their identification was not requested and instead an automatic unique identification was assigned for each student in each session.

The KC system includes a knowledge ranking mechanism (Alamán and Cobos, 1999; Cobos, 2003), which is called "knowledge catalyzing", that makes possible to index documents by order of relevancy based on users access and explicit votes to the documents. This mechanism has been validated previously (Cobos, 2003) and has been used now for checking the new ranking procedure based on "Interaction Intensity Degree" (IID) described in this paper. This way, once the documents indexing was carried out by means of the KC mechanisms, the Web server log files were processed to establish a classification on the documents according to the interaction intensity that was detected on the client side. In order to estimate the relevancy of each document, the following data were used: the number of active cycles registered by MC, the periods in which activity had been detected on each document and the intensity of this activity, according to the quantity of each kind of events detected during these periods.

Finally, the ranking obtained by this new procedure based on IID on the client side has been compared with the ranking obtained by KC original catalyzing mechanism.

The first experience involved 300 students from the "Artificial Intelligence" course, which is a mandatory subject in the third year of the Computer Engineering degree. This experience was a voluntary project that could represent up to 15% of their mark in the course. A more detailed description of the experience can be found in (Cobos and Diez, 2005). The participating students were distributed in three groups, each one focused on one of the three topics proposed by the lecturers. Each student contributed a document to his/her group topic before the deadline. Then they had one month to express their personal evaluation on the documents prepared by their partners. After this, a catalyzing process was carried out to select the best document in each topic. By the end of the first part of the year, the final exam included a question on all of the contents in these "best" documents. The results obtained in this experience were very satisfactory, since most of the participating students obtained good marks in the questions related to the documents selected by the system.

The second experience was carried out with 110 students from the "Operating Systems" (OS) course, which is a mandatory subject in the second year. In this case, the experience was also voluntary for the students, and could represent up to one extra point on top their mark. In this activity, the students were distributed in three groups focusing on two or three topics, according to the number of students assigned. Each student chose one of the topics in his/her group, prepared a paper on the topic and inserted the corresponding document in the system. Then, each student had to evaluate his/her partners documents on his/her topic, by means of votes and annotations. After this, a catalyzing process was carried out to produce a ranking index in the documents. This index made possible the selection of the papers that would be exposed in class at the end of the activity.

4.   RESULTS

The first of the two experiences, AI, was the most interesting, because of its size in number of users and documents, and because of the motivation achieved by participating students.

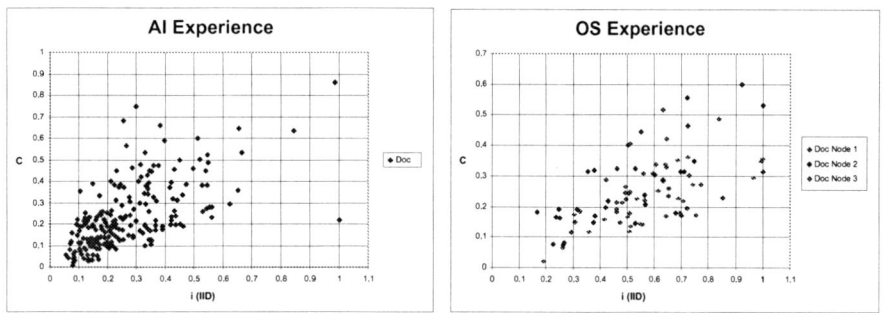

Figure 11-2. C versus I on the AI experience and on the OS experience

The graph on Figure 11-2 shows the documents in the system in both experiences. The y-axis represents the "Knowledge Catalyzing Degree" (C) of each document. The x-axis is represents the "Interaction Intensity Degree" (I) of each document.

These charts show a high correlation between both parameters (C and I): the points are reasonably concentrated along the diagonal. The coincidence between documents with high C degree that also have high level of I is significant, as shown in the right superior quadrant. In the same way, it is interesting to observe that documents with low level of both parameters -that are located in the left bottom quadrant- are quite numerous.

Some documents, however, keep C index low in spite of having been used actively; these are shown in the right bottom quadrant. This is a reasonable possibility for documents that, in spite of having aroused great interest, are finally not very much appreciated. The cases without – apparently- a logical explanation are those documents that maintain low IID but have high C degree, and can be found in the left top quadrant of the AI experience chart. These are documents that, in spite of having been insufficiently consulted and scarcely used through the experiments, have nevertheless received enough support from the users to catalyze. A plausible interpretation is that users have sometimes voted arbitrarily.

To illustrate the OS experience, the graph on the right of Figure 11-2 superimposes the results of the three nodes used in the experiment. Again, as in the AI case, a high correlation between the two indexes is found: the concentration of documents in the right top quadrant and in the left bottom is very significant. It is also interesting to observe that very few documents appear on the left top quadrant, as should be expected.

5.   CONCLUSIONS

An index based on the user interaction intensity on the client side seems to show the user interest in the elements of knowledge management systems such as KnowCat (KC) or Semantic KnowCat (SKC). An index of these characteristics could be used to detect anomalies in knowledge relevance measurements -such as the "knowledge catalysing degree" of KC- and to contrast its results. But also, an index defined in this way could be useful to approximate a good indexation of relevant documents, without the need for explicit expression of user opinions regarding these elements, such as SKC intends to do. However, interaction monitoring on the client side is only possible under certain conditions and under important restrictions that cannot always be assumed or imposed.

ACKNOWLEDGEMENTS

This work has been partially funded by the Spanish Ministry of Education and Science, projects UCAT (TIN2004-03/40) and MOSAIC-Learning (TSI2005-08225-C07-06).

REFERENCES

Alamán, X. & Cobos, R., 1999, KnowCat: A Web application for knowledge organization, in: *LNCS 1727*. Eds. Chen, P.P. et. al. (Springer), pp. 348-359.

Cobos, R., 2003, *Mecanismos para la Cristalización del Conocimiento, una Propuesta Mediante un Sistema de Trabajo Colaborativo*. Ph.D. Thesis. UAM.

Cobos, R. & Diez, F., 2005, Descripción de una experiencia docente de trabajo colaborativo en IA, in: *Proacs. VI Congreso Nacional de Informática Educativa (SINTICE'2005)*. Granada, Spain.

Fenstermacher, K. & Ginsburg, M., 2002, A lightweight framework for C/S monitoring, in: *IEEE Computer*. Vol. 35, No. 3. March, 2002.

Hilbert, D. & Redmiles, D., 2000, Extracting usability information from user interface events, in: *ACM Computing Surveys*. Volume 32 , Issue 4, 384 - 421.

Moreno, J., 2003, *Una Propuesta para la Gestión de Conocimiento Colaborativa Mediante Información Semántica*. Doctoral research project. UAM.

Moreno, J. & Alamán. A., 2005, Proposal of design for a collaborative knowledge management system by means of semantic information, in: *HCI Related Papers of Interacción 2004*. Springer, pp. 307-319.

Srivastava, J., Cooley, R., Deshpande, M. & Tan, P. N., 2000, Web usage mining: Discovery and applications of usage pattern from Web data, in: *SIGKDD Explorations*, 1(2):1-12.

Chapter 12

SWAD: WEB SYSTEM FOR EDUCATION SUPPORT

Cañas A., Calandria, D. J., Ortigosa E. M., Ros E., Díaz, A. F.
Dpt. Computer Architecture and Technology, University of Granada

Abstract: This chapter presents a platform for supporting education tasks; we call it SWAD (in Spanish, it stands for Web-System for Education Support). This platform has been gradually developed during the last 7 years and is currently used at the University of Granada in more than 578 different subjects of different degrees. We describe here the various web services provided by the platform for students and educators, such as electronic index card, class photograph, document downloading, student self-assessment through multiple-choice exam, online checking of grades, internal web mail, discussion forums and electronic blackboard. The chapter also gives details about its implementation and provides evaluation statistics about its use and users' opinions after testing the platform.

Key words: e-learning, b-learning, LMS, educational tool, self-assessment.

1. INTRODUCTION

The use of LMS (Learning Management Systems) is interesting because they help teachers accomplish some educational and management tasks —for example, to distribute documents, consulting students data,...—, but mainly because it favors students autonomy and self-training, since the students may use such services at any time and from any place. Some services that a university web portal should offer are presented by Bernier et al. (2002).

In recent years, the use of E-learning and B-Learning platforms, both commercial and free, that agglutinate the software services necessary to give support to a complete infrastructure of teleeducation through the Internet, has begun to extend. Examples of commercial platforms are WebCT (WebCT, 2001-2006), Blackboard (Blackboard Inc, 1997-2006) and IBM Lotus

B. Fernández-Manjón et al. (eds.), Computers and Education: E-learning, From Theory to Practice, 133–142.

Learning Management System (IBM Lotus, 2001-2006). As examples of free distribution platforms we can mention Moodle (Dougiamas, 2006), ILIAS open source (ILIAS, 2006), dokeos (dokeos, 2006) and Claroline (Claroline, 2006). These and other platforms are analyzed and compared in literature (Li et al., 2000; Schneider, 2004; Cane, 2004; Cane and Leitner, 2005; SIGOSSEE/JOIN, 2005; EduTools, 2006). These environments allow even the experimentation of advanced methods based on artificial intelligence techniques (Andriessen and Sandberg, 1999; Murray, 1999; Cumming and McDougall, 2000; Brusilovsky, 2001). In general, these systems allow the creation of courses or subjects that can be designed and managed like a whole by educational staff, with no need for technical knowledge. Their main disadvantages are the high price (in the case of commercial platforms), the dependency on an external company, and the difficulty of adaptation to the needs and particularities of each educational organization.

As an alternative, several universities use their own developments for their specific requirements —for example, AulaWeb (García-Beltrán and Martínez, 2004) in the Polytechnic University of Madrid (Spain)—. One of these tools is SWAD (Cañas, 1999-2006), developed by the University of Granada (Spain).

SWAD platform includes features of learning support, teaching and students' data management. In former reports (Cañas et al., 2002; Cañas, 1999-2006) of this platform, students showed very positive evaluations. At the moment, SWAD is developed within the framework of two educational innovation projects supported by the University of Granada (Spain), and is used by 623 teachers and 27,859 students in 578 subjects of 115 degrees.

This chapter presents the platform SWAD beginning by the description of the services that it offers, continuing with a summary of its implementation and a report on the use of the system by the students, and finalizing with a section comprising conclusions.

2.   DESCRIPTION OF THE PLATFORM

SWAD allows the access to different types of users, mainly students, teachers and administrators, each one with a different vision of the system. In order to facilitate navigation, we have cared over the homogeneity of the interface and the permanent accessibility to the different tabs and menus (see Figs. 1 and 2). In the upper part of the screen the name of the selected subject and the identified user are shown. In the left part there are a calendar, a virtual notice board, and menus that allow the access to any subject. The right part shows the currently logged users, and a direct access to diverse services of the university. The central zone presents the following six tabs:

- Information and documentation of subjects.
- Student's assessment.
- Information and administration of users.
- Communication between users.
- Statistics and consult of accesses.
- Personal information.

Each tab offers a different menu to enter the services that will be presented in the following subsections.

2.1   Information and documentation of subjects

In the "Subject" tab, there is information related to the selected subject, structured in the following sections:

- Subject description.
- Academic calendar, showing important dates.
- Timetable. Theory or lab sessions, duration, group, classroom...
- Theory and practice programs.
- Bibliography. It is a page with the recommended text books.
- FAQ. Answers to the questions formulated more frequently by students.
- Links to web resources related to the subject.
- Download area with documents like slides, exercises, tutorials,...
- Common zone of storage, for both students and teachers.

2.2   Student's assessment

The "Assessment" tab presents diverse options related to the evaluation of the students:

- Information about the assessment system.
- Customized card of the student in each subject.
- Work submission (see Fig. 12-1).
- Student's self-assessment by means of questions randomly chosen from a test bank edited by teachers. This is one of the services best rated by students, since it allows them to assess themselves and to arrive at the actual examination with greater confidence. In addition, a sensible improvement in the academic results has been stated after its implantation (see section 4).
- Examinations announcements.
- Grades online (visible only for the identified student).

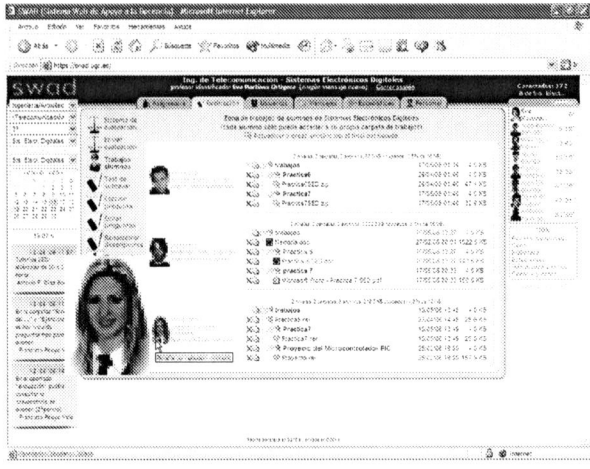

Figure 12-1. Works submitted by three students.

2.3   Information and administration of users

In the "Users" tab, there is information about the students and teachers in the subject:

- Class photograph (see Fig. 12-2).
- Student's list with links to their web pages, e-mails, etc.
- Students data in the form of a traditional card.
- List of teachers in the subject.
- Groups' management.
- Common storage area for each group.
- Assignment and elimination of users to/from groups or subjects.

2.4   Communication between users

The "Messages" tab offers the following communication services between users:

- Notices edited by teachers.
- Electronic mail to all or to selected students of a subject.
- Internal web mail between users within the platform. The addresses are selected from a small class photograph. This service facilitates a spam free communication between students and teachers.
- Discussion forums for each course or degree, and for the university.
- Graphic virtual whiteboard and chat.

2.5 Statistics and consult of accesses

Whenever a user accesses a service, the time of the access and the selected action are logged. In the "Statistics" tab, it is possible to check all the accesses or those of selected users:

- Access statistics for a course. Consultation by user, date, action…
- Global access statistics for the university or a degree. Consultation by user, date, action, degree, subject…
- Detailed listing of accesses for particular users.
- Global use of the system. Number of subjects, students, teachers...

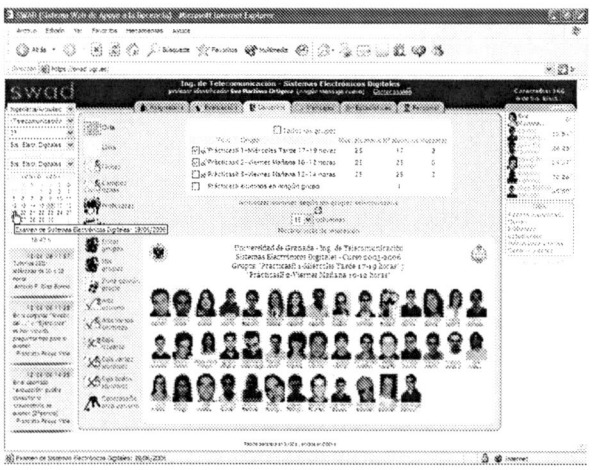

Figure 12-2. Class photograph.

2.6 Personal information

The "Personal" tab includes services related to the identified user:

- User index card (shared by all courses).
- Photograph upload. The users can send their photographs through a form. As opposed to other systems where the user is treated in a depersonalized way, in SWAD, a special emphasis is placed on having available the photographs of students and teachers in the different services. A remarkable characteristic of SWAD is the use of a combination of classic algorithms and neural networks to improve or reject the photographs of low quality or those that do not correspond to a human face (Rodrigo et al., 2005).
- Personal briefcase. Each user has a storage space, useful to keep backups or to move information between different physical locations.

3.   IMPLEMENTATION DETAILS

The platform runs in an Apache web server on Linux. Most of the services are implemented in the form of a single program that uses the CGI standard and integrates the actions that normally should be carried out by about 330 CGI programs. The distinction between different actions is implemented by means of a parameter sent to the server. This solution is interesting because it facilitates the reusability of functions, the maintenance of the code, and the compilation. Although the language more used to program a CGI is Perl, for speed and clarity reasons we have chosen ANSI C, coded according to the GNU standard. The main module source code of SWAD has about 36,000 lines in the current version (November 2006). The size of the executable file is 1.95 MB and, in most services, it generates the web page in a few milliseconds.

The platform uses the well-known database management system MySQL to store the data, although certain elements are maintained in XML archives. For the encryption of passwords and other elements, we have used the implementation of Philip J. Erdelsky (2002) of the Rijndael algorithm (AES) (Rijmen, 2004). The photograph processing is made by a separate module written in C++. The whiteboard/chat server is programmed in Java, and the client uses a combination of Java Applets, ActionScript, JavaScript, and HTML. More details are given in Cañas (1999-2006).

4.   EVALUATION

After the end of the second semester of academic year 2003-2004, students made an evaluation of the system by means of a survey which enquired them regarding the interest in each one of the services that were provided (Cañas, 1999-2006). The most valued services were the file downloading, the consultation of grades and the self-assessment exams. The least valued were those that affected the privacy of the users.

The real frequency of visits to each service has been recently analyzed (see Fig. 12-3). Apart from the authentication and navigation through tabs and menus (not shown), the more accessed services are, in descending order, messages between users, document downloading, forums, grades consultation, theory and practice programs, and work submission.

The platform is widely used now at the University of Granada. There are currently 56,715 undergraduate students at the university and the platform has now 28,482 users (623 of them are teachers). This represents about 50% and allows to address more specific usage analysis which is being done in

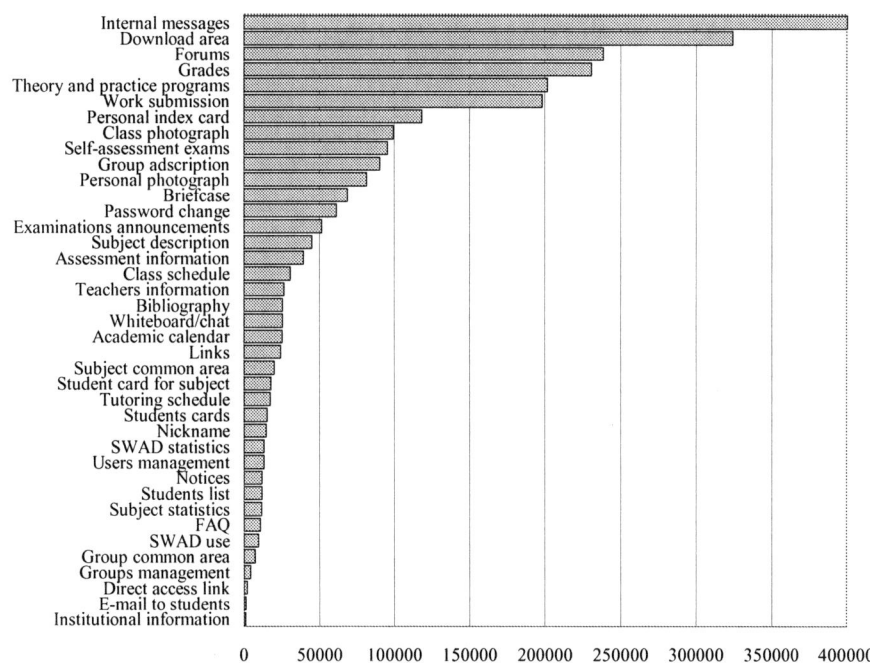

Figure 12-3. Number of visits to each service in academic year 2005-2006.

different subjects. The large number of users from very different careers makes the platform a very valid tool to address pedagogic studies. Since everything is installed on a single server, the extraction of statistics across different careers is easy. Quantitatively measuring the "learning capabilities improvement" due to the use of the platform is difficult. Only indirect performance indications can be extracted from the analysis of the tool usage. Lecturers seem to find SWAD as a valid tool as it is indicated by the increase number of subjects in which the platform is used. Note that professors are not even recommended to use the platform (the institution does not bias their interest in such a tool). Therefore, the increase of subjects that become supported is a result of its capability of facilitating material exchange, evaluation, learning, monitoring, etc. More concretely, in 2005-2006 16,467 documents were made available to the students through the SWAD. Besides, 14,342 documents were made available by the students to their teachers.

In Fig. 12-4 we show the evolution in the platform usage from January of 2005 until November 2006. We can see the dramatic increase in the activity from last year. Holiday periods can be clearly seen as intervals of low activity (summer and winter holidays, as well as the holly week).

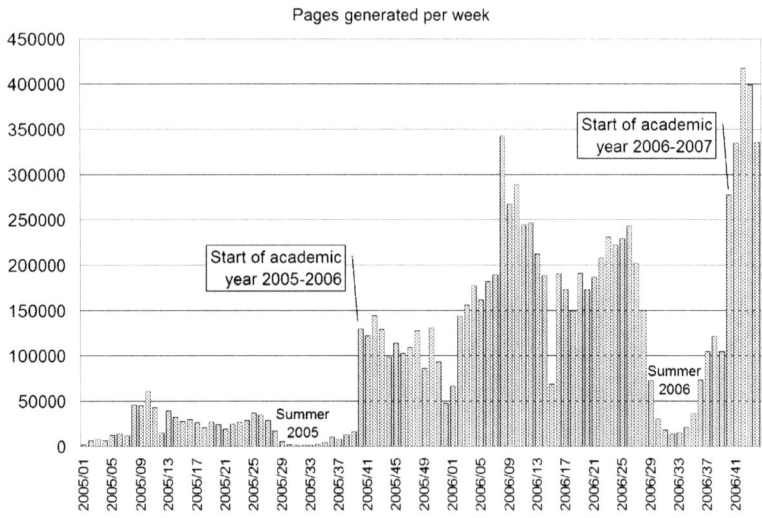

Figure 12-4. Visits from January 2005 till November 2006.

Fig. 12-5 represents the visit ratios along a day. The statistics have been extracted averaging the data collected from January of 2005 until November 2006. It is very interesting to see that both teachers and students actively work within the platform even very late at night. This is a good example that illustrates that the tool can be accessed "every time and everywhere". Furthermore, this kind of graphs can be used to model student behaviors such as the high activity at very late hours in the night, which are not very productive and can be monitored by the professor. For instance a high level of night activity close to an exam or a deadline.

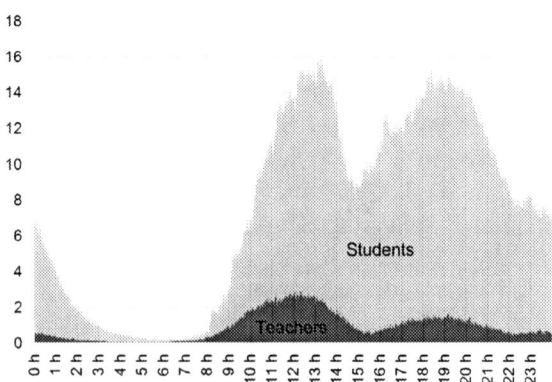

Figure 12-5. Activity of students vs. teachers during a standard day. The representation has been extracted using the average activity (pages generated per minute) during 2005 and 2006.

Currently we are addressing specific studies to evaluate the impact of the platform on the learning enhancement. Concretely, we have compared the marks (grades) obtained by the students on two specific subjects in a test exam before and after the tool allowed the students to check out their subject knowledge through "on-line tests". The improvement obtained was approximately 21%. This has been estimated comparing the marks of six years (24 tests) in which online tests where not available (average qualification of 4.54 ± 0.55 in the interval [0-10]) with the marks obtained in the last four years (16 tests) making available the tests tool to be done online (obtaining an average mark of 5.49 ± 1.08).

5.   CONCLUSIONS AND FUTURE WORK

The educative change necessary in Europe to adapt to European Higher Education Area (EHEA), which focuses more in learning than in education, forces the teachers to modify their educational function, ceasing to be mere transmitters of knowledge and becoming tutors of their students. In the same way, the role of the students changes from passive subjects to an active part in their learning process. With this philosophy, the platform SWAD has been created as an innovative educational resource. It is a website where the students have not only access to download information, but rather they become an active part of the own system, because the platform offers them the possibility of participating actively with all the users (their teacher and the rest of implied teachers, their classmates and other students of their same or different university degree) through different services integrated in the platform.

The tool counts on a very good acceptance from students and teachers. Students frequently use most of the offered services and hardly need instructions of use. As regards teachers, we can emphasize that the use in the web pages of their subjects of sections such as links, FAQ, student's self-assessment, grades consultation or discussion forums, represents an appealing idea contemplated in some occasion by almost all but not often developed. The fact that these services are included in a shared platform encourages teachers to use it. With the incorporation of SWAD, the image of a course improves, in spite of not requiring too much effort on the part of the teacher.

In the short and mid term, our objectives are: to extend the functionality of the platform —adding new services and improving the present ones—, to adapt the platform to LMS standards, and to develop a free, installable version for other educational universities or institutions.

REFERENCES

Andriessen, J., and Sandberg, J., 1999, Where is Education Heading and How About AI? International Journal of Artificial Intelligence in Education (IJAIED).**10**,130–150.

Bernier, J. L., Barchéin, M., Cañas, A., Gómez-Valenzuela, C., and Merelo, J. J., 2002, The services a university website should offer, *Information Society and Education: Monitoring a Revolution. Education Society Series* **9** (3), 1746–1750.

Blackboard Inc., 1997-2006, Blackboard Academic Suite™, http://www.blackboard.com/products/as/

Brusilovsky, P., 2001, ELM-ART: An Adaptive Versatile System for Web-based Instruction, International Journal of Artificial Intelligence in Education. **12**, 351–384.

Cane, J. W., 2004, Measuring Performance of Web Applications: Empirical Techniques and Results, Southeast Con. IEEE Proceedings, ISBN 0-7803-8368-0, 261–270.

Cane, J. W., and Leitner, L., 2005, A virtual network laboratory for instruction and research, Southeast Con. IEEE Proceedings, ISBN 0-7803-8865-8, 651–655.

Cañas, A., Díaz, A. F., Rodríguez, M., Bernier, J. L., and Prieto, A., 2002, Development and Evaluation of a Web-based Tool to Support University Education and Administration, Information Society and Education: Monitoring a Revolution. Education Society Series **9** (1), 473–477.

Cañas, A.,1999-2006, SWAD platform, http://swad.ugr.es/, http://www.swad.es/

Claroline, 2006, Claroline.net Open Source E-Learning, http://www.claroline.net/

Cumming, G., and McDougall, A., 2000, Mainstreaming AIED into Education?, International Journal of Artificial Intelligence in Education (IJAIED). **11**, 197–207.

dokeos, 2006, dokeos Open Source E-Learning, http://www.dokeos.com/

Dougiamas, M., 2006, Moodle: A Free, Open Source Course Management System for Online Learning, http://moodle.org/

EduTools, 2006, Course Management Systems, http://www.edutools.info/

Erdelsky, P. J., 2002, Rijndael Encryption Algorithm, http://www.efgh.com/software/rijndael.htm

García-Beltrán, A., and Martínez, R., 2004, Spread of an e-Learning System in a Polytechnical University, Proceedings of the IADIS International Conference e-Society, 895–898, http://www.dii.etsii.upm.es/aulaweb/

IBM Lotus, 2002-2006, IBM Lotus Learning Management System, http://www.ibm.com/software/sw-lotus/lotus/offering6.nsf/wdocs/homepage

ILIAS, 2006, ILIAS open source, University of Cologne, http://www.ilias.de/

Li, S. F., Spiteri, M., Bates, J., and Hopper, A., 2000, Capturing and indexing computer-based activities with virtual network computing, Proceedings of the 2000 ACM symposium on Applied computing, ISBN 1-58113-240-9, 601–603.

Murray, T. Authoring Intelligent Tutoring Systems: An analysis of the state of the art, International Journal of Artificial Intelligence in Education. **10**, 98–129 (1999).

Rijmen, V., 2004, The Rijndael Page, http://www.esat.kuleuven.ac.be/~rijmen/rijndael/

Rodrigo, A. E., Cañas, A., Masegosa, A. R., Álvarez, J., and Calandria, D. J., 2005, Detección de rostros y mejora de la calidad de imagen en fotografías de tipo carné enviadas a una plataforma web. SICO2005 (IEEE Computational Intelligence Society, SC), Thomson, ISBN 84-9732-444-7, 387–394.

Schneider, T., 2004, ECMS.-.Educational Contest Management System for Selecting Elite Students, Electronic Journal of e-Learning, **2** (2), ISSN 1479-4403, 257–262.

SIGOSSEE/JOIN, 2005, Catalogue of Open Source Learning Management Systems, http://www.ossite.org/join/en/lms/catalog.htm

WebCT, 2001-2006, WebCT.com, http://www.webct.com/

Chapter 13

TOWARDS THE EVERYDAY COMPUTING IN THE CLASSROOM THROUGH RFID

J. Bravo, R. Hervás, S. Nava, G. Chavira, J. Parras, M. Luz Delgado,
A. Vazquez, F. Terán, I. Sánchez, U. Viñuela, & J. Sanz
Castilla-La Mancha University – Spain

Jose.Bravo@uclm.es

Abstract: Many educational scenarios are based on the learning process itself using computers as a tool to aid teachers and students. However new forms of interaction arise making possible to solve daily activities in the classroom. In this work we present a tool to support a cooperative work scenario through the identification process by Radio Frequency Identification technology (RFID). With this technology, the environment identifies users and reacts properly showing information through that we called "Mosaic of Visualization". This process requires only the natural interaction embedded in the users' activities.

Key words: Ubiquitous Computing, Ambient Intelligence, RFID, Context-Awareness.

1.   INTRODUCTION

Ambient Intelligence (AmI) is a vision from the ISTAG in the six Framework Program of the European Community (ISTAG 2001). In it a detailed document expresses the guidelines in all areas of society in terms of intelligent environments and how to serve the users. This vision promotes the learning paradigm based on the active learning approach (to learn by doing) with all the senses (eyes, ears, hand, etc.), with all methods (at school, on the network) and access to knowledge anywhere and anytime. So, it is obvious that the learning process becomes more flexible in an ubiquitous learning environment.

B. Fernández-Manjón et al. (eds.), Computers and Education: E-learning, From Theory to Practice, 143–153.

However, for this vision to become a reality it is necessary to handle the context-aware information. There are some definitions of context: "*Context is any information that can be used to characterize the situation of an entity. An entity is a person, place, or object that is considered relevant to the interaction between a user and an application, including the user and application themselves*" (Dey 2001). This author defines a context awareness system as "*a context to provide relevant information and/or services to the user, where relevancy depends on the user's task*". In order to use context effectively, designers need to identify certain types of context-aware information as being more relevant than others (Brooks 2003). The user profile and situation are essential.

Once the context and their important features are defined, it is time to study new interaction forms proposing the approach to the user by means of more natural interfaces. At this point Albrecht Schmidt proposes a definition of Implicit Human Interaction (iHCI): "*iHCI is the interaction of a human with the environment and with artifacts, which is aimed at accomplishing a goal. Within this process the system acquires implicit input from the user and may present implicit output to the user*" (Scmidt, 2000, 2005). Schmidt also defines implicit input as user perceptions interacting with the physical environment. At this moment, the system can anticipate the user, offering services with explicit output. In addition this author defines embedded interaction in two terms. The first one embeds technologies into artifacts, devices and environments. The second one, on a conceptual level, is the embedding of interactions in user activities (tasks or actions) (Schmidh 2005b). These concepts allow users to concentrate on the task and not on the tool, according to the principles of the Ubiquitous Computing paradigm. If our main goal is to achieve a natural interaction as the implicit interaction concept proposes, we should complement system inputs with sensorial capability.

In this work we focus on the search of context awareness situations, allowing users to obtain system outputs through implicit and natural interactions. We try to solve daily activities in the classroom particularly in a cooperative work activity. In it, students in groups transmit information to each other in a simple and natural way by an intelligent meeting scenario. For that we apply the Radio Frequency Identification technology (RFID). With this it is possible to identify users wearing little devices called tags, offering visualization services without any explicit interaction. The system reacts properly showing the presentation according to the summary made by every student.

Under the next heading a proposal with new challenges, a scenario and the "who model" is presented. In section three a proposal for context-awareness by identification architecture in the classroom is studied. The next point a cooperative work real experience with the format of the information and visualization mosaics is presented. Finally, conclusions are set out.

2.   NEW CHALLENGES

New forms of interaction are important to solve daily activities in the classroom. As researchers mentioned before argue about implicit or embedded interaction it is possible to talk about disappearing interaction. In this sense it is a complement to the disappearing computers initiative.

As we have mentioned before, in order to improve the user-interaction, we have adapted the RFID technology by embedding it in different objects such as credit cards, watches, key rings, etc. The simple action of walking near an antenna allows the system to read and write information contained in the tags. We have focused the context aspects mentioned before on the identification process (Bravo et al, 2005a, 2005b, 2006a, 2006b). We are therefore placing these concepts strategically in order to obtain services for the user as is shown in figure 1. We aim to make the interaction transparent, non-intrusive and included it in everyday activities for the user. Thus, a user wearing tags and walking through a building can interact with the environment without any explicit interaction. The user can also obtain typical identification services such as location, access, presence, inventory, phone call routing, etc. All of these are obtained with a combination of "who", "where" and "when" concepts of context. We have called it the "who model". Through this it is possible to handle non-intrusive services without any interaction.

With this model we try to solve the matching between these kinds of inputs and outputs. Both of them in a non-intrusive way allow the user to concentrate on the task, not on the tool.

To understand ambient intelligent environments it is important to illustrate different context scenarios and processes which are going to occur. Next we describe a cooperative scenario to discuss the effort made by the members of a group of students.

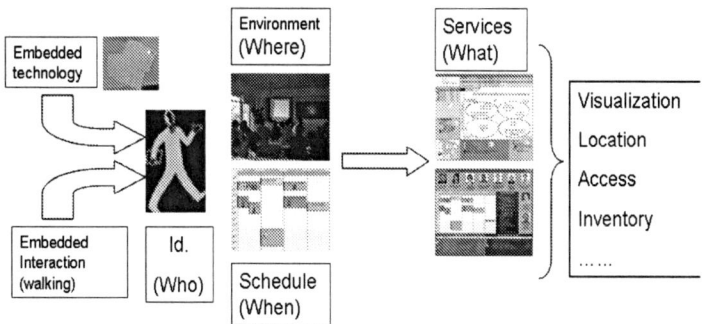

Figure 1. The "who" model

2.1   A scenario

Ruth is preparing the Geology cooperative work at home. For that she uses a single tool in order to prepare a summary that will be presented to other members of her group. With this tool Ruth formats the information according to the advice that the teacher gave her some days ago. She introduces, in a structured manner, with main and secondary texts what she will present to her colleagues, connecting contents to graphics and pictures trying to make her presentation comprehensible. When Ruth has finished she passes her tag near a device (reader) placed next to the computer to store this summary in it. To do this she uses a contact RFID set. Once in the group meeting, Cristina approaches the board and automatically her summary appears on it as in a mosaic format. Also, a plan for this session can be seen. It is surprising to her that only by passing near an antenna it is possible to identify her and start her presentation in a good form of visualization. All the students enclose these summaries using the same method trying to explain their piece of the group work.

3.   THE ARCHITECTURE

3.1   RFID Technology

We have adapted RFID technology with the purpose of identifying people. In this technology three kinds of objects are clearly differentiated: the reader (reader or transceiver) connected to the computer, the antenna and the label (tag or transponder). The last one is a small device containing a transponder circuit that takes, in the case of the passive tags, the wave energy that the reader continually emits and reads and writes the information that these may include. Figure 2 shows two RFID sets. The one on the top right presents a reader and an antenna with a read-and-write capability reach of over 75 cm. This has been specially designed for its location on room doors, or near boards. The one on the top left is a contact reader including an antenna with a reach of only 10 cm. A model of the tag is also shown. This identification system is ideal for individual use.

We are trying another kind of RFID set, offering more distance between reader and tags (2 or 3 meters) see Figure 2 bottom. Entry to and exit from each environment will also be controlled. This system is called HFKE (Hands Free Keyless Entry) and has a semi-passive tag using a battery along with 32 Kbytes of EPROM memory for the user's data. The reader

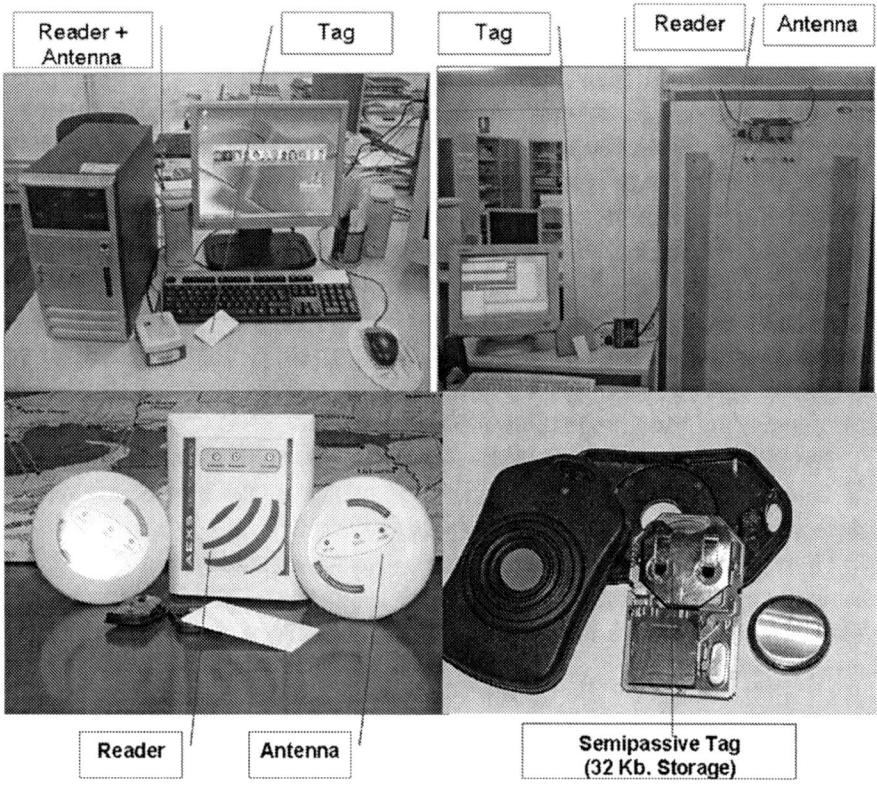

Figure 2. RFID devices

(HFRDR) transmits waves of low frequency, 125 Khz, continuously. When a tag detects this wave it activates the microcontroller sending the required information in UHF frequency. The communication between reader and computer is by Bluetooth.

3.2 The Classroom

The classroom is equipped with readers, a computer and antennas. These antennas are placed on the door and next to the board. In the classroom, teachers and students wearing tags mean they can be identified and located, thus allowing them access to the system and to services, all in an implicit way.

When teachers and students enter the classroom the location (attendance) and access control services are automatically activated. These are typical services that RFID technology offers. In addition to this, the visualization service comes up on the board. It is a mosaic of information which varies according to the context (classroom) and time (schedule). This mosaic is different for each attendance profile. In the time between classes the information is about news and announcements to students. In the actual class-time, the mosaic is transformed and presents information prepared by the teacher for the session see Figure 3.

The second activity in the classroom is to get information onto the board by means of proximity of a person to its surface. When the teacher approaches the board, his lesson presentation, the problems proposed, solutions, documentation, etc. are shown. In order to control the order of these activities, the teacher has a plan for each class. If the student is the one approaching the board, the answer he has given to the problem posed previously can be displayed. On the other hand, some presentation, or any other kind of information may be shown,

The third activity consists of the storage of information on the content of the lesson or lecture in tags. Teachers and students have this information when they go through the door as they leave the classroom.

These activities are completed by work at home. Teachers and students, helped by a contact reader, are able to read the information included in tags and/or rewrite more for the next class. All transactions are managed by the classroom server.

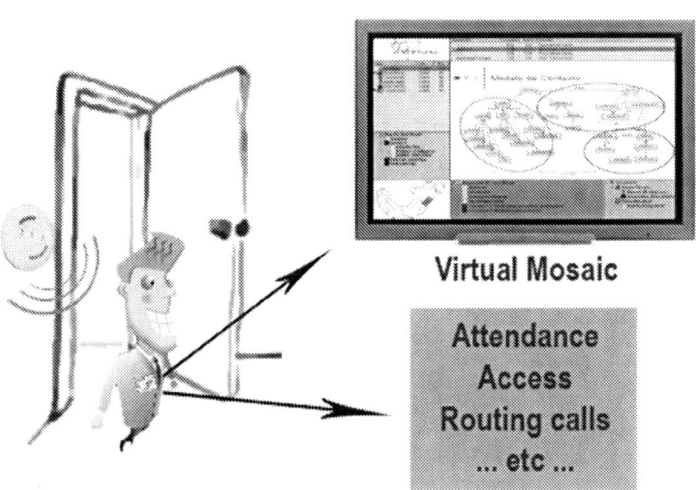

Figure 3. Identification at Classroom

4.   A COOPERATIVE WORK EXPERIENCE

This experience is based on the new paradigm mentioned before. On the one hand keep in mind the disappearing computers initiative and, on the other hand, with the new forms of interaction that some researchers propose. With these perspectives we have experimented with two different groups of students that have to do a cooperative work. The first ones uses the computer tool to prepare the presentations and, the second ones, with the traditional cooperative way without computers but evaluating this experience as external evaluators.

In figure 4 the evaluation process can be seen. The first one, on the left, the student actually present passes near an antenna and his presentation appears automatically on the board. The picture in the middle shows the audience for this evaluation process. Finally, the third picture on the right shows the presentation itself with the mosaic that the system generates automatically starting from the student's summary arranged before the session.

It is obvious that some kind of additional interaction is expected. For that we have placed a number of sensors below the display with different functionalities (next slide, previous slide, finish, etc.). By only passing a hand near each sensor the user can obtain answers from the system. The interaction required for each hand movement is a combination of identification and sensors. So, control of different information for each student and the functionality of each sensor can be adapted to them according to their needs in every mosaic.

Figure 4. A cooperative work experience

4.1   Formatting the Information

The subject for this experience has been Geology. The requirement for the initial information is simple. We have built a tool for students with the purpose of doing the summaries. With this tool, see figure 5 left, the students can introduce main and secondary texts. They can also attach pictures and graphics. In addition, the control of slides is considered.

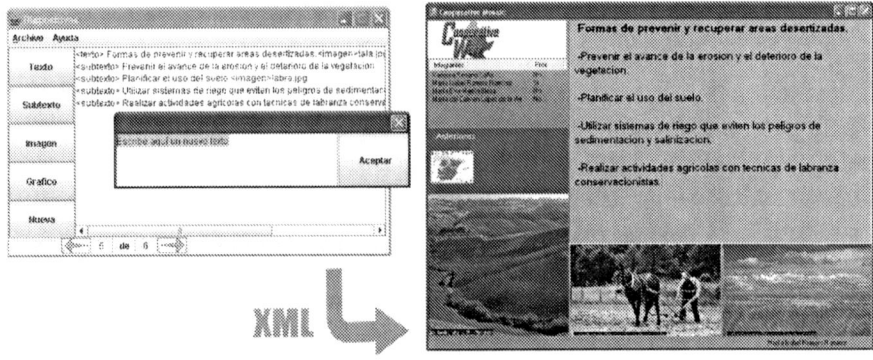

Figure 5. Formatting students' information

When the student has finished the summary, this tool converts it to an XML-based language. Then, the system generates the mosaic for every student's summary automatically. See Figure 5 on the right. Every main or secondary text can be shown with a picture or graphics attached.

4.2   The Visualization Mosaics

The presentation of information is important without needing the user's request. This presentation and the independence of the display device are important factors to be considered. We are trying to regard every visualization component as a puzzle piece. For that, the visualization service is structured as a mosaic of information. For the representation of each mosaic, we have applied a XML-based language. In it, the pieces of the mosaic, the size and the kind of each element are considered. In Figure 6 the XML representation of a mosaic is shown.

Every mosaic is generated automatically from the students' summaries. Some aspects such as size, situation, distribution, etc are contemplated. All of these concepts have been grouped in the corresponding ontology. It is important to keep in mind that to every main and secondary text some pictures and graphics can be attaches, so the concept of slide is significant. The distribution of the space and the link between texts and figures has to be optimized.

The visualization service involves three modules which are clearly differentiated: The Analysis Context Module, responsible for the changes of the context and the managing of a Data Base. The Mosaic Generation Module which obtains data that will be presented in the selected mosaic. Finally, the Mosaic-Composer Module that executes the mosaic and generates the user interface automatically.

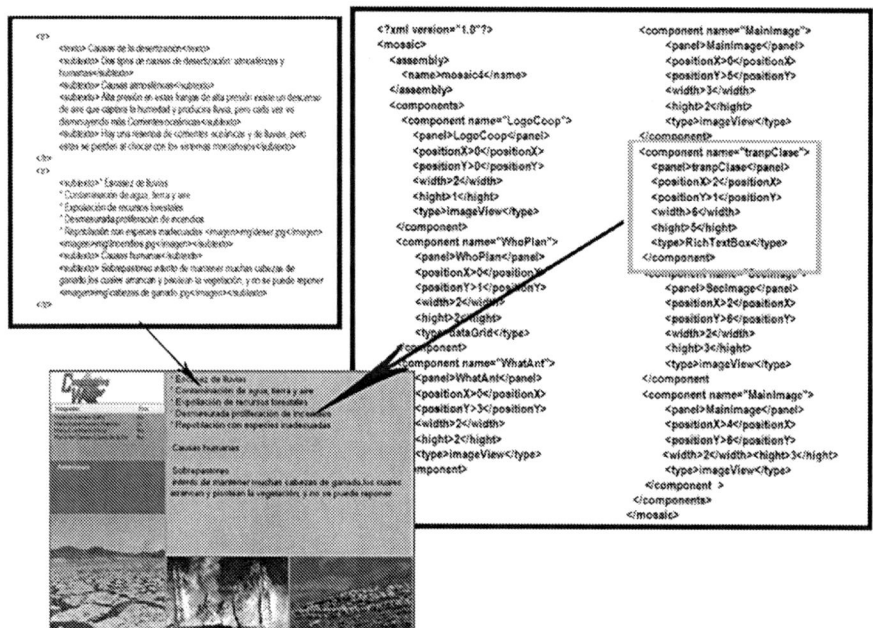

Figure 6. Mosaic XML Structure

4.3   The evaluation

In order to make this experience more real, the students, at the beginning, only know the tool to format the information. Later, in the meeting room, everyone understands the effect of the mosaic and the functionality of sensors below the board. We think this impact is important and this gave us a clearer idea about the acceptance of the new computational situation.

We have evaluated this experience with the students of the School of Education at the University. In it, two groups of students are clearly differentiated. The first one, at the top of Table 1, corresponds to the groups taking part actively in the experience. The second one, at the bottom of the table, is the data from students that have carried out the usually experience of collaborative work of this school.

In this evaluation different features have been clearly contemplated. In a general aspect of the experience, that is, the interest in the experience and the global evaluation, have a good result (33% excellent, 71% and 66% good, 28% average). In the interaction aspects, the results are good by proximity (85% and 66% excellent, 14% and 33% good) and average and by sensors (28% and 44% good, 43% and 44% average, 28% and 11% fair). It is obvious that the last aspect should be improved.

Table 1. Cooperative Experience Evaluation

Aspect	Excellent	Good	Average	Fair	Poor
Interest in the experience		71%	28%		
Interaction by proximity	85%	14%			
Interacting with sensors		28%	43%	28%	
Appropriateness of the mosaic	28%	56%	14%		
Global evaluation of the experience	42%	56%			

Aspect	Excellent	Good	Average	Fair	Poor
Interest in the experience	33%	66%			
Interaction by proximity	66%	33%			
Interacting with sensors		44%	44%	11%	
Appropriateness of the mosaic	33%	55%			
Global evaluation of the experience	44%	44%			

Globally the experience was satisfactory and it encourages us to continue with our investigations in this field.

5.   CONCLUSIONS

We have put into practice the ideas of the Ambient Intelligence vision trying to create an environment in which computers and interactions disappear. With this vision it is possible for users to concentrate on the task not on the tool.

This real experience has been possible to connect implicit inputs and outputs trough RFID technology and visualization mosaics. In this sense we need to move towards real intelligent environments that serve users without any extra interaction, just carrying out daily activities.

REFERENCES

ISTAG, Scenarios for Ambient Intelligence in 2010. Feb. 2001. http://www.cordis.lu/ist/istag.htm.

Dey, A. (2001). "Understanding and Using Context". Personal and Ubiquitous Computing 5(1), 2001, pp. 4-7.

Brooks, K. (2003). "The Context Quintet: narrative elements applied to Context Awareness". In Human Computer Interaction International Proceedings. Crete (Greece) by Erlbaum Associates, Inc.

Schmidt, A. (2000). "Implicit Human Computer Interaction Through Context". Personal Technologies Volume 4(2&3) 191-199

Schmidt, A. (2005). "Interactive Context-Aware Systems. Intering with Ambient Intelligence". In Ambient Intelligence. G. Riva, F. Vatalaro, F. Davide & M. Alcañiz (Eds.).16 José Bravo, Ramón Hervás, Inocente Sánchez, Agustin Crespo. "Servicios por identificación en el aula ubicua". In Avances en Informática Educativa. Juan Manuel Sánchez et al. (Eds.). Servicio de Publicaciones – Universidad de Extremadura. ISBN84-7723-654-2.

Schmidt, A., M. Kranz, and P. Holleis. Interacting with the Ubiquitous Computing – Towards Embedding Interaction. in Smart Objects & Ambient Intelligence (sOc-EuSAI 2005). 2005. Grenoble, Francia.

Bravo, J., Hervás R., Nava, S & Chavira, G. "Ubiquitous Computing at classroom: An Approach through identification process". Special Issue on Computer and Educations. Journal of Universal Computer Science. Vol. 11_9. September 2005. p.1494-1504.

Bravo, J., Hervás, R., Chavira, G., Nava, S. & Sanz, J. (2005). "Display-based services through identification: An approach in a conference context". Ubiquitous Computing & Ambient Intelligence (UCAmI'05). Thomson. ISBN:84-9732-442-0. pp.3-10.

Bravo, J., Hervás, R., Chavira, G. & Nava, S. "Modeling Contexts by RFID-Sensor Fusion". Workshop on Context Modeling and Reasoning (CoMoRea 2006), PerCom 2006. Pisa (Italy)

Bravo, J., Hervás, R., Delgado, M.L., Parras, J., Teran, F., Chavira, G., Nava, S.(2006) "Enabling and Ambient Intelligence Educational Scenario by Identification Process". Mobile Learning Conference. Dublin (Ireland)

Chapter 14

USING JAVA AND C# FOR EDUCATIONAL SIMULATORS: THE CASE OF SIMPLE-2

Ramón-Ángel Fernández, Luis Panizo and Lidia Sánchez
Department of Electrical Engineeering and Electronics. University of Leon
Campus de Vegazana s/n, 24071-León (Spain)

Abstract: Due to the impact of the new technologies in our Society, special efforts to use them for teaching-learning computer architectures have been done. This work presents a simulator of a simple architecture (Simple-2) using two different technologies: Java and C#. In the one hand, the Java version is an applet which runs inside a web browser; in the other hand, the C# version runs as an application that needs a virtual machine be installed in the system. The impact of both technologies on first year Computer Science students has been analyzed, as well as the degree of learning achieved when using the simulator for learning an architecture in a semi-autonomous way.

Key words: computer architecture simulation; educational simulator.

1.   INTRODUCTION

One of the core fields of Computer Science education at the University consists on learning those concepts related to computer structure and organization, as well as the interactions among computer components in order to run sequences of instructions. The result of this learning is a key matter in order students can successfully progress with their studies.

To complete this learning, a first stage may be considered to let the student acquire a global vision of computers, recognizing their functional units and the operation of every single unit. After that, the student has to assimilate the different ways in which those functional units interact. During this stage, ability to relate concepts and integrate them into a higher abstraction level is required, which involves a considerable difficulty, especially for first year students.

B. Fernández-Manjón et al. (eds.), Computers and Education: E-learning, From Theory to Practice, 155–162.

To help the students during this second stage, the concepts explained in the lectures should be reinforced. Solving exercises and doing practices in the laboratory usually are not enough, and other additional tools to stimulate the students to learn should be used. Several software solutions have been developed that allow the students to interact in order to simulate computer behavior and to observe program execution events[1]. There is also software that graphically represents the activity of every component of a computer and the way those components interact[2,3]. Students, in general, and Computer Science students, in particular, find quite attractive the possibility of working and learning through the Internet. That is one reason to explain the efforts in developing network learning tools and checking their efficiency in the learning process.

In the department of Electrical Engineering and Electronics at the University of Leon, a simulator of a simple processor (Simple-2[4]) has been developed so as to be used by the students through a web server. There are two available versions: a Java applet, which runs in a web browser; and a C# application that must be downloaded and runs locally in the student's computer. Anyway, both versions have the same interface and provide the same functionality. After using the software, its influence on the learning has been analyzed on the basis of the results of written tests fulfilled by the students.

2.   JUSTIFICATION OF THE WORK AND OBJECTIVES

Computer Organization and Technology is one subject that students learn during their first year of the degree in Computer Science at the University of Leon (Spain). This subject involves two main blocks: the basics of *Analogical and Digital Electronics*, and, based on those fundamentals, *Computer Organization*.

The block related to Computer Organization begins with the description of the main functional units present in Von Neumann architecture based computers: Central Processing Unit, Memory Unit and Input/Output Unit. Next, the operation of the datapath is analyzed for a subset of one RISC processor, the MIPS, as described by Patterson[5]. The lectures are complemented with animated slide presentations that can be downloaded from the departmental website. Those presentations show the paths the data follow as well as how the control unit manages those paths. In the last part of the course, the concept of memory system is presented, including the possibility of using hierarchies to improve the performance. Finally, basic input/output techniques are studied.

In the laboratory, students learn to develop software using the MIPS assembly language and the *xspim* emulator under the Linux operating system. This software helps the student to assimilate the utility of the banks of registers, to understand how the information is stored in the memory system, and to test several input/output techniques. Anyway, *xspim* does not include any utility for datapath visualization, nor shows the operation of the control unit during program execution. Hence, students cannot check in the laboratory some of those concepts explained in the lectures and required for solving exercises. Therefore, we have decided to develop an additional simulator to provide the students a graphical tool to observe the operation of the computer components altogether.

With the objective of evaluating the impact of the use of a simulator in the learning process, we have decided to use an architecture different to the one described in the lectures. Then, the influence of the lecturer on the first approach to the architecture is bypassed, although students may talk to the professor and make questions (in the office, by e-mail, instant messages or Internet forums). The chosen architecture is the pedagogical computer Simple-2[4], that is used for teaching Computer Organization and Structure II at the *Escuela Universitaria de Informática* at the *Universidad Nacional de Educación a Distancia* (UNED, Spain).

Then, the students have to learn the Simple-2 architecture by themselves, just from a paper with an explanation and with the help of the simulators they can access through the Internet. In order to increase the motivation of the students, an extra bonus over their final qualifications is offered by means of a test about that architecture.

3.   SIMPLE-2 SIMULATOR

As mentioned above, two identical versions of the Simple-2 architecture simulator have been developed[1] using platform independent technologies. The first version is a Java applet, which runs in any Internet browser. The other one is an application developed using C#. The use of this second version needs the user install a C# virtual machine as *mono* (http://www.mono-project.com).

---

[1] The two versions of the simulator have been developed as Final Projects by Jesús A. Fernández and Montserrat Sotomayor, students of Computer Science at the University of Leon.

3.1   User Interface

The graphical user interface has three different panels: one to edit the source code, one to visualize the machine status, and another one to visualize the datapath activity.

The panel for the source code (figure 14-1) lets the user write assembly code and also has a tool for detecting and displaying errors. Once the source code has no errors, the machine code is displayed for every instruction. This panel has three main objectives: students learn to write assembly code correctly, they check whether they are able to translate source code to machine code, and they also test their skills in using the hexadecimal representation for binary information.

The panel that displays the machine status (figure 14-2) shows the values of every register and also the values of the main memory cells during a program execution. This module helps the students analyze the evolution of the machine status as long as a program is executed.

The third panel (figure 14-3) graphically displays the activity in the datapath while the instructions are executed. This module provides a view of the functional units, the mechanisms they use to interact and the paths followed by the data to carry out the execution of each instruction. One Simple-2 instruction consists in a sequence of micro-instructions that need one clock cycle to finish. As one instruction is composed of a set of micro-operations, Simple-2 architecture divides each cycle into 4 sub-cycles. At every moment, the simulator shows the micro-instruction that is running and the values of its fields. In addition, those functional units that are involved in the current micro-operation are highlighted in the datapath.

To make easier the analysis of both, the machine status and the flow of data through the datapath, both versions of the simulator allow pausing and resuming the execution.

4.   EXPERIMENTS

The experiments have been designed in order to analyze the influence of the simulator over a population of 190 students of Computer Organization and Technology at the University of Leon.

The questions used to evaluate the learning have the following objectives:

1. Finding out the version of the simulator used by the student: the Java applet or the C# application.

2. Evaluating the student skills in writing assembly code for the Simple-2 architecture.
3. Evaluating the student skills in identifying the computer functional units.
4. Evaluating the ability of the student for relating the functional units working altogether to the execution of instructions.

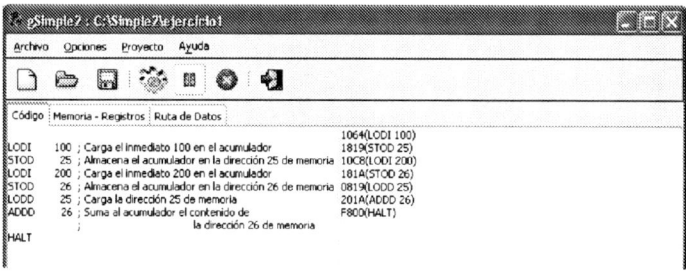

Figure 14-1. Graphical User Interface: Panel for Simple-2 assembly code edition and machine code visualization.

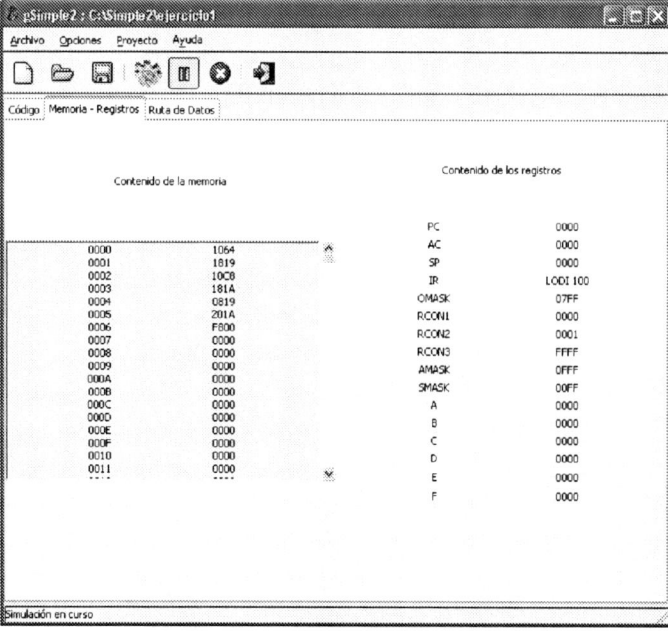

Figure 14-2. Graphical User Interface: Values of memory and registers during execution.

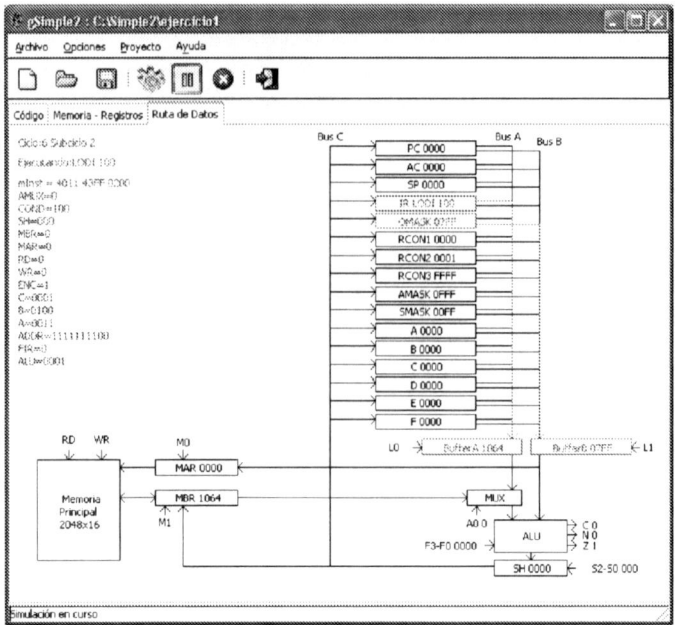

Figure 14-3. Graphical User Interface: Datapath status during program execution. At every moment, the involved microinstruction is displayed. In each sub-cycle, the functional units that execute the current micro-operation are highlighted.

5.   RESULTS AND CONCLUSIONS

The results of the experiments are shown in table 14-1. They show that most of the students (85.8%) preferred using the Java applet, much easier to access and that does not require any additional effort to be run. Anyway, although only a few students chose the C# application (14.2%), all of them passed the tests. As both versions are identical, the main reason for this variation in the success rates may only reside in the initial auto-motivation of the students. At the beginning of the experience, those who chose the C# application knew that they should do an extra work in order to install a virtual machine that was not included in any operating system. Therefore, as they were interested in learning how to install *mono* and how to run a C# application, we can assume that they were also more motivated to learn the details of the architecture than most of the rest of their partners.

Table 14-1. Results of the experiments with students of first year in Computer Science. The qualifications belong to [0,100]

| | SOFTWARE VERSION | | | |
| | Java Applet | | C# Application | |
Results of the evaluation	Students	%	Students	%
Programming skills				
≥75	15	7.9	14	7.4
[50,75)	92	48.4	13	6.8
<50	56	29.5	0	0.0
Sum	163	85.8	27	14.2
Functional units identification				
Correct	134	70.5	27	14.2
Incorrect	29	15.3	0	0.0
Sum	163	85.8	27	14.2
Ability for relating functional units work to instruction execution				
≥75	21	11.1	25	13.2
[50,75)	102	53.7	2	1.0
<50	40	21.0	0	0.0
Sum	163	85.8	27	14.2

In former years, the students have also studied the Simple-2 architecture by themselves, but without the help of any additional software, being the success rates of below 50%. From table 14-1, we can see that more than 70% of the students passed the tests (70.5% passed the programming test, 84.7% passed the functional units test, and 79.0% passed the instruction execution one). Hence, we can see that the success rates are quite bigger with the use of the simulators, and we can conclude that they improve the learning of the students with low costs. Furthermore, the analysis of the software version the students choose is useful for finding out the initially most auto-motivated ones and also for paying special attention to the others. Naturally, for the first semesters, simple computer architectures should be used in order the students to be able to identify their components and analyze their functionalities. In addition, the use of simulators increases the interest of those students with lower motivation, although those with higher initial motivation get the best results.

6. FUTURE WORK

Future work pretends to increase the possibilities of the simulator in order to allow the user to define new instructions. The graphical user interface is to be improved and also a language selection option is going to be included.

The experimental future work will try to develop an evaluation system that provide some measure of the rate students' efforts/learning when using software simulators and comparing them to those rates obtained without the simulators.

REFERENCES

Moure, J.C., Rexachs, D.I., and Luque, E., 2002, The Kscalar simulator, *ACM Journal of Educational Resources in Computing (JERIC)*, **2**(1): 73-116.

Campos, A.M., García, D.F., Entrialgo, J., and Díaz, J.L., 2002, Simulador educacional de un computador elemental basado en la arquitectura Von Neumann, *Actas de las XXIII Jornadas de Paralelismo*, Lleida, 95-98.

Brorsson, M., 2002, MipsIt - a simulation and development environment using animation for computer architecture education, *Proceedings of the Workshop on Computer Architecture Education*. Anchorage, Alaska, 65-72.

Dormido, S., Canto, M.A., Mira, J., and Delgado, A.E., 2000, *Estructura y Tecnología de Computadores*, Sanz y Torres, Madrid.

Patterson, D.A., and Hennesy, J.L., 1997, *Computer Organization and Design: The Hardware/Software Interface*, 2nd ed., Morgan-Kaufmann, San Mateo, Ca.

Chapter 15

ITERATIVE DESIGN OF LEARNING PROCESSES

Telmo Zarraonandia, Juan Manuel Dodero, Camino Fernández, Ignacio Aedo y Paloma Díaz
Universidad Carlos III de Madrid, Departamento de Informática, Escuela Politécnica Superior

Abstract: The aim of this work is to bring together the traditional way of teaching and working using a computer-supported environment. This means, increasing the flexibility of the learning processes application, giving instructors the chance to introduce variations on runtime. Besides, learning processes are refined through its use, by making permanent the modifications which have shown to improve the learners' performance on the different learning objectives. This approach is similar to the one followed for the development of user interfaces, where the interface design is obtained by an iterative process of prototyping, testing, analyzing and refining. This chapter describes the lifecycle of the iterative design of learning processes and proposes an architecture for implementing its runtime stages for processes described by means of the IMS Learning Design specification.

Key words: Learning Design, adaptation, runtime, iterative.

1.   INTRODUCTION

When describing an educational process it is not always possible to know all its elements properties at design time. Many of them as, for instance, the ones related to synchronization and temporization of the activities cannot always be established before the proper execution of the learning process begins.

On the other hand, regardless of how careful and precisely a learning process has been defined, its application to actual educational settings is all but rigid, since it is very difficult to foresee all the potential reactions from

B. Fernández-Manjón et al. (eds.), Computers and Education: E-learning, From Theory to Practice, 163–177.
© 2007 *Springer.*

learners. In practice, teachers take the learning process as a starting base, not to be followed blindly. They observe the evolution of the learners during its execution, introduce the appropriate adaptations afterwards in order to solve specific problems, reinforce the learning of some particular concepts and, more generally, guarantee the achievement of the original learning objectives. Furthermore, the adaptations proven to improve the original process results will be part of future applications. Due to the above, the learning process is traditionally refined through its use.

This work aims at increasing the degree of freedom of the teachers when applying a learning process on a computer-supported environment, offering the instructors the possibility to introduce modifications in the learning process definition during its proper execution. Those adaptive actions introduced could be evaluated against their original goal, measuring its influence on the learning objective achievement and, accordingly, giving the teacher a chance to automatically include them in the original process. This way, instructors would imitate the way teachers work in real life: the gain obtained by the use of the process is kept within the process and, at the same time, is also used to refine it.

The rest of the paper is organized as follows. First, the iterative design of learning process lifecycle will be defined, describing the purpose and characteristics of each of its different stages. Next, notations for the specification of the process evaluations and adaptations will be provided. Following, the architecture of a system able to implement the runtime phases of the iterative composition of an IMS Learning Design (IMS Global Learning Consortium, 2003) specified process will be outlined. The paper will conclude with an example of the whole late modeling process and the presentation of some conclusions and future work lines.

2.   ITERATIVE DESIGN OF LEARNING PROCESS

The application of a learning process is in practice quite flexible as it is not possible to foresee all the potential reactions from the learners. Instructors take the learning process as a basis, and after observing the learner reactions, they may response providing extra examples, explanations to reinforce particular concepts, repeating activities, tuning the time-limits for completion of the assessments, etc. However, the more the instructors play the course, the less adaptation are required to be applied as the process is refined through its use. The experience gained from prior plays is comprised within the process definition and a wider range of learner reaction response is captured. This means that the course model definition does not

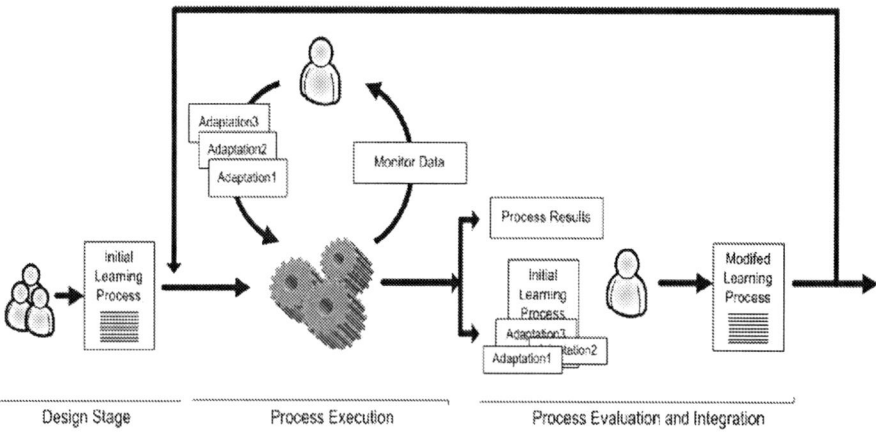

Figure 15-1. Phases of the iterative design of a Unit of Learning

conclude until no more modifications are required to be applied. This approach is similar to the one followed for the development of user interfaces, where the interface design is obtained by an iterative process of prototyping, testing, analyzing and refining (Gould et al., 1991).

Figure 15-1 illustrates the different activities of the iterative design of a learning process carried out on a computer-supported environment. The process starts once an initial model of the course has been defined and its execution begins. Instructors observe learners interactions and introduce the appropriately tagged adaptations. The success of the applied adaptations will be evaluated, and once the process is finished, the learning objective achievement will be measured. Based on that information, a new version of the learning process will be generated, including the successful modifications introduced. This new version will go through the same cycle on its next plays until no more adaptations are required to be applied.

This section provides a description for each of the different activities that compose an iterative design process: monitor the execution, adaptations introduction, adaptations evaluation, process evaluation, and finally, adaptation integration.

2.1 Monitor the execution

In order to detect potential problems and introduce the appropriate adaptive actions, it is fundamental for the instructors to be able to monitor the learner's interactions and progress during the learning process.

The more information instructors can obtain from the process execution, the better they will identify causes of problems during the learning process. For instance, if they can only retrieve information about the learner's score on the different activities, they may only be able to conclude that her/his performance is not being adequate. Otherwise, if they could retrieve information about which resources the learner has visited and how much time she/he has spent on each of them, they may be able to extract more accurate conclusions and produce appropriate recommendations and adaptations.

On the other hand, the comparison of information from the different learning process instances of the different participants facilitates the identification of the nature of the problem.

2.2   Introduction of Adaptations

Based on the information retrieved from the monitoring activities, instructors will describe the process variations required to guarantee the process success.

Jacobson et al (1997) defined variation point as "places in the design or implementation that identify locations at which variation can occur". Variation points can be bound to the system at different stages of the product lifecycle. Svahnberg (2002) presented a taxonomy of variability realization techniques which defined different ways in which a variation point can be implemented. One of these techniques is the code fragment superimposition, where a software solution is developed to solve the generic problem; code fragments are superimposed on top of this software solution to solve specific concerns. This superimposition can be achieved by means of different techniques; as for example the Aspect Oriented Approach (Kiczales et al. 1997), and provides the designer with the possibility to bind the modifications during the compilation phase or even at runtime.

We can take these concepts into the adaptation of learning process area. The authors can describe the desired adaptations on auxiliary specification files that could be processed together with the original Unit of Learning (UoL) (IMS Global Learning Consortium, 2003) and applied at runtime giving the user the feeling that they were included in the original UoL. This way, we can maintain a single UoL definition and a number of descriptions for adaptations. Those files tie together all the changes involved in a particular adaptation and keep that particular concern separated from the main UoL functionality and the rest of adaptations.

An overview of the process is shown in figure 15-2. From several possible adaptations defined for a particular UoL, the designer chooses the one which best fits the current situation and applies it to the UoL. The introduction of the adaptive action can be carried out at design time (adaptation 1) or at runtime (adaptation 2, 3, 4). In the last case, adaptation could be applied to all the running instances of a UoL (adaptation 2), to all the users of a particular running instance (adaptation 3) or only to the personalized view of a particular user (adaptation 4).

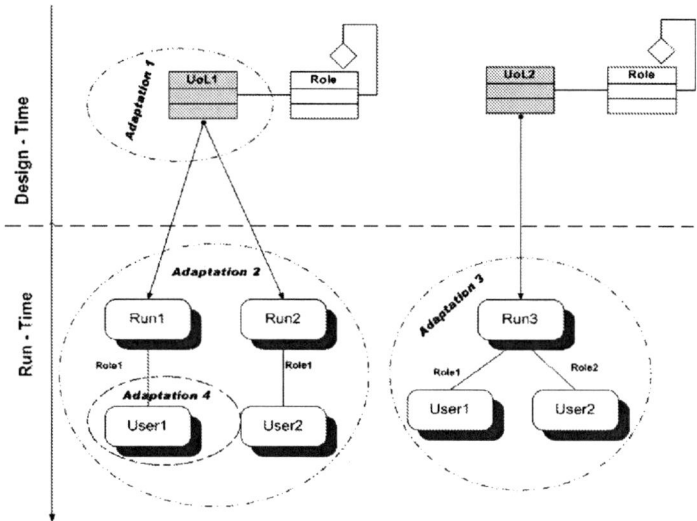

Figure 15-2. Different moments of adaptations introduction on UoL instances

We define *adaptation poke*s the description of a small modification of some elements in a learning process. A notation for the *adaptation pokes* description is provided in section 4.

2.3 Evaluation of Adaptations

To measure the success of the adaptive action it is not only necessary to evaluate the grade of satisfaction of the adaptation objectives but also check possible interactions with other parts of the course and the introduction of collateral effects. Note that the evaluation is not directly based on the learners results but on comparing the expected consequences of the adaptation with the actual ones. Hence, the difficulty lies on the identification of what is a real consequence of the adaptation and what is not. Correlation between adaptations effects must also be considered at this stage.

2.4 Evaluation of the Process

Once the learning process is finished, its results must be evaluated to identify its strengths and weaknesses. This evaluation is mostly based on the information about the performance of the learners for each learning objective obtained once the process is finished. If most of the learners score low for a particular learning objective, designers may consider including complementary material, reviewing the pedagogical approach or reviewing the calibration of the difficulty of the assessment activities. However, causes of low performance may also lay on external circumstances or incorrect learner profiles. It is necessary then, to establish the grade of reliability of the process results by comparing them with other plays of the course data.

2.5   Integration of Adaptations

Once the process results have been analyzed, the integration phase takes place. This way, adaptive actions which have proved to mean an improvement of the process become a permanent part of it. This is a two step process: fist, instructors thoroughly examine all the adaptation results and select the ones to be integrated, and second, the system applies them to the original process design following their introductory order. Each of the adaptation introductions is validated separately. This method facilitates the identification of dependencies with rejected adaptations in case of failure.

3.   LEARNING PROCESS EVALUATIONS SPECIFICATION

In order to evaluate learners' progress and process success it is necessary to explicitly specify what is going to be evaluated and how that evaluation should be performed. This specification can be provided using an XML notation for the purpose of automating its processing by the appropriate engine. Following this approach the authors present an XML schema for the learning process evaluations definition, whose graphical representation is shown in Fig 15-3. The evaluations are the core of the schema, each of them will be composed of a combination of values related to performances on process elements and learning objectives, plus another information data. An evaluation element must be provided for each learning objective. Optionally relations between the learning objectives and the process elements which contribute to their achievement can also be provided.

Three different types of elements may be required to fully specify a learning process evaluation:

- Process components: They represent elements of the learning process that contribute to a learning objects acquisition. Their definition will be composed of an identification, a reference to the corresponding learning process element and an expression to be used to estimate the learner performance for that element. This expression can be either a monitor command, for obtaining a learners' test score, for instance, or an expression where references to other components and information elements are combined to produce a value.

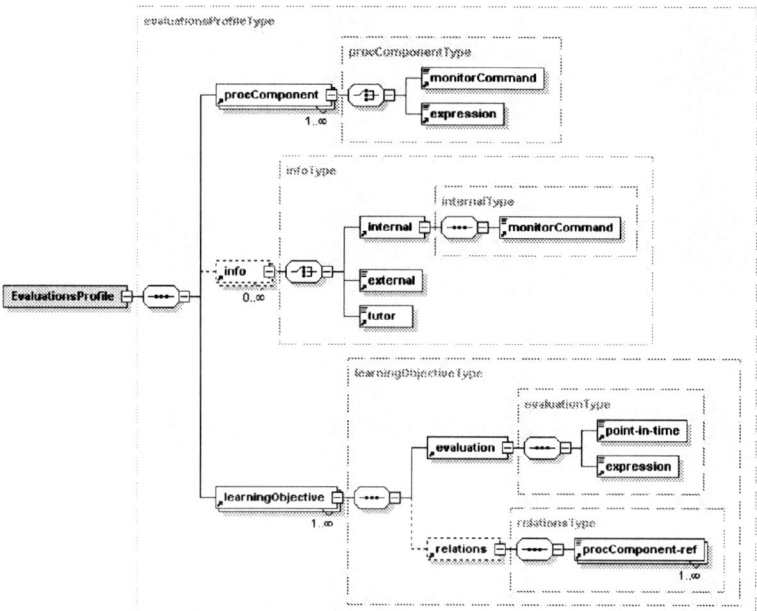

Figure 15-3. Evaluations Schema

- Information elements: Definitions of information not related with learners performance on a particular element but required for the learning objectives evaluations. This information can be obtained by monitoring the learning process, read from an external resource or introduced by the process instructor directly. This way, for instance, the number of learner's messages in the learning process's forums can be used to estimate her/his grade of interaction with other learners; results on previous learning process stored in the learner profile can by used to rate her/his improvement in a particular subject, or the instructor can be inquired regarding her/his opinion about the learner's collaborative skills.
- Learning objectives: Each of the learning objectives will be related with an evaluation and a list of process components that contributes to the learning objective achievement. The evaluation will contain the specification of the moment in time in which it should be performed and an expression which combines references to components, information elements and learning objectives with mathematical and logic operators. Once the time limit specified by the *moment-in-time* element is reached, the system engine will parse the formula, retrieve the actual value for each of the referred elements and produce the evaluation's score.

4.   PROCESS ADAPTATIONS SPECIFICATION

In previous work authors (2006) defined adaptation pokes as descriptions of small modifications of some elements in a learning design process. The set of elements whose modification could be subject of description by an adaptation poke were also defined. Authors also introduced the three different types of files which could be required to fully specify an adaptation poke: an adaptation command file - describing the adaptive actions-, adaptation manifests files - containing the definition of new learning process elements-, and resource files -corresponding to new content files-.

Alternatively, the adaptation command file can be described by means of an XML notation and increased with new elements for supporting the evaluation of the adaptations. Fig 15-4 shows a graphical representation of an XML schema developed for this purposes. The schema defines three different types of elements which can be provided for the description of an adaptive poke:

- Adaptation action: It is the only mandatory element of the file. It describes the adaptive actions to be performed by the engine in charge of the adaptation interpretation. There are only three possible adaptive actions:
  - Set a value of a learning process element's property.
  - Add a new element to the structure: In this case it may be necessary to indicate the new element's parent in the structure and to provide the corresponding adaptation manifest file including its definition.
  - Remove an element from the structure.

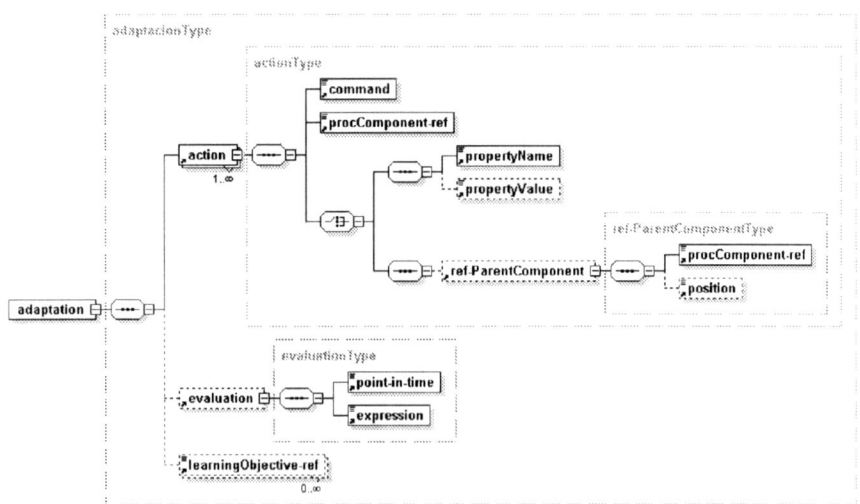

Figure 15-4. Adaptations Schema

- Adaptation evaluation: Contains a formula, similar to the ones used for the objective evaluations, which will be used to estimate the adaptation success.
- Learning objectives: As the introduction of an adaptation may influence the learner's performance of some of the learning objectives, it is convenient to specify them in this section if they are known. This will help to the adaptation influence analysis when examining the process results.

The definition of the adaptation evaluation may require the specification of new elements of the evaluations profile as process components, information elements or even learning objectives. Besides, as a result of the adaptive action, elements of the learning process may be removed and new ones added. Therefore, some of the objective evaluations may require to be updated. In these cases, it will be necessary to introduce a new type of adaptation poke file together with the above mentioned three. This file will follow the same schema as the evaluations profile definition and, as well as the specification of new elements, it can also include updates in the existing one's definitions.

5. IMPLEMENTATION OF ITERATIVE DESIGN OF IMS LEARNING DESIGN PROCESS

This section covers the proposed architecture for implementing the runtime phases for the iterative composition of learning design specified process. The core of the architecture is a Learning Design Player able to interpret *adaptation pokes* descriptions and to introduce the specified modifications at runtime. A mechanism to guarantee the integrity of the modified UoLs must also be defined.

5.1 LD Player

An Learning Design Player (LD Player) is the program that interprets a UoL. It presents the different activities and resources to the involved roles and controls their interactions. In a previous work authors (2006) outlined the structure of a LD Player capable of combining, both prior and during the execution time, the original UoL information with adaptations' descriptions included in the adaptation pokes. The proposed structure (Fig. 15-5) followed an Object-Oriented design, establishing a correspondence between the elements of the Learning Design specification and the class concept from an OO approach. It also made use of design patterns and an Aspect Oriented Approach (Kiczales et al., 1997). This allows a separate specification of the elements of the structure and the definition of the operations that can be

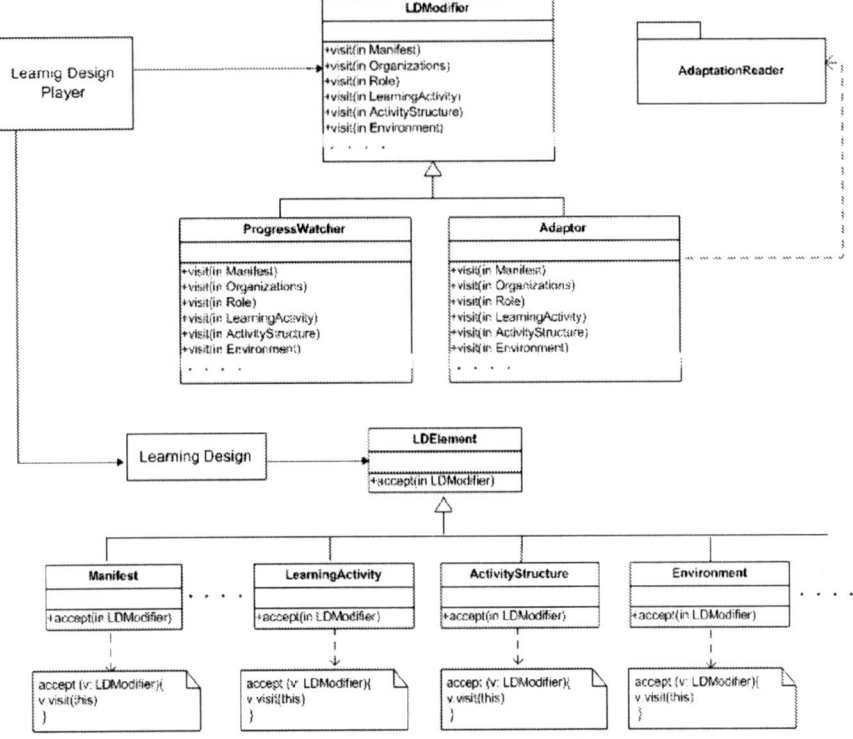

Figure 15-5. LD Player Structure

applied. Two of the possible operations that could be implemented were the modification of the elements definition (*Adaptor class*) and the retrieval of information about their stage (*ProgressWatcher*).

The *adaptation pokes* could be included in the content package or uploaded to a running instance indicating the user or UoL instances which should be adapted. The *AdaptationReader* generates the appropriate *Adaptor* object and passes it to the execution engine to perform the required adaptations.

Following the same approach, a set of commands were defined to specify the elements' characteristics whose value could be retrieved at runtime. The designer introduced the appropriate command at runtime indicating the element identifier and the UoL running instance she/he desired to observe. A *ProgressWatcher* instance was then generated and the appropriate values obtained.

The adaptive LD Player was implemented as an extension to the CopperCore IMS Learning Design engine (CopperCore, 2005) and can be used to implement the main stages of the iterative composition of learning design specified process: to introduce adaptations and to monitor the execution. The former clearly match the adaptive LD Player operational way and the later can be performed using monitor service implementations (IMS Global Learning Consortium, 2003), complemented with *ProgressWatcher* actions. Besides *ProgressWatcher* actions can be used for the definition of the process components and information elements of the evaluations profile. The engine will generate the corresponding *ProgressWatcher* instances and the values will be retrieved when the time for the evaluation is reached.

5.2   Adaptation Validation

Some considerations must be taken into account to ensure that the adaptation by the LD Player previously described does not compromise the integrity of the original UoL. Every time a UoL is published in a particular player, a validation process is launched to guarantee its compliance with the IMS LD language definition and the availability of the referenced resources. Consequently, after the introduction of runtime adaptations, the same validation process should be repeated to ensure that the UoL definition remains valid.

Lama (2005) and Amorin (2006) described an IMS LD-based ontology which captures the semantics of the IMS LD specification as well as the restrictions to be verified between the LD concepts. As this ontology model defines formally these restrictions, it is possible to use it for the detection of inconsistencies on adapted instances of a learning design, because the detection of inconsistencies will happen when these restrictions are not verified. The IMS LD ontology was implemented in Frame-based Logic (F-Logic) (Kiefer et al., 1995), and the FLORA-2 reasoner (Yang et al., 2005) was used to check the axioms of the ontology when the concepts instances were introduced.

The process for detecting the inconsistencies can be resumed as follows: first, an *adaptation poke* is introduced into UoL instance, and, as a consequence, its LD description is changed; then, the ad-hoc translator is executed to transform the XML-schema representation of the adapted learning design into the F-Logic description; and finally, the FLORA-2 reasoner is invoked to answer the queries associated to the axioms that must be verified.

5.3   Evaluation and Adaptation Example

In order to make a clear understanding of the above described process, authors illustrate some adaptations and evaluations of an example course.

Consider a unit of learning which covers different topics on the *Data Structure & Algorithms* subject (Fig 15-6). The course is composed by theoretical activities and autoevaluation exercises. On an scheduled date tests and problems become available for the learners final evaluation.

```
<EvaluationsProfile>

<internal id="i-AutoTest"  monitorCommand="getPropertyValue Auto.SCORE"></internal>
<internal id="i-InsDel"  monitorCommand="getPropertyValue Final.SCORE"></internal>
<tutor  id="i-Exercise" Text="Introduce the score for the exercise:"></tutor>

<procComponent id="e-Definition" design="LD-Definition"  monitorCommand="getPropertyValue Basics.SCORE"/>
<procComponent id="e-Insertions"  design="LD-Insertion" expression="i-InsDel / 2"/>
<procComponent id="e-Deletion"  design="LD-Deletion"  expression="i-InsDel / 2" />
<procComponent id="e-Rotation"  design="LD-Rotation"  datatype="integer"
                                            monitorCommand="getPropertyValue Rotations.SCORE"/>
<learningObjective id="lo-Theory" description="AVL trees theory understanding">
  <evaluation>
    <point-in-time command="LD-Final on-completion"/>
    <expression expresion="e-Definition*0.2+i-InsDelTest*0.4+e-Rotations*0.4" />
  </evaluation>
  <relations>
    <procComponent-ref ref="e-Definition"/>
    <procComponent-ref ref="e-Insertion"/>
    <procComponent-ref ref="e-Rotations"/>
    <procComponent-ref ref="e-Deletions"/>
  </relations>
</learningObjective>

<learningObjective id="lo-Practice" description="AVL trees practical application">
  <evaluation>
    <point-in-time command="LD-Final on-completion"/>
    <expression expresion="i-Exercise" />
  </evaluation>
  <relations>
    <procComponent-ref ref="e-Insertion"/>
    <procComponent-ref ref="e-Rotations"/>
    <procComponent-ref ref="e-Deletions"/>
  </relations>
</learningObjective>

</EvaluationsProfile>
```

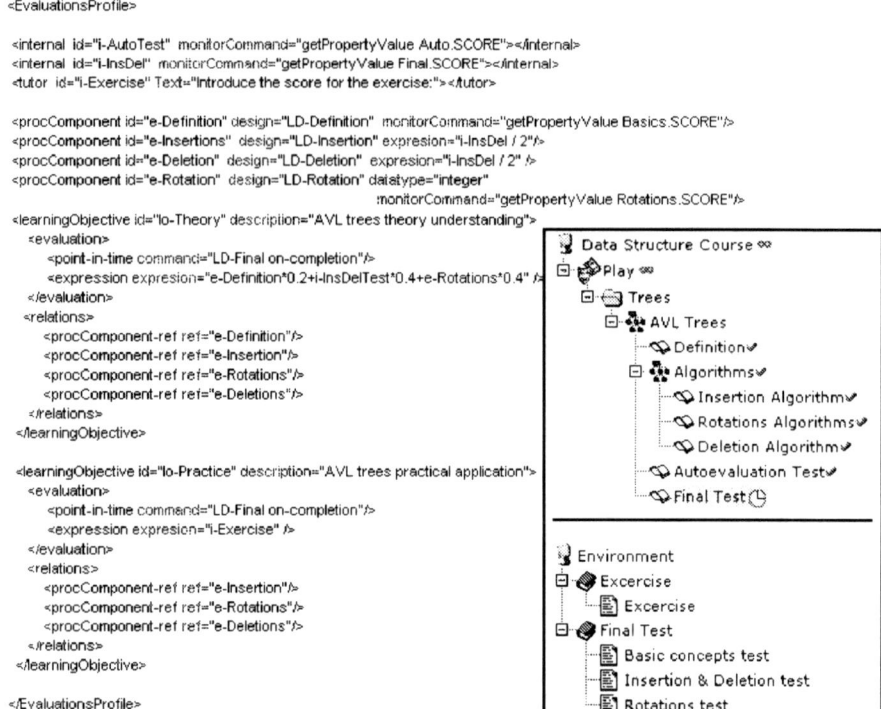

Figure 15-6. Evaluations Profile and Course Structure

The evaluation profile shown in Fig 6 has been defined for the course. The process components correspond to the activities that cover the theoretical aspects of the course. The information elements in turn, retrieve information about the learners test and exercise scores by using ProgressWatcher commands or directly inquire the tutor. Finally, two learning objectives are defined: theoretical understanding and practical application. Their estimation is obtained using the previously described elements and should be calculated after the completion of the latest activity of the course.

During the course execution two adaptive pokes (Fig. 15-7) are required to be executed. The first one is included as a result of the poor performances in the autoevaluation test. It introduces a new environment including a set of applets containing visual animations of the presented algorithms. The adaptation goal is to improve learners understanding of the subject. To measure this goal achievement the results on the final exercise and tests will be used. The adaptation introduction should be considered when analyzing the two learning objectives of the course.

Figure 15-7. Adaptation Pokes Examples

The second adaptive poke is introduced after detecting that most learners have not been able to complete the evaluation on the scheduled time. Therefore, the estimated time for the activity completion is not accurate and should be adjusted. The adaptation will be considered as successful if values for the latest test are obtained, meaning learners finished the task. The adaptation does not contribute to the process learning objectives achievement as such.

Once the process is finished the integration process takes place:

- Learners' results are evaluated: scores on both learning objectives are over 7 out of 10 for the 70% of them. Instructors consider the results as satisfactory.
- The two adaptations are also evaluated:
  - The fist one was marked as related with both learning objectives. The adaptation evaluation is satisfactory and therefore instructors label it to be integrated.
  - Values are obtained for the latest test from most learners. Therefore the evaluation of the second adaptation results *true* for most of them. Accordingly instructors label this adaptation for the integration process.

6.   CONCLUSIONS AND FUTURE WORK

This paper has introduced the concept of *adaptation poke* as the specification of small adaptive actions that can be applied, even at runtime, to a previously defined learning process. The adaptive actions introduced are evaluated against their original goal, measuring its influence and, consequently, giving the instructor a chance to automatically include them in the original process. The cyclic process of refine the learning process definition by its use is called iterative design.

An architecture of a Learning Design Player that provides the means to implement the runtime stages of the iterative composition in IMS Learning Design specified process has been described. The player was designed as an extension to the CopperCore runtime engine and implemented with the help of different design patterns and an Aspect Oriented Programming approach. Once the UoL has been adapted, it must be validated in order to guarantee its compliance with the IMS LD specification. For that purpose an ontology that captures the semantics of the elements of the Learning Design specification is used. To help on the evaluation of both the introduced adaptations and the process results, an evaluation model which works on top of the learning process definition can be used. A notation for this evaluations specification has also been provided.

An application to aid on the iterative design process is currently being developed. On one hand, the application will facilitate the authoring of process evaluation profiles and adaptations. By using a GUI interface, designers will be able to select elements of an IMS LD specified process and connect them with evaluation profile elements. Templates to facilitate the adaptation definitions and new learning process components specification will also be provided. On another hand, the application will communicate with a CopperCore engine increased with adaptation capabilities in order to directly introduce the described adaptations into running UoL instances. The retrieval of data to populate the evaluation profiles will also be possible by means of a *ProgressWatcher* implementation. This will simplify the process progress monitorization tasks.

ACKNOWLEDMENTS

This work is part of the MD2 project (TIC2003-03654), funded by the Ministry of Science and Technology, Spain.

REFERENCES

IMS Global Learning Consortium, 2003, IMS Learning Design information model, version 1.0-final specification; http://www.imsglobal.org/learningdesign/ldv1p0/imsld_infov1p0.html

Gould, J. D., Boies, S. J. and Lewis, C., 1991, Making usable, useful, productivity: enhancing computer applications *Communications of the ACM*. **34**(1), pp. 72-85.

Jacobson, I., Griss, M. and Johnson, P., 1997, *Software Reuse. Architecture, Process and Organization for Bussiness Success* (Addison Wesley).

Svahnberg, M., Gurp J. van and Bosch. J., 2002, A taxonomy of variability realization techniques, Blekinge Institute of Technology, Technical paper, Sweden

Kiczales, G., Lamping, J., Mendhekar, A., Maeda, C., Lopes, C., Loingtier, J., and Irwin, J., 1997, Aspect-Oriented Programming, *Proceedings of the European Conference on Object-Oriented Programming*, 1241, pp. 220–242

Zarraonandia, T., Dodero, J. M. and Fernández, C., 2006, Crosscutting runtime adaptations of LD execution, *Journal of Educational Technology and Society*, 9 (1), pp. 123-137

CopperCore, 2005, CopperCore v2.2.2 (OUNL) release; http://coppercore.org/

Lama, M., Sánchez, E., Amorim, R. and Vila, X.A., 2005, Semantic description of the IMS Learning Design Specification. *AIED-Workshop on Semantic Web technologies for E-Learning (SW-EL 05)*, Amsterdam, pp. 37-47.

Amorim, R., Lama, M., Sánchez, E., Riera, A. and Vila. X.A., 2006, An ontology to describe semantically the IMS Learning Design Specification. *Journal of Educational Technology and Society*, 9 (1), pp. 38-57.

Kiefer, M., Lausen, G. and Wu, J., 1995, Logical foundations of object-oriented and frame-based languages, *Journal of ACM*, **42**(4), pp. 741-843

Yang, G., Kiefer, M., Zhao, C. and Chowdhary, V., 2005, FLORA-2: users' manual; http://flora.sourceforge.net/docs/floraManual.pdf.

Chapter 16

Design by Contract-Based Selection and Composition of Learning Objects

Salvador Sánchez-Alonso[1], Miguel A. Sicilia[1], José M. López-Cobo[2], Sinuhé Arroyo[1]

[1] University of Alcalá, Computer Science Department, Madrid, Spain {salvador.sanchez, msicilia}@uah.es , sinuhe.arroyo@alu.uah.es

[2] iSOCO, Madrid, Spain ozelin@isoco.com

Abstract: Selection and composition of learning objects are two essential activities in automated approaches to Web-based learning. Such activities require high-quality metadata records that are not only conforming to current specifications and standards, but that provide clear system-oriented run-time semantics that support automated decision processes. In this paper, the *Design by Contract* paradigm is described as a method to formally specify and drive selection and composition of contents aimed at concrete learning requirements. In addition, an architectural mapping for such approach to Web Service technology is described, which provides a flexible integration mechanism in a context of heterogeneous and dynamic learning content-providers.

Keywords: Learning Management Systems, Learning Objects.

1. INTRODUCTION

Learning Management Systems (LMS) are a concrete category of *Web-Based Information Systems* aimed at delivering diverse kinds of learning experiences. A number of evolving specifications and standards for learning contents have fostered consistency in format and description of Web learning contents (Anido *et al.*, 2003), but they still lack a level of semantic specification enough to enable consistent runtime automated semantics. This has lead to loose metadata creation practices resulting in learning content that doesn't meet the required completeness (Pagés *et al.*, 2003) and consistency (Kabel *et al.*, 2003) to serve as the basis for common automated LMS-initiated behaviours –like selection and composition. In addition, the

B. Fernández-Manjón et al. (eds.), Computers and Education: E-learning, From Theory to Practice, 179–191.
© 2007 *Springer.*

roles of relationships are not free of ambiguity (Farance, 2003), which seriously hampers the possibilities of consistent composition.

Selection of learning objects requires complete enough metadata records to allow an LMS to decide for inclusion of a given object in the ongoing composition. In addition, the composition itself requires compatibility of the metadata records of the aggregate and the parts (Sanchez-Alonso & Sicilia, 2004a), so that some properties are "propagated" between them, resembling well-known properties of aggregations in object-oriented modelling. From a technical point of view, learning object repositories can be accessed through Web services in order to provide them with the essential infrastructure to be effectively reused (Blackmon & Rehak, 2003) (Ternier & Duval, 2003). This approach provides learning objects with a number of benefits, as expanded searching capabilities, better management of usage fees, accurate access and usage statistics and so on. But before publishing Web service-based learning object repositories, a common way of specifying what a final user can expect from a given learning object and the conditions under which it can be used is needed. Learning object *Design by Contract* (Sicilia & Sanchez-Alonso, 2003), a notation based on the *Learning Object Metadata* specification (IEEE LTSC, 2002) and enhanced with richer semantics, can be used for that purpose. In previous works, design by contract (Meyer, 1997) has been applied to the description of machine-understandable learning object metadata in the form of learning object contracts. Learning object contracts essentially allow the specification of a set of preconditions (circumstances under which the object can be used) and post-conditions (learner expected outcomes) for each learning object, which can also be used to clearly specify relationships between learning objects.

In the rest of this paper, the use of learning object-contracts to drive selection and composition processes is described, focusing on the interpretation of aggregations as the main compositional relationship. In addition, a concrete, flexible architecture based on Web Services is sketched to illustrate the actual behaviour of contract-based composition services. Section 2 describes learning object contracts as a content design method for learning objects. Section 3 focuses on the specifics of the aggregation relationship, and on its consequences in the process of learning object composition. In Section 4, a Web Service-based architecture is used to illustrate the behaviour of contract-based composition services. Finally, conclusions and future research directions are provided in Section 5.

2.   SPECIFYING LEARNING OBJECT CONTRACTS

The concept of 'learning object' represents an attempt to enhance the design of Web-based educational contents, focusing on their reusability in diverse learning contexts (Sicilia & García, 2003). The key to reusability is the provision of metadata in standardized formats for fine-grained content items. But reusability requires precisely specified metadata records, especially if "machine-understandability" is required to build software modules that automatically retrieve and combine learning objects to form higher-level units of instruction. Unfortunately, current learning object metadata specifications do not address this and other important issues (Farance, 2003). In consequence, previous work (Sanchez-Alonso & Sicilia, 2003) (Sanchez-Alonso & Sicilia, 2004a) (Sicilia & Sanchez-Alonso, 2003) has proposed design by contract –a technique borrowed from the object-oriented paradigm– as a way of formalizing learning object metadata records. A learning object contract can be expressed as follows:

```
rlo <URI>
    require <list_of_preconditions>
    ensure <list_of_postconditions>
```

provided that both pre- and post-conditions are expressed through assertions according to a syntax like the following:

```
[level] preconditionId.element <relationallOperator> requestedValue
        postconditionId.element <relationalOperator> value [θ]
```

Where pre- and post-condition *identifiers* correspond to either the learner (`lrn`), the learning context (`ctx`), or the system where the learning object is due to be executed (`sys`); *element* maps to a metadata element (e.g. one of those defined in LOM); and θ refers to a certain degree of credibility. This level is a way to express the fact that some learning objects may be credited to be "more appropriate" than others, due to authoritative revisions or evaluation processes (like, for example, the peer-review assessments being carried out in the MERLOT learning object repository[1]). Finally, *level* indicates the strength of the precondition (mandatory, recommended or optional). The following example uses this syntax to describe a metadata instance corresponding to an introductory lesson on the use of the genitive case in English. It is intended for an Italian speaking audience, and includes the time of work required to complete the lesson (*Typical Learning Time* in LOM):

---

[1] http://www.merlot.org

```
rlo <http://.../GenitiveCaseForItalians>
   require
      ctx.language = en ;   ctx.time = 2h ; lrn.language = it
```

Regarding postconditions, learner knowledge is obviously the principal outcome of learning activities, but other products may also be considered. For example, social relationships among learners are an important issue according to sound theories of learning (Lave & Wenger, 1990), and learning resources that foster social activities may be considered to strength those relationships. Nevertheless, most preconditions will refer to expected learning outcomes, showing absolute or relative outcomes on the learner side. Relative outcomes compare to the learner's previous knowledge –denoted by a '–1' value–, while absolute outcomes can only be noted provided that a taxonomy for the specific knowledge domain has been defined. Following our previous example, we might come upon a RLO ensuring that the learner's knowledge will grow (relative outcome).

```
rlo <http://.../GenitiveCaseForItalians>
   ...
   ensure
      lrn.knows(genitive_case) > lrn.knows(-1)(genitive_case)
```

Learning object contracts can be used as a machine-understandable source of information for selection and composition, since they state requirements and outcomes in a semantically interpretable way. Nevertheless, not only self-descriptions but also relationships influence selection and composition decisions. Concretely, aggregations are critical in the interpretation of composition, as described in the following section.

3.   LEARNING OBJECT AGGREGATION AND ITS ROLE IN COMPOSITION

Aggregation is in the very nature of reusable learning resources: most of them are composed of others. Composition implies, among other commitments which will be examined later, that the contract of a learning object that is an aggregate of others has necessarily to be affected by the contracts of its parts. Consider for example a LOM-conformant learning object whose *1.8:AggregationLevel* is equal to 3 (course). Let's imagine that it is written in Italian. As it is a composition of lower-level objects, the language of its parts must be Italian. In cases like this, the contracts of the parts must conform to what the aggregate contact states. This way, the representation of aggregation relationships in metadata records may entail dependencies on information in other objects metadata records.

An important question is whether the parts should conform to the aggregate contract or not. If not, then the aggregate metadata value items should be inferred from its constituent parts. As a matter of fact, this should be a two-way process. Before the aggregate "physically" exists, the "composer agent" (the software or human who is in fact carrying out the composition) relies on a few directions on what the target system expects from the parts. These directions are formalized into the shape of a contract, thus creating a learning object contract blueprint specification that we call *the archetype*. This is step one. Then, an automated system looks for tentative parts (candidates) in learning object repositories, by focusing the search on the needs and restrictions expressed in the archetype. As the result of this search, a list of candidate learning objects is made up. The best candidate in the list –according to selected criteria– will be the one that will integrate the final aggregate.

Another important issue to consider is whether the information on aggregation should be set in a learning object metadata record or not. Reusability asks for the components of an aggregation to be built without any knowledge about any aggregation they might be part of, in order to facilitate its future reuse, so it should be the aggregate responsibility to compose all the parts and to keep the track on them. We suggest stating this information only in the aggregate by using the IEEE LOM metadata item *hasPart*, thus avoiding the use of *isPartOf* in the parts. This approach forces systems to check the related resources to a given one that is composed by others, but preserves the individual reusability levels of simple educational resources. Besides all the mentioned issues, the fact that aggregation relationships entail *runtime commitments* that affect the objects that participate in the relationship has also to be considered. The most important of these commitments is *availability*, which means that the referenced resource has to be available whenever the current learning object is used or delivered. This can be achieved in two different forms: a) the referenced object being effectively available, or b) the learner providing evidence of a level of knowledge greater or equal than the stated in the learning outcomes published in the learning object contract. Apart from availability, other commitments are *propagation* (some properties propagate from the aggregate to the parts), *acyclicness* (chains of aggregate links must not form cycles) or *reference validity*, a weak form of availability (Sanchez-Alonso & Sicilia, 2004b).

In the following example, a learning object *MyLO* that displays a Flash-animated example of the *Quicksort* algorithm is in the list of candidates returned by an automated search engine, and it is consequently under consideration by a composer agent in order to integrate it to a Java course object:

```
rlo <http://... /MyLO>
  require
    mandatory    sys.browser >= V6_browser
    mandatory    sys.requirement = FlashPlugIn
    mandatory    ctx.cost = true ; recommended ctx.time = 0.5h
  ensure
      lrn.knows(qSort)[90]
```

The mentioned commitments affect the given object in the following way. *Propagation* requires the aggregate learning time to remain unknown until the total number of pieces is assembled, since it is calculated from them. *Availability* asks for MyLO to be publicly accessible whenever the aggregate is being delivered or used, but also for its usage fee to be paid. As MyLO is not composed by other learning objects (it is a leaf in the aggregation tree), *acyclicness* is guaranteed given that all the potential cycles would end here. So, if MyLO was finally chosen in the ongoing composition after the selection process the aggregate contract would be affected by the data in MyLO metadata record. The aggregate contract could be:

```
rlo <http://... /AgentGeneratedAggregate>
  require
    mandatory    sys.browser > V6_browser
    recommended ctx.time = 10h;  mandatory    ctx.cost = true
    mandatory    ctx.hasPart = "MyLO"
    ...
  ensure
      lrn.knows(qSort) [90]
```

As this example shows, MyLO design is not constrained by pre- or post-conditions in the aggregates it would be part of. It is the responsibility of the author of the aggregate to check the consistency of the parts with the aggregate contract, and to make use of some features to calculate the final values to be set in some assertions (as the *learning time* in our example). The new precondition *hasPart* appears after choosing MyLO and as a consequence of the relationship.

4.   EXAMPLE ARCHITECTURE AND PROCESSING

In our model, contracts are the basis for searching and retrieving learning objects from a repository. We define *Learning Web Services* (LWSs) as Internet services that use a standard SOAP communication interface to expose learning objects that are described by metadata in the form of contracts. The LWS SOAP interface provides the clients with a) discovery of learning objects, based on their contracts, b) download of learning objects, using learning object packaging technologies (IMS Global Learning Consortium, 2001), and c) learning object metadata retrieval. In what follows, a concrete design of LWS is described as a general-purpose architecture fulfilling the requirements of contract-based selection and composition. A declarative XL-like syntax (Florescu *et al.*, 2002) is used for the sake of obtaining a high-level architectural description.

When searching for learning objects, the query operation encodes a search request as a learning object contract archetype that will be in turn compared to the contracts of the RLOs stored in the repositories. Going back to our first example, let's suppose that an Italian-speaking learner is following a course of English as a foreign language; learning resources that are not locally available are required for the full course. As a lesson on the genitive case is needed, the LMS will need to locate a learning resource that fits to the current learner profile and system settings. A contract archetype will then be created from the course needs (which will form the postconditions in the contract) and limitations about both the system and the learning context (preconditions in the contract), e.g.:

```
rlo <CONTRACT_ARCHETYPE>
    require
        sys.browser <= v6_browser;
        ctx.time < 3h ;
        lrn.language = it
    ensure
        lrn.knows(genitive_case) [80]
```

This contract archetype asks for a RLO providing the learner with knowledge on the genitive case over 80 percent confident. It limits the valid objects to those that can be displayed in a version 6 browser or lower, with a duration shorter than 3 hours, and intended to Italian-speaking audiences. A composer service can be used to provide the full selection and composition request through an interface like the following:

```
service <http://../Composer>
    history;
    let compositionRules rules;
    context let archetype arch;
    invariant archetype validates as contract;
    context let learningObject rlo;
    operation <http://../Composer>::compose
        precondition $input validates as contract;
        postcondition $output validates as learningObject;
        postcondition conforms($input, $output);
        body   ...
            <<divide in c_i>>
            c_i,rules -> <http://../ContractSearcher>::lookFor⇒rlo_i
            <<combine rlo_i>>
        endbody
    endoperation
endservice
```

The above XL-like syntax specifies a type called *archetype* for the `arch` context variable of the service, which is instantiated in a per-conversation basis. The `rlo` variable represents the ongoing composition. The type *compositionRules* is intended to reflect the global knowledge of the service regarding the constraints on composition required as those described in the previous examples. Such declarative specification can be easily expressed in XML, with a syntax similar to that of RuleML[2]. The *history* clause entails the automatic recording of conversations, which is useful to cache repeating requests. The combination of RLOs entails the definition of a new aggregated learning object with metadata reflecting the contracts of the parts. In this model, not only RLOs can be retrieved, but also their contracts. Contract retrieval is particularly useful when choosing among RLOs offering similar outcomes, since the assessment criteria is the contract. Repositories of RLOs and contracts can be accessed through separate services with a minimal interface like the following:

```
service <http://../ContractRepository>
  operation <http://../ContractRepository>::query
     precondition $input validates as contract;
     postcondition conforms($input, $output);   ...
  endoperation
endservice
service <http://../RLORepository>
  operation <http://../RLORepository>::get
     precondition $input validates as LOMid;
     postcondition $output validates as learningObject;   ...
  endoperation
endservice
```

A software agent working on behalf of the end-user application (called Proxy agent) interacts with another software service called Composer. Composer takes an archetype contract from the expressed needs of the learner and will hand parts of it (c_i) over to searching services conforming to ContractSearcher. This intermediation allows for quality assessments and other criteria to be located on searchers, so that the repositories are simply persistent storages. ContractSearchers may also implement a subset of combination rules not included in Composer, allowing for extensibility of the approach to new sub-schemas. The requirements for searchers is that they should be able to provide an ordered collection of RLOs conforming to the given (sub-)contract, so that results are "explainable" according to the ordering criteria of searchers.

```
service <http://../ContractSearcher>
  let contractRepositoryCollection sources;
  let compositionRules rules;
  operation <http://../ContractSearcher>::lookFor
    precondition $input$ validates as contract, compositionRules;
    postcondition conforms($input[contract], $output);
    body
       $input$[contract]→ <http:../ContractRepository>::query → lo_i
       <<sort lo_i>>   ...
    endbody
  endoperation
endservice
```

---

[2] http://www.ruleml.org/

The communications between the Composer and the searchers is typically asynchronous, resembling Request-for-Quote business processes, while queries to repositories typically require a synchronous, immediate response. The decomposition described carries out the essential composition and selection tasks. Additional supporting services can be added to deal with repository discovery and assessment. The complex conditions contracts impose on LO metadata require some form of logics-based support if maximum flexibility is desired. The *Web Services Modeling Ontology* framework[3] is an ideal candidate for such kind of effort. WSMO could be used to provide the description for *lookFor* implementation. An example fragment of an ontology definition in WSML could be:

```
concept learningObject
    nonFunctionalProperties
      dc#description hasValue "Any digital entity that may be
      used for learning, education or training"
    endNonFunctionalProperties
    aggregationLevel impliesType  (1 1) aggregationLevel
    languages impliesType humanLanguage
    isClassifiedInto impliesType classification
    hasRights impliesType rights
    hasTechnicalRequirements impliesType technicalRequirement
    locationURI impliesType _iri
    hasEducational impliesType  (1 1) educational
    identifier impliesType  (1 1) learningIdentifier
    title impliesType _string
    structure impliesType  (1 1) structure
    hasRelations impliesType relationship
concept educational
    nonFunctionalProperties
      dc#description hasValue "Educational aspects of the LO"
    endNonFunctionalProperties
    descriptionOfEducational impliesType _string
    interactivityType impliesType interactivityType
    learningResourceType impliesType learningResourceType
    hasInteractivityLevel impliesType interactivityLevel
    hasDifficulty impliesType difficulty
    contextEducational impliesType contextEducational
    intendedEndUserRole impliesType intendedEndUserRole
concept orCompositeTechnicalRequirement
    nonFunctionalProperties
      dc#description hasValue "Define the possibilities of a
      choice for a technical Requirement of a LO"
    endNonFunctionalProperties
    minimumVersionOfTR impliesType _string
    maximumVersionOfTR impliesType _string
    typeOfRequirement impliesType _string
    nameOfRequirement impliesType _string
concept technicalRequirement
    nonFunctionalProperties
      dc#description hasValue "A Technical Requirement that a LO
             has to comply"
    endNonFunctionalProperties
    installationRemarksOfTR impliesType  (0 1) _string
```

---

[3] http://www.wsmo.org

```
      formatOfTR impliesType  (0 1) _string
      sizeOfTR impliesType    (0 1) _string
      locationOfTR impliesType  (0 1) _iri
      durationOfTR impliesType  (0 1) _duration
      hasOrCompositeRequirements impliesType
orCompositeTechnicalRequirement
  concept learningIdentifier
      nonFunctionalProperties
        dc#description hasValue "An unique and unambiguous
            identifier for a LO"
      endNonFunctionalProperties
      entryCatalog impliesType _string
      catalogIdentifier impliesType _string
  concept resourceInRelation
      nonFunctionalProperties
       dc#description hasValue "Describes the Resource (LO) which
       is related with other LO"
      endNonFunctionalProperties
      descriptionOfResource impliesType _string
      identifiedResource impliesType learningIdentifier
  concept kindOfRelation subConceptOf _string
      nonFunctionalProperties
        dc#description hasValue "Defines one kind of Relation
            between two LO"
      endNonFunctionalProperties
  concept relationship
      nonFunctionalProperties
        dc#description hasValue "Describes one relationship between
        the LO owner and other LO"
      endNonFunctionalProperties
      kindOfRelationship impliesType kindOfRelation
      resourceInRelationship impliesType resourceInRelation
  concept structure subConceptOf _string
      nonFunctionalProperties
        dc#description hasValue "Defines the LO structure"
      endNonFunctionalProperties
  concept aggregationLevel subConceptOf _integer
      nonFunctionalProperties
        dc#description hasValue "Describes the LO granularity"
      endNonFunctionalProperties
```

Such shared formal definitions could be used to specify Web Services that provide a concrete kind of learning objects, as illustrated by the following WSML fragment that describes the capability to provide LO with concrete language, aggregation level and content classified according to certain taxonomy elements:

```
webservice _"http://www.uah.es/ontologies/ws.wsml"
nonFunctionalProperties
  dc#title hasValue "Algorithm for Internet Applications Learning
Object Web Service"
  dc#description hasValue "Web service for access the content of a
  Learning Object on Algorithms and purchase it"
endNonFunctionalProperties
importedOntologies _"http://www.wsmo.org/ontologies/purchase"
capability _#
 precondition
    axiom _#
    nonFunctionalProperties
```

```
      dc#description hasValue "The input to the Web Service has to be
a user with an intention to select a Learning Object"
      endNonFunctionalProperties
definedBy
   ?Buyer memberOf po#buyer.
  postcondition
     axiom _#
     nonFunctionalProperties
     dc#description hasValue "The output of the service is a
  Learning Object about Internet Algorithms."
      endNonFunctionalProperties
definedBy
?LO memberOf lom4WSMO#learningObject[
   isClassifiedInto hasValues {?Classifications},
   languages hasValues {lom4WSMO:englishUK},
   aggregationLevel hasValue 3
   identifier hasValue ?Identifier,
   title hasValue "Algorithms for Internet Applications (WS2001/02,
lecture 14)"] and
?Identifier memberOf learningIdentifier[
   entryCatalog hasValue lom4WSMO#ARIADNE,
   catalogIdentifier hasValue "V3VIROR_v_3.1_nr_22"] and
?Classifications memberOf lom4WSMO#classification[
   purpose hasValue lom4WSMO#discipline,
   taxonPath hasValues {?Paths}] and
?Paths memberOf lom4WSMO#taxonPath[
   hasSourceTaxonPath hasValue lom4WSMO#ARIADNE,
   hasTaxon? hasValues {
      idTaxon hasValue "000000001",
      valueTaxon hasValue "Exact, Natural and Engineer Sciences",
      fatherOfTaxons hasValues {
       idTaxon hasValue "000000002",
       valueTaxon hasValue "Informatics & Information Processing",
       fatherOfTaxons hasValues {
          idTaxon hasValue "000000003",
          valueTaxon hasValue "General"}},
      idTaxon hasValue "000000004",
      valueTaxon hasValue "Internet Algorithms"}].
  effect
     axiom _#
     nonFunctionalProperties
     dc#description hasValue "there shall be a trade for the
Learning Object of the postcondition"
      endNonFunctionalProperties
  definedBy
   ?someTrade memberOf po#trade[
      po#items hasValues {?LO},
      Po#payment hasValue ?acceptedPayment]
   and ?acceptedPayment memberOf po#creditCard.
```

In order to match the user desire with the Web Service capability, namely the access to the learning object described in it, we need to define the desired learning facility required by the user by means of a WSMO Goal, as in the WSML fragment written below.

```
goal _"http://www.uah.es/ontologies/goals/goalLO.wsml"
nonFunctionalProperties
   dc#title hasValue "Searching for a Learning Object about Internet
Algorithms"
   dc#description hasValue "Express the goal of buying a Learning
Object for learn Internet Algorithms"
endNonFunctionalProperties
importedOntologies {_"http://www.uah.es/ontologies/lom4WSMO"}
postcondition
```

```
axiom purchasingLearningObject
nonFunctionalProperties
  dc#description hasValue "This goal expresses the general desire
of purchasing a Learning Object"
endNonFunctionalProperties
definedBy
  exists ?LearningObject, ?Classification, ?Paths(
  ?LearningObject memberOf lom4WSMO#learningObject[
       lom4WSMO#isClasssifiedInto hasValue Classification?] and
  ?Classifications memberOf lom4WSMO#classification[
       taxonPath hasValues {?Paths}] and
  ?Paths memberOf lom4WSMO#taxonPath[
       hasSourceTaxonPath hasValue lom4WSMO:ARIADNE,
       hasTaxon? hasValues {valueTaxon hasValue "Internet
Algorithms"}]
  ).
```

In consequence, both the decomposition of selection and composition in sub-activities and the expression of contracts in terms of a formal ontology can be interpreted in terms of a contract-based approach in which goals and Web services logically match to serve the user with the desired set of Learning Objects required by his learning needs.

5.   CONCLUSIONS

Learning object contracts can be used to drive the process of selection and composition of learning resources in a consistent way. Pre- and post-conditions can be used as search criteria, and aggregation relationships can be used to derive aggregate metadata. Such processes can be properly devised following a service-oriented approach, as illustrated by the high-level specification provided. Future work should detail the influence of each concrete metadata element in such processes, following the lines of recent work (Sicilia *et al.*, 2004), and the process itself (or a set of alternative configurable processes) should be specified to guarantee a standardized, common and predictable behaviour. It should also deal with implementing intelligent agents to carry out the selection and composition processes, capable of changing their goals at runtime by introducing a more interactive approach.

ACKNOWLEDGEMENTS

The research reported in this chapter is funded by the European Commission 6th Framework (IST) Project LUISA (FP6-027149).

REFERENCES

Anido, L. E., Fernández, M. J., Caeiro, M., Santos, J. M., Rodríguez, J. S. and Llamas, M., 2002, Educational metadata and brokerage for learning resources, *Computers & Education*, 38(4): 351–374.

Blackmon, W.H., Rehak, D., 2003, Customized learning: a Web services approach, in: *Proceedings of Ed-Media '03*.

Farance, F., 2003, IEEE LOM standard not yet ready for 'prime time. *IEEE LTTF Learning Technology Newsletter*, 5(1).

Florescu, D., Grünhagen, A., Kossmann, D., 2002, XL: An XML programming language for Web service specification and composition, in *Proceedings of the International World Wide Web Conference*, 7-11.

IEEE LTSC, 2002, *Learning Object Metadata (LOM)*, IEEE 1484.12.1.

IMS Global Learning Consortium, 2001, *Content Packaging Final Specification*.

Kabel, S., Hoog, R. and Wielinga, B., 2003, Consistency in indexing learning objects: an empirical investigation, in: *Proceedings of the learning objects symposium*: 26-31.

Lave, J., Wenger, E., 1990, *Situated Learning: Legitimate Peripheral Participation*, Cambridge University Press, Cambridge, UK.

Meyer B., 1997, *Object Oriented Software Construction*, Prentice Hall, pp. 331-410.

Pagés, C., Sicilia, M.A., García, E., Martínez, J.J. and Gutiérrez, J.M., 2003, On the evaluation of completeness of learning object metadata in open repositories, in: *Proceedings of 2nd Int. Conf. on Multimedia, Information & Communication Technologies in Education*: 1760-1764.

Sánchez-Alonso, S. and Sicilia, M.A., 2003, Expressing preconditions in learning object contracts, in: *Proceedings of 2nd International Conference on Multimedia, Information & Communication Technologies in Education*, 1656-1660.

Sánchez-Alonso, S. and Sicilia, M.A., 2004a, How learning object relationships affect learning object contracts: commitments and implications of aggregation, in: *Proceedings of Ed-Media '04*.

Sánchez-Alonso, S. and Sicilia, M.A., 2004b, On the semantics of aggregation and generalization in learning object contracts, in: *Proceedings of the 4th IEEE International Conference on Advanced Learning Technologies*: 425-429.

Sicilia, M.A. and García, E., 2003, On the concepts of usability and reusability of learning objects, *Int. Review of Research in Open and Distance Learning*, 4(2).

Sicilia, M.A. and Sánchez-Alonso, S., 2003, On the concept of learning object "Design by Contract", *WSEAS Transactions on systems*, 2 (3): 612-617.

Sicilia, M.A., Pagés, C., García, E., Sánchez-Alonso, S. and Rius, A., 2004, Specifying semantic conformance profiles in reusable learning object metadata, in: *Proceedings of the 5th International Conference on Information Technology Based Higher Education and Training*.

Ternier, S. and Duval, E., 2003, Web Services for the ARIADNE knowledge pool system, in: *Proceedings of the 3rd ARIADNE International Conference*.

Chapter 17

ONLINE EVALUATION AT HIGHER AND SECONDARY EDUCATION
A teaching and learning experience

Joglar, N., Risco, J.L., Díaz, A., Colmenar, J.M.
Ingeniería Técnica en Informática de Sistemas

Centro de Estudios Superiores Felipe II, C/ Capitan, 39, 28300 Madrid, Spain

Abstract: This chapter describes the experience of developing and testing a tool for online evaluation in academia. The tool was firstly built as a result of a collaboration project among several subjects in the Computer Science Department at the college C.E.S. Felipe II (Aranjuez, Spain). A later beta-version of the application was tested in the evaluation of students from five different courses like *Music* at the middle school level or *Calculus* at college level. We include here a brief summary with the results of all tests. The absence of some features detected in those tests and the complexity of the tool, which was coded by students, guided the people in charge of the research team to decide the development of a new tool starting from scratch. The features of this new tool, called *iTest*, are also shown in this chapter, detailing the differences it presents in relation to the previous tools.

Key words: Online Evaluation, New Technologies in the Classroom, Mathematics Education, High School Education, Teacher Education.

1. INTRODUCTION

The instructional films of the 1940's were expected to radically change the educational delivery system, as were instructional radio and television. While each one of these technological innovations had some impact on educational programs, they did little to change the fundamental nature of education. The Internet and computer technology, as the next generation of

193

B. Fernández-Manjón et al. (eds.), Computers and Education: E-learning, From Theory to Practice, 193–204.
© 2007 *Springer.*

technological innovation to impact distance education, appears to have the power to alter the education landscape significantly (Aragon and Johnson, 2002).

The Internet offers the possibility of providing a stimulating environment to engage students in meaningful learning through reflection, application and interaction (Macdonald et al., 2001). In addition, web-based quizzes provide teachers and students with several advantages as the technology for self-assessment (Chapman, 2004). For these and other reasons, the number of web-based or online courses has increased rapidly over the past few years to become a significant constituent of educational pedagogy worldwide. Online learning or e-Learning is stimulated primarily by using new technologies (Suanpang et al., 2003).

Conformance to e-Learning standards, such as IMS (Instructional Management System) (IMS, 2006) and SCORM (Sharable Content Object Reference Model) (SCORM, 2006), is increasingly seen as the way forward in the development and deployment of e-Learning frameworks. The standards use XML technology for the specification and are released by the IMS consortium. One of these standards is Question and Test Interoperability (QTI), developed for constructing and exchanging tests and assessment information.

Our research team in the Computer Science Department of the higher education institution called CES Felipe II in Madrid, has always been conscious of the importance of the integration of e-Learning technologies. In this direction, we are developing a tool called *iTest*, which is a subset of a *Virtual Learning Environment* (VLE) or *Learning Management System* (LMS). In this chapter we present iTest giving all the details from its motivation to its technical features. iTest is an online management software that allows instructors to configure exams and students to take them. The tool was started with the aim of improving the current strategies to implement mathematical formulas for online exams on the web. The scope of iTest has been enlarged in order to store multimedia contents and to allow the design of *Music* course tests and animated tests using Flash. Our idea is also to include the feature of importing and exporting from IMS QTI 2.1. iTest is aimed to be part of a research project between our Institution and the Education Department of Aranjuez City Council. This project includes developing courses to instruct secondary school teachers on the usage of this tool next academic years.

The rest of the chapter is organized as follows: firstly, we describe the motivation of our work, then we give all the details of the development of the tool; after that, we present the results obtained using the tool in higher and secondary education. Finally, we give the conclusions of this work.

2. MOTIVATION

With the availability of course management software such as Blackboard (Blackboard, 2006), WebCT (WebCT, 2006) and many others, most of educators are converting conventional tests into web-based tests. As an example, the state of Virginia, USA, required all public schools to have the capability of online testing. Virginia students took over 226,000 online tests in 2004. The state of Indiana (USA) developed online end-of-course assessment in *Algebra I* and *English* for 11th grade students. About 91,000 students took the tests, and their schools received the results within 48 hours. Teachers appreciated the speedy feedback and the absence of test booklets (Rodriguez, 2005).

In Spain the situation is not the same. In spite of the rapid growth in the accessibility of new technologies, for example, the program *one computer per two students* in the Spanish region of Extremadura, the new facilities for online evaluation are not being used (Guijarro, 2005).

Commercial systems are usually very expensive to be implemented on a large scale and development costs are very high. Since they all use different formats, test libraries cannot be easily integrated or accessed hence reducing reuse and portability. In addition, teachers are often discouraged because they do not have time to learn how to use platforms with so many features.

In view of all these problems, one of the goals of our research team is to develop a new non-commercial tool, called iTest, which is easy to use and does not require any commercial software to run. Besides, formation as well as continuous assistance for teachers using the tool will be provided by our team members.

Through an innovative application and combination of open Web technologies such as MathML, Java active pages (JSP), webservices (J2EE) and database access (MySQL), iTest aims to create a website for online exams where contents and support services are interoperable. Contents and support services can also be created, deployed and maintained on a distributed basis. The iTest website is organized to systematically supplement complete courses curricula in any given school.

The idea of developing this project was suggested by the Mathematics lecturers at our Department. There was a strong need for a new teaching and learning methodology using new technologies to increase the motivation of the students. Different versions of a preliminary tool were developed in collaboration with some of our students during the academic years 2003-05 (Díaz et al., 2005; Joglar at al., 2006). iTest not only allows them to self-test their knowledge in a specific area at a given point, but it also increases the motivation for the students to study abstract and difficult concepts. This idea is clearly extensive to all levels of education.

2.1   Higher Education

Based on our experience, Computer Science students seemed to be highly interested in using this kind of tool, in particular during the first semester of their first year at the university, since they have not had the opportunity to work at a university computer laboratory yet. Besides, these students in particular are not scared to turn on a computer. In fact, they are really eager to work with one even to learn mathematics.

We find these tools essential to help us motivate our students to learn cold and abstract topics such as *Calculus*, *Discrete Mathematics*, *Linear Algebra* and *Statistics*. It is important to remark here that iTest lets us not only to visualize graphs of functions and to reproduce sound files, but it also allows us to properly display mathematical formulas without using screenshots. This issue is a real plus of the tool.

2.2   Secondary Education

Another goal of the project is to modernize the educational process in the secondary education system where the knowledge growth is rapid, and it demands constant curriculum redefinition and implementation of new methods for efficient learning.

The original idea to implement e-Learning in order to modernize the educational process, is growing as the new hardware and software tools are now available at school and it is expected that the teachers are motivated to use new technologies to improve their teaching. It has also been expected that the educational process can be significantly improved by creating new educational resources with visually appealing multimedia contents that include interactive elements and up-to-date reusable information, as in (Smothers et al., 2004).

3.   DESCRIBING THE TOOL

In this section we explain the history of the development of the tool, its different features, the exam configuration management and some other technical details.

3.1   Development History of the Tool

In the next paragraphs we would like to carefully specify all the development stages of the tool and the different versions obtained.

During the 2003-2004 academic year, an online application that allows random generation and automatic grading of exams was developed through an educative experience between several subjects at our Department (Díaz et al., 2005). Some students had the opportunity to develop a medium size project instead of small exercises for each class working together and closely supervised by a group of professors from our Department. We think this is a very interesting aspect of our tool; it has been developed by students, and it is conceived to be used by the students themselves. In order to complete this first stage, a group of students voluntarily developed a first simplified operative version. They named the first version *ExaNet* (Díaz et al., 2005).

In May 2005 a first evaluation of this initial version is performed in the *Statistics* course at our Department. After this first evaluation, some problems were detected: low usability in the interface of the student taking an exam, administrator interface too simplified and mathematical formulas not supported.

The tool was partially improved by a second group of students again assisted by professors from our Department during the first semester of the academic year 2005-2006. Students were granted some free configuration credits for their work (Joglar et al., 2006). This second version of the tool will be referenced along the article as the beta-version of the tool.

In January 2006 and May 2006, tests were performed in the *Calculus* and *Statistics* courses, respectively. Exams at secondary school level are also carried out (one in an *Algebra I* course and another one at a *Music* course). The results obtained are very encouraging. Students are satisfied with the new evaluation system but some usability problems are detected in the administrator's interface. The teachers using the tool could not work independently. They had to prepare their questions and answers in a separate document, and then the general administrator user was in charge of transferring all the data to the database. This general administrator was also the only user able to register new students, to configure exams and to access the statistics of the results.

After our experience with the beta-version over the past two academic years, we are nowadays developing a new application with all the features that have been detected as necessary for an optimum functionality (see next subsection). This new tool is being developed from scratch and it has been named *iTest*.

The development of iTest has been integrated in a project with the Aranjuez City Council in order to systematically use the tool at all local high schools and middle schools. We have also obtained financial support from the *Universidad Complutense de Madrid* through their program for *Special Actions in Research*.

In the next subsections we will present the features of iTest emphasizing the differences with the beta-version.

3.2   Features of iTest

Our tool considers three kinds of users: instructors, students and a general administrator user.

Instructors have to structure the subjects they teach in different didactic units. They may add, edit or delete any question or answer for each didactic unit within each subject. A level of difficulty can be assigned to each question. They may also configure any number of exams and visualize different types of statistics of the exams performed by the students.

Students may choose to start an exam from the list of courses that have any exam configured for the current date within the set of subjects the student is currently enrolled in. Once the student selects the subject, the tool randomly generates the exam for the chosen subject by using the configuration held at the database. If the assigned time length for the exam expires, the tool automatically finishes the exam and alerts the user with a message. The student is also able to finish the exam at any time. In both cases, the tool grades the exam and it automatically shows the user's grade on the screen right after completion. The tool saves the information corresponding to each generated exam to allow the student to revise his exam during the correction period, which starts the day after the exam is not available. The students may check different aspects about the exams they did: generated questions, given answers, correct answers, grade per question and final grade.

The general administrator user is able to add, edit or delete information stored at the database. Currently, we use the administrator features to add students, instructors and subjects to the database and to include the relationships between them.

The main difference between the beta-version and iTest is that the beta-version did not have instructor users. As we have already mentioned in the previous subsection, this is a crucial aspect of the tool in order for the teachers to be able to work almost independently from the general administrator.

3.3   Exam configuration and statistics

The instructors can configure more than one exam for the same subject during a course period. The configuration of each exam has the following configurable parameters: time to solve the exam in minutes, points per right answer, penalization for each wrong answer, dates in which the exam will be available for the students and information about the didactic units that are covered by the exam. The configuration for a didactic unit consists of the next parameters: number of questions, number of answers per question and maximum and minimum difficulty of the questions. In this way it is possible to generate an exam that contains questions only from the chosen didactic units and within the selected difficulty level.

The beta-version did not have the possibility to decide which didactic units were covered by a given exam. However, the tool selected a balanced number of questions per didactic unit using all the didactic units included in the particular subject. This version did not have either the possibility of assigning a level of difficulty per question.

Given that the tool randomly generates each exam, it is very difficult that two students get the exact same exam at the same time. In spite of this fact, when using the tool via Internet without any supervision, it is difficult to control all the factors involved to avoid cheating. Thinking in a non-supervised use of this tool, the final version will register the IP address, time of starting the test and time of answering a given question.

The instructor user can also fix the specific grades assigned to each question at a given exam. When a question has more than one correct answer, the exam might be set up to only penalize the student with wrong answer if none of the correct answers is selected. If a student does not select all the correct answers for such a question, the penalization is proportional to the number of correct answers selected compared to the number of correct answers. For example, if a student selects one correct answer in a question with two correct answers from an exam where 1 point is given for a full correct answer and -0.3 per wrong answer, the final the penalization is -0.15 (-0.3/2). It might also be interesting to study giving partial credit for wrong answers even if there is only one correct answer per question. For that, one would have to think of an ordering in the set of possible answers for a particular question from *totally wrong to totally correct* (Ashton et al., 2006).

Finally, the tool also provides statistics like averages, standard deviations, percentages of correct answers for a given question, etc. In particular, the tool computes the ratio of success for a given question, that is, number of students who got the right answer divided by the number of students who had that question on the exam. These ratios are important because they allow the instructor to detect misunderstandings by the students in a particular point of the course syllabus.

3.4   Technical details

All the tools described above were developed as Java applications, based on a MVC (model-view-controller) architecture. The database support has been developed according to the SQL standard.

Going a step further, the Java application was converted into a dynamic web application, using J2EE platform. Since it was developed according to MVC paradigm, only view and controller had to be redesigned using J2EE technologies: JSP and servlets. The web application was deployed into a Tomcat application server.

The most innovative aspect of the tool is the support for visual representation of mathematical formulas. This feature was implemented using MathML. Instructors are able to include, in questions and answers statements, mathematical formulas written in a LaTeX-like notation. Then, we reused a JavaScript code written by Peter Jipsen to transform this notation into MathML (AsciiMathML, 2006). Client browsers can then display the formulas if they have the appropriate plug-in (MathPlayer, 2006). Other resources, such as sound tracks or flash animations can also be included in questions and answers. For these cases the tool just stores the file and embeds it into the HTML presentation in order to be described by the adequate plug-in of the client browser.

4.   TESTING THE BETA-VERSION OF THE TOOL IN HIGHER EDUCATION

The beta-version of the tool described above has been successfully tested with first and second year Computer Science students at our university since May 2005. All our students have taken the online tests in Math courses voluntarily. They also took the test in computer laboratories at our Institution supervised by their instructors, except for one test in the *Calculus* course. *Calculus* students took the test online at home without any kind of supervision in January 2006.

All students who took an online test filled in an evaluation form right after finishing their tests. All participants agreed that their experiences had been very interesting and motivating for them. The most appreciated feature of the tool was the fact that the tool gave them their grades immediately. Many of them suggested a methodic and continuous use of the software to help them self-test their knowledge of a given topic at any given time.

We remark that we are not in the position of making a formal statistical study of the usage of this tool yet because we have conducted only one basic test with each participating group of volunteered students. Once we check the well-functioning of the final version, we will be ready to design formal usages of the software.

In Table 1 we include significant data from the three tests we have conducted with our students from May 2005 until May 2006. Two of them

Table 1 Description of different tests at university level

Course	#questions; #answers; time	Didactic units	Participation	Grading	Passed
Statistics (May 05)	4; 5 per question; 15 min.	2	17% (18/105)	0,25;-0,1	100%
Calculus (Jan. 06)	5; 5 per question; 30 min.	3	60% (58/98)	0,2;-0,1	43%
Statistics (May 06)	5; 4 per question; 25 min.	3	42% (44/104)	0,2;-0,1	48%

were given at the end of the *Statistics* course during two academic years. *Statistics* is a mandatory 2nd year course covering 7.5 credit hours work (75 course hours) during the Spring semester. Students took these tests voluntarily at our computer labs supervised by their instructors. The grade obtained by each student in this exam was agreed to be add up to the grade in the final exam (grading scale of the final: from 0 to 10). On the other hand, *Calculus* students took their tests voluntarily at home without any supervision. *Calculus* is also a major course for our first year students with 6 credit hours work (60 course hours) during the Fall semester.

All these tests were design with only one correct answer per question. Partial credit was not given for wrong answers. Students were penalized for wrong answers to avoid random responses and students were not penalized for leaving a question blank. In the grading column of Table 1, we specify the number of points given per correct answer and the number of points subtracted per wrong answer. All questions of a given exam had the same level of difficulty.

5. USAGES OF THE TOOL IN SECONDARY EDUCATION

The beta-version of the tool has also been tested at secondary education level in collaboration with two secondary schools of our geographic area. Since one of the main functionalities of the tool includes the editor for math formulas, we decided to design at least one test for 11th grade *Algebra I* students from the *Instituto de Enseñanza Secundaria Fortuny*. All students involved in this particular test were science majors. They all were enthusiastic with the experience. Students appreciated especially the fact that the tool was developed by computer science students at a nearby college. They all affirmed that they would like to use this software in a continuous way to help them self-test their knowledge in a given subject at any time during the semester. This feedback gave us the idea to prepare an experiment to be completed during the academic year 2006-2007 with 12th grade students adapting questions from the national exams to access public universities in Spain.

On the other hand, given that it is also possible to include sound files in the data base of our system, we decided to run a test for a *Music* course. We design a simple test for 8th grade students with the help of the *Music* teachers of a local middle school (*Instituto de Enseñanza Secundaria Las Salinas*). Again, students were very satisfied with their performances in the exam, except for two of them who misunderstood the rules for validating their answers.

In these two experiments at local secondary schools, we decided not to penalize students for getting a wrong answer. To do so, we set up the tool so that it added 1 point per correct answer and 0 points per wrong or blank answer to the student grade.

The results of both tests are included in Table 2 following the same structure as Table 1:

Table 2 Description of different tests at secondary school

Course	#questions; #answers; time	Didactic units	Participation	Grading	Passed
Algebra I (Mar. 05)	8; 4 per question; 50 min.	4	90% (28/31)	1;0	82%
Music (May 06)	6; 4 per question; 20 min.	3	100% (24/24)	1;0	92%

It is worth mentioning that the passing rate was extremely high in both cases. Despite the lack of statistically significant data at this level, all the parties involved in the experiments agreed on the positive educative aspects of the usage of this tool as an assessment tool.

The teachers were a little concerned at the beginning with their lack of knowledge of the management of the tool. They all overcame this feeling with the continuous support offered by the members of our research team.

We deeply believe that it is crucial to engage students in critical thinking especially at the secondary education level nowadays. For that it is important that they get used to different evaluation systems as well as to the progressive integration of new technologies in the classroom.

There are a lot of improvements to make in this direction. Teachers at primary and secondary schools in our country feel often discouraged when it comes to the use of new technologies in the classroom. It is true that there are many tools available for them through the Spanish Ministry of Science and Education. However, it is very hard, some times even impossible, for them to use these applications without close supervision and permanent personalized assistance. Many tools are too wide and complicated to use. They offer functionalities that the teacher might not need and this fact makes its practical use in the classroom even harder for the instructor.

We believe that it is important to study how to build an effective system of preparation and professional development for general teachers concentrating on their continuous formation and technical support.

6.   CONCLUSIONS AND FUTURE WORK

After all the preliminary study described above with the beta-version of the tool including the five tests that have been run, we are developing iTest, the new tool that implements all the extra features discussed in section 3.

We are also in the position of designing a formal study of an extensive use of the system to obtain statistically significant results.

In order to do so, we are establishing a cooperation agreement between our Institution and the Education Department of Aranjuez City Council. This agreement includes a project with the regional resource center (*Centro de Apoyo al Profesorado*) in Aranjuez to develop courses to instruct secondary school teachers on the use this tool this coming academic year 2006-2007. The courses will be taught by professors from our research team at our Computer Science Department. There will also be technicians working full time to be sure that the tool always works properly and to implement the new needs that could arise while the teachers are extensively using the software with their students. They will also provide continuous assistance to the teachers using the tool.

The flexibility of this type of systems is so big that its use at other educational levels (primary education, adult education, students with special needs, etc) could be easily given with the appropriate equipment and with the adaptation of the formation courses for the teachers to the precise educational level.

Signing this kind of institutional agreements will build affiliations and promote dialog among individuals from different statements to affect positive change in the academic community of the city of Aranjuez.

ACKNOWLEDGEMENTS

The authors would like to express their gratitude to all the students and instructors involved in all the tests mentioned in this article. The nature of our project allowed us to work effectively from the geographic distance with lots of people from different institutions without necessarily meeting in person.

We would especially like to thank the following people:

Former student advisors: D. J. Bodas, R. Sánchez and F. J. Soltero, instructors at the Computer Science Department, CES Felipe II.

Student development Groups: J. Barba, B. Blanco, D. Jiménez, F. Pérez, V. Sánchez, D. Sanz and J. Fernández.

Secondary education teachers: V. Díaz from IES Las Salinas, Seseña, Toledo, Spain and A. Corbato from IES Fortuny, Madrid, Spain.

This work has been partially supported by the program *Acciones Especiales AE-5/06-15073 del Vicerrectorado de Investigación de la Universidad Complutense de Madrid.*

REFERENCES

Aragon S., and Johnson S., 2002, An Instructional Strategy Framework for Online Learning Environments, in: *Proceedings of World Conference on E-Learning in Corporate, Government, Healthcare, and Higher Education* edited by G. Richards (Chesapeake, VA: AACE), pp. 529-536.

Macdonald C. J., Stodel E. J., Farres L. G., Breithaupt K., and Gabriel M. A., 2001, The demand-driven learning model: A framework for Web-based learning, Internet and Higher Education 4, 9-30.

Chapman N. S., 2004, Various ways of Using Online Testing in a Virtual Learning Environment, Brookes eJournal of Learning and Teaching, 1(1), 1-5.

Suanpang P.,Petocz P., and Kalceff W., (2003) Student Attitudes To Learning Business Statistics Online Vs Traditional Methods, in: HERDSA 2003 Learning for an Unknown Future (Christchurch, New Zealand).

IMS, 2006; http://www.imsglobal.org

SCORM, 2006; http://www.adlnet.gov/scorm/index.cfm

Blackboard, 2006; http://www.blackboard.com

WebCT, 2006; http://www.webct.com

Rodriguez N. C., 2005, State to try some CATS exams online, hopes for quicker results, in: The Courier-Journal.

Guijarro J. V., 2005, The global project on the information society in Extremadura: a free step towards future, in: Information Technology Interfaces, pp. 347- 351.

Díaz A., Colmenar J. M., Risco J. L., Joglar N., Sánchez R., Bodas D. J., and Soltero F. J., 2005, Experiencia educativa entre varias asignaturas, in: Actas de las XI Jornadas de Enseñanza Universitaria de Informática (Thomson).

Joglar N., Risco J. L., Sánchez R., Colmenar J. M., and Díaz A., 2006, Experiencia en el desarrollo y utilización de una herramienta de corrección automática de exámenes, in: Actas de las XII Jornadas de Enseñanza Universitaria de Informática.

Smothers V., Greene P., and Cohen C., 2004, Implementing an E-Learning Strategy, in: Strategic Reports from MedBiquitous Consortium.

Ashton H. S., Beevers C. E., Korabinski A. A., and Youngson M. A., 2006, Incorporating Partial Credit in Computer-Aided Assessment of Mathematics in Secondary Education, British Journal of Educational Technology 37(1), 93-119.

AsciiMathML, 2006; http://www1.chapman.edu/~jipsen/asciimath.html

MathPlayer, 2006; http://www.dessci.com/en/products/mathplayer

Chapter 18

GAME IMPLEMENTATION: AN INTERESTING STRATEGY TO TEACH GENETIC ALGORITHMS

José M. Chaves-González, Noé Otero-Mateo, Miguel A. Vega-Rodríguez, Juan M. Sánchez-Pérez and Juan A. Gómez-Pulido

Dept. Informática, Univ. Extremadura, Escuela Politécnica, Campus Universitario s/n, 10071 Cáceres, Spain, {jm, noe, mavega, sanperez, jangomez}@unex.es, Fax: +34-927-257-202, http://arco.unex.es

Abstract: This chapter captures the experience acquired in the development of applications based on genetic algorithms. Specifically, we implemented two games that show an intelligent behaviour by executing genetic algorithms. They both show good results as well, because they are able to play successfully against human players. Moreover, the genetic algorithms parameters are user-configurable; so, the user can modify the number of individuals per generation, the number of generations, the mutation probability of each individual, the crossover function to generate new individuals, etc. This is very useful because the applications developed also generate statistical reports that show how individuals evolve in each generation. Therefore, the user can understand the evolution and analyze results easily. With this approach the user can test several combinations of parameters to study and compare them by analyzing their behaviour, speed, etc. In conclusion, as we are going to see in this chapter, the implementation of these two genetic games is an interesting strategy in order to teach and learn genetic algorithms.

Key words: Educational Strategy; Genetic Games; Genetic Algorithms; The Rabbit and the Dogs; Ten and a Half.

1. INTRODUCTION

Bio-inspired algorithms are a set of design methodologies based on how some natural or social systems work. They are vastly applied to several fields. Specifically, evolutionary algorithms are a sort of bio-inspired

205

B. Fernández-Manjón et al. (eds.), Computers and Education: E-learning, From Theory to Practice, 205–223.
© 2007 *Springer*.

algorithms based on the evolution mechanism. Species arise, then evolve and finally disappear. While they evolve, only some individuals survive. They are usually the individuals best adapted to the environment (Mitchell, 1998).

In evolutionary computing, genetic algorithms are one of the most complete and theoretically developed paradigms (Mitchell, 1998; Goldberg 1989), based on Neo-Darwinism and aimed to solve complex problems. Figure 18-1 shows the classical working schema for a genetic algorithm.

A genetic algorithm works over an initial population of individuals. Some of them, the best ranked by a fitness function, are selected to be parents for the next generation. This next generation is obtained by crossing and merging the parents' features that made them to be the best individuals. Some mutation probability is usually introduced to add new features in the new generation of individuals. These new features are not shown in parents, so the population evolves easily. The offspring is the new generation in the population, and the old individuals die (sometimes not all of them, but most). The fitness function will evaluate again each individual in the new generation, which is supposed to be better suited for the environment (new individuals are better problem solvers) than the old ones. Anyway, they are worse than individuals in the next generation, so the genetic algorithm can keep producing new generations until the stop criterion is reached.

If we select the individuals among the potential solutions for a problem (a move in a game, for example), only the best solutions of each generation are chosen to produce more individuals. For this reason, if there are generations enough, an optimal solution will be achieved at the end of the process.

On the other hand, it is known that the best way to understand, learn and study in depth a computational model is to build it in practice (Vega-Rodríguez et al, 2001; Granado-Criado et al, 2006). If students implement a model, they discover and learn fine details that the model has. Sometimes it is impossible to see these details if some complex concepts are only studied in a theoretical way.

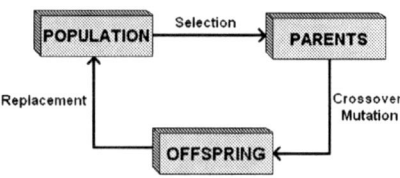

Figure 18-1. Genetic algorithm working schema.

Moreover, not only the practical application is relevant. It is also important that the topic which is going to be studied is attractive for the students (Gallego et al, 2006; Aznar et al, 2006; Overmars, 2004) because only if the students are motivated, their involvement will be increased and they will develop very good jobs (Garris et al, 2002; Martens et al, 2004). As a consequence, both students and the teacher will obtain a pleasant and nice sensation of a well-done job.

In this chapter, we present our experience in teaching and learning genetic algorithms by means of the development of two games:

- Sam, Coyote and Tazmanian Devil vs. the Road Runner - a funny variation of the game "the rabbit and the dogs" (Paredes-Juárez et al, 2006).
- The ten and a half game (a variation of the Spanish card game "Seven and a half" which is played with British cards).

In the following sections we explain in depth the implemented applications and their genetic components, as well as the results obtained with them and the educational conclusions that we have reached with the development and use of both games.

We want to emphasize that in both games the user can configure the different genetic parameters and then he/she can run the game with the chosen configuration. Both applications generate reports about the genetic behaviour of the games which the user can analyze and work with. For example, the reports are very useful if they are used to find an optimal genetic combination or to study the influence that the configuration of different parameters has on the artificial intelligence of the games: very important aspects from an educational point of view.

2.   THE RABBIT AND THE DOGS GAME

The game "the rabbit and the dogs" (Paredes-Juárez et al, 2006) or the version developed for this work: "Sam, Coyote and Taz versus the Road Runner" is a board game that consist in 3 dogs (the characters of the Sheep Dog Sam, Wile E. Coyote and Tazmanian Devil in our case) that try to catch a rabbit (the Road Runner) in a board with a particular dimensions and characteristics. We can see in figure 18-2 the game board and the places which are taken by the different characters when the game starts.

2.1   Game description

The user can play both in the dogs' team and in the rabbit team. The application controls, using a genetic algorithm, the team which is not selected by the user. The goal of the dogs' team is to trap the Road Runner, or in other words, the dogs have to force the Road Runner to go to a square in the board where he can not do any movement. Only three cells in the board make this possible (see figure 18-3). On the other hand, the Road Runner goal is to get rid of the dogs. If the Road Runner gets to be on the left side of the three dogs, or the dogs move 17 times without catching the Road Runner, he wins the game.

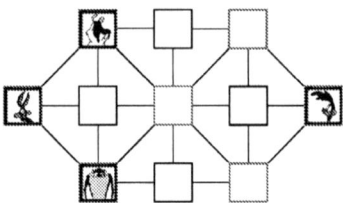

Figure 18-2. Game board for "Sam, Coyote and Taz vs. the Road Runner".

The game board has 11 positions and the connections which are drawn in figure 18-2. When the game starts, the dogs are on the left side of the board, one in each row, and the Road Runner is just on the opposite side, in the central row on the right-hand side. The game always starts with the persecution team (Taz, Coyote or Sam), and they swap the turn with the Road Runner alternatively until the match ends.

During the dogs turn, any of them can move, with neither restriction of repetition nor order among them. They only have some movement limitations: Taz, Coyote and Sam only can move towards empty adjacent cells which are connected with a line in the board and which are on the right,up or down to their position (dogs can not move back). On the other hand, the Road Runner can move to any empty adjacent cell (no matter if he goes up, goes down, goes forward or goes backward).

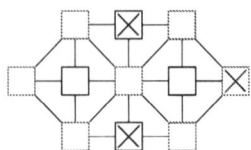

Figure 18-3. Places where the Road Runner can be trapped.

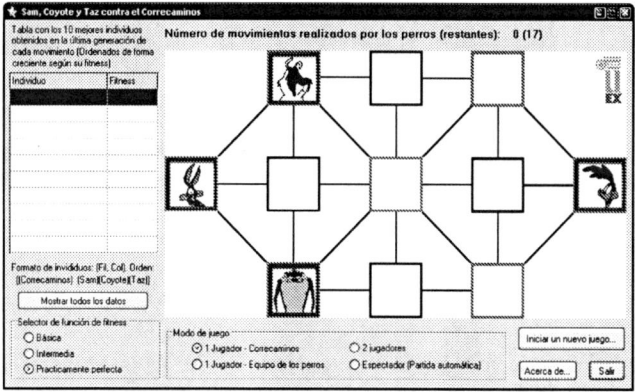

Figure 18-4. Main window of the game.

The main window of the game (see figure 18-4) has the following important parts:

- Just in the middle the board game is located. To move the characters in their appropriate turns, the user uses the mouse.
- In the top right corner there is a counter with the number of movements that the dogs have done until that moment to catch the Road Runner. If this counter reaches 17, the dogs lose the game.
- In the bottom right corner there are 3 buttons for the application management (Start a new game, quit the program and show the credits).
- In the bottom left corner, there is a control to select the fitness function which is going to be used during the game. The user can choose three different levels. Depending on the level of the fitness function, the individuals of each generation will have a better or worse behaviour.
- Down and in the centre of the window, a box to configure the game mode is placed. There are 4 different modes: the user can play with the dogs' team, or with the Road Runner team, but also it is possible that two users play a game between them, one controlling the dogs and another playing with the Road Runner (no genetic algorithm is working in this case). Finally, the program can be configured to play with no users. In this last case the application manages (by using genetic algorithms) the two teams and the user only sees how the game is performed and how it finishes.
- In the top left corner, there is a table with the 10 best individuals obtained in the last generation of the current movement, ordered from the lower to the upper value according to their calculated fitness. So, the individual placed in the first row of the table is the one which is selected to perform the actual movement. The individual is situated on the left column

(following a specific format that we will explain later) of the table and the value of the fitness function for that individual in that concrete movement is located on the right column.

- Just under the table described in the previous point, there is a button to open the file where all the genetic information about the game is saved. The format of the file that contains such information is explained in the *Results* subsection.

2.2   Genetic configuration of the game

The configuration of the game parameters is the first step to start a new game. These parameters are: *the fitness function* (there are three different functions, one for each level of difficulty in the game: easy, intermediate and advanced), *the game mode* (we have to decide which team is going to be controlled by the computer), and *the genetic parameters* of the game. These genetic parameters are fixed using the window shown in figure 18-5.

The configurable genetic parameters are the following:

- The number of individuals for each generation. This parameter can take values from 1 to 50. If the user does not change this parameter, it takes the value 16. We have checked the genetic algorithm and we know that 16 individuals in the population are enough to obtain good results. In case that the user selects only 1 individual per generation, no crossover is done (the individual will only change its genes from the mutation process). Therefore, it makes nonsense to select a population of only one individual, but the application allows it for didactic purposes (to compare different genetic configurations, even extreme values). The highest number of individuals is 50, because we have tested the game and we know that a higher number is useless for the genetic algorithm used.

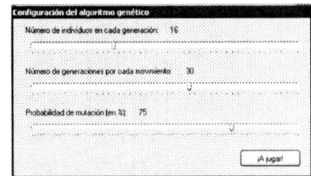

Figure 18-5. Window for the configuration of the genetic algorithm.

- The number of generations for each movement in the game. This parameter takes values from 1 to 50. As we explained with the previous parameter, it does not make a lot of sense to configure the number of generations with only one generation, but that can be useful to do some comparative studies. Besides, less than 30 generations are enough to produce the best movement in a game (but it depends on the number of individuals, which is configurable), so if the user does not touch this parameter, it takes the value 30.
- The mutation probability (in %). The mutation process consists in a random change in one of the genes of the genome of an individual. The default percentage is 75%, which means that the 75% of the new individuals in a generation suffer a mutation.

As we pointed out, both the genetic parameter ranges and the concrete default values have been obtained with the experience, making a lot of tests with lots of different values. We have specially taken care that the extreme values are wide enough to make comparative studies with even extreme configurations.

In the following sections we explain the representation of the genome, the correspondence between genotype and phenotype, how the initialization of the population is done, how we perform the individuals evaluation, which are the crossover and mutation operators, the selection and replacement strategies and the termination condition for the genetic algorithm.

2.3 Genome description

The design of the genome is very important in the development of a genetic algorithm. The genome contains the characteristic information which is inherited and improved from a generation to the next one. As we can see in figure 18-6, the genome for this game is made up with an array of 8 genes (1 byte per each cell), where the two first cells are the coordinates (row and column) of the Road Runner on the board. The following two cells are the row and column of Sam in the board, the two next ones are the coordinates (row and column) of Coyote and the two last are the row and column where Taz is situated in the board.

We have to point out that although the dimensions of the game board are 3x5, we do not consider the four corners (see figure 18-2). So, the rows of the board are 0, 1 and 2 (from the up to the down side of the board) and the columns are 0, 1, 2, 3 and 4 (from the left side to the right side). The positions (0,0), (0,4), (2,0) and (2,4) do not exist in the board.

Road Runner Row	Road Runner Column	Sam Row	Sam Column	Coyote Row	Coyote Column	Taz Row	Taz Column

Figure 18-6. Genome format used in the game.

The relation between the phenotype and the genotype is quite easy. The genotype is the array which is described in figure 18-6, and the phenotype is the game board. The genotype which represents the initial state of the board (figure 18-2) is: [1,4,0,1,1,0,2,1], or if it is shown as a list of coordinates: [(1,4), (0,1), (1,0), (2,1)]. This means, according to figure 18-6, that the Road Runner is situated in the position (1,4) on the board, Sam in the coordinate (0,1), Coyote in the (1,0) position and Taz' devil in (2,1). When we started the work, we thought that a good genome could be the full game board, which means to consider an array with 11 genes (one byte per each cell in the board), but we have chosen a representation that allows to hold all the necessary information with less bytes, so we think it is a quite better structure for the final representation of the genotype.

2.4   Fitness function

This game has two different evaluation functions. One is for Sam, Coyote and Taz and another different one is for the Road Runner. It can not be the same, because the two teams have different objectives. An individual which is good for the dogs, because for instance, it almost traps the Road Runner, probably will be bad for the Road Runner; so the evaluation functions have to be different. We start studying the fitness function for the dogs.

One of the most difficult tasks in this work was to get that the dogs' evaluation function works perfectly. It is proved that if the dogs' team plays with no errors, they win the game, so the fitness function has to be perfectly fixed to obtain this result. However, the user probably is going to get boring if the dogs always win; so, we have developed three different versions for the evaluation function. But it is not only important the evaluation function, a right genetic configuration is also very important for the right behaviour of the characters. With too few generations per movement or too few individuals in the population, the artificial intelligence of a character will not be very high, although the evaluation function is very good. We can observe the pseudo-code for the full fitness function used for the dogs' team in figure 18-7.

```
int FitnessForDogs (TSIndividual *individual)
{
      fitness = 0;
      nMovRabbit = NumberMovementsRabbit (individual);

      //We give a lot of influence to the winner movement
      if (!nMovRabbit) fitness += 50000;

      fitness -= 1000 * RabbitOvertakesDogs (individual);
      fitness += DogGetsCentre (individual) ? 500 : 0;
      fitness -= RabbitCanGetCentre (individual) ? 3000 : 0;
      fitness -= 100 * RabbitNumMovements (individual);
      fitness -= RabbitRowEmpty (individual) ? 50 : 0;
      fitness += OneDogPerRow (individual) ? 20 : 0;
      fitness += RabbitAlmostTrapped (individual) ? 1000 : 0;
      fitness += Conditional3InARow (individual) ? 1000 : 0;
      fitness -= BadCase3InARow (individual) ? 2000 : 0;
      fitness += GoodStart (individual) ? 120 : 0;
      fitness -= EmptyColBetweenDogs&Rabbit (individual) ? 10000 : 0;
      fitness -= TwoDogsInARowInFinalCols (individual) ? 600 : 0;
      fitness -= LooserRhombus (individual) ? 10000 : 0;
      fitness -= StartALoop (individual) ? 10000 : 0;
      fitness += WinningCover (individual) ? 30000 : 0;
      return fitness;
}
```

Figure 18-7. Pseudo-code for the fitness function when the computer plays with dogs.

The value of the fitness is initialized to 0 at the beginning of the fitness function. The final value can be positive or negative, because, as we can see in figure 18-7, some functions add something to the final result and another subtract something from the final fitness. The number of movements that the Road Runner has is the first value which is calculated. If the result of this function is 0, the Road Runner is trapped, so, that individual makes the dogs win the game. For this reason, we give a lot of points (+50000) to this function (this individual has to be chosen if it appears). If this winning individual does not appear, the fitness function has 15 more little functions. The first of them is very valuable, because it is very important for the dogs that the Road Runner does not overtake them (because this would mean that he wins the game). So, for each dog overtaken by the Road Runner, 1000 points will be taken away from the fitness. Moreover, it is very important for the dogs to get the central square, because it is the cell which gives more freedom of movements. If the Road Runner gets this cell, he will very probably win the game. So, if an individual represents that one of the dogs is in that cell, that individual adds 500 points to its fitness. On the other hand, if an individual represents that the Road Runner is in the central cell, that individual subtracts 3000 points to its fitness value, because that individual makes the Road Runner wins the game (and for this reason is a very bad individual for the dog team).

The common sense and the experience acquired doing tests have been the principal rules that we have used to create all the expressions of the fitness function. It is true that some functions control little details of the game, but the fitness function shown in figure 18-7 supplies an almost perfect behaviour for the dogs team, so, it is important to take into account little details.

To sum up, the fitness for a dog individual is calculated with all the considerations that can be observed in figure 18-7. With the fitness obtained in the last generation of a movement, it is evaluated which move is performed when the dogs play in their turn. The higher value of the fitness, the better movement for the dogs, so, the individual with the highest value will be the selected one for the movement that the dogs' team will do in their turn.

On the other hand, the Road Runner fitness function is quite easier than the function for the dogs, because there are fewer parameters to consider in this case. It is easier to decide the movement for a single character than for three characters, and besides, in this game, the heuristic to escape is simpler than the heuristic to trap (because of the characteristics of the game). Figure 18-8 shows the evaluation function code for the Road Runner.

Similar to the dogs, when the Road Runner plays, its fitness function is calculated for each individual type "Road Runner". In this case, the criteria to calculate the fitness change, because the objective is that the Road Runner escapes from the dogs. As we can see in figure 18-8 the evaluation function

```
int FitnessForRR (TBoard *board, TSIndividual *individual)
{
    fitness = 0;
    nMovRabbit = NumberMovementsRabbit (individual);
    nDogsOverTaken = RabbitOvertakesDogs (individual);
    //We give a lot of influence to the winner movement
    if (nDogsOverTaken == 3) fitness += 6000;

    if (!nMovRabbit) fitness -= 1000;
    if (nMovRabbit == 1 && !RabbitProgressLevel (board, individual))
        fitness -= 2000;
    fitness += 100 * RabbitNumMovements (individual);
    fitness += EmptyColBetweenDogs&Rabbit (individual) ? 50 : 0;
    fitness += LooserRhombusForDogs (individual) ? 1000 : 0;
    fitness += RabbitGetsCentre (individual) ? 1000 : 0;
    fitness += RabbitProgressLevel (board, individual) ? 300 : 0;
    fitness += RabbitInLevel1or2 (individual) ? 500 : 0;
    fitness += 500 * NumDogsSameLevel0rHigher (individual);
    return fitness;

}
```

Figure 18-8. Pseudo-code for the fitness function when the computer plays with the Road Runner.

gives a lot of points to the movement that makes the Road Runner win (+6000). It is penalized that the Road Runner does not have movements (-1000). It is good that he has a lot of possibilities of movement, or also that an empty column is between the dogs and the Road Runner, etc. To summarize, the individuals that represent good movements add more or less points depending on how good is the movement. A movement is good if the Road Runner has a possibility to escape from the dogs, although if they play with no mistakes, it is impossible for the Road Runner to win the game.

2.5   Description of the genetic operations

In the first generation, all bytes of all individuals in the population are randomly initialized (with correct values) and the fitness of each individual is calculated. New generations are created from the previous ones. From a generation to the next one, not all the individuals are replaced, because the elitism policy is applied between the individuals of a generation and the individuals of the following. It depends on the number of individuals configured, but approximately, the 25% of the individuals of a generation pass to the next one due to the elitism mechanism. The other 75% of the new population is created from the crossover of two random parents chosen from the old population. After the crossover, some mutation is done over the new offspring (depending on the configuration that the user made up for the mutation). The mutation is done so that not all descendants come from the cross between individuals of the previous population. The process consists in the random selection of a concrete gene inside the genome of an individual and the random change of this gene (taking the new value from a valid range). Once the processes of crossover and mutation are done, the fitness for the new generation of individuals is calculated and the cycle starts again until we arrive to the last generation. The termination condition is established by the user when he/she sets the number of generations for each movement (in figure 18-5 we can see the window to configure the genetic parameters). When the algorithm gets the last generation, the best individual, according to the fitness value, is selected to perform the most appropriate movement. This movement will be the best one that the team which is playing can do in that moment of the game.

2.6   Results

All the genetic information of the game is saved in a file of results. The structure of this file is described in figure 18-9.

```
FILE OF STATISTICAL RESULTS OF THE GAME

Game configuration:
    Game mode: {which team is managed by the computer}
    Fitness function behaviour: {basic, intermediate, almost perfect}
    Number of individuals for each generation: {1..50}
    Number of generation for each movement: {1..50}
    Mutation probability: {0..100}%

Results obtained in the game:
    Game movement: 0
        Generation: 0
            Individual 0 → Genome: [(1,4) (0,2) (1,0) (2,1)] and Fitness: x
            ... ... ... ...                    ...           ...
            Individual n → Genome: [(1,4) (0,2) (1,1) (2,1)] and Fitness: x+y
        ...        ...      ...      ...       ...       ...       ...       ...        ...
        Generation: m
            Individual 0 → Genome: [(1,4) (0,2) (1,0) (2,1)] and Fitness: x
            ... ... ... ...                    ...           ...
            Individual n → Genome: [(1,4) (0,2) (1,1) (2,1)] and Fitness: x+y
    ...      ...       ...       ...       ...       ...       ...       ...       ...        ...       ...
    Game movement: Last movement of the game
        Generation: 0
            Individual 0 → Genome: [(2,3) (0,3) (1,0) (2,1)] and Fitness: x
            ... ... ... ...                 ...           ...              ...          ...
            Individual n → Genome: [(2,3) (1,2) (0,1) (2,1)] and Fitness: x+y
    ...      ...      ...      ...              ...              ...             ...       ...
        Generation: m
            Individual 0 → Genome: [(2,3) (0,3) (1,0) (2,1)] and Fitness: x
            ... ... ... ...                 ...           ...              ...          ...
            Individual n → Genome: [(2,3) (1,2) (0,1) (2,1)] and Fitness: The highest one
```

Figure 18-9. General structure of the results file.

The file of results, which structure is shown in figure 18-9, is very important, because it makes possible to study in depth the behaviour of the genetic algorithm used in the game (for each generation) and to compare different genetic configurations in a quantitative way. The file is divided in two parts. In the first part is detailed the configuration of the game (the configurable parameters are explained in the previous subsections and can be briefly explored at the beginning of the file -figure 18-9-). However, the most relevant information in the file appears in its second part (in the subsection "Results obtained in the game") because in this subsection, all the genetic data generated during the game are detailed. The file of results contains each single individual (with the specific genome) and the value of the fitness for that individual. Besides, they are ordered by the fitness value from the worse to the best individual. So, the last individual is the best in that generation. Moreover, the information is detailed for all generations of each movement in the game. So, the last individual of the last generation in a movement is the individual chosen to perform the movement, and the last individual of the last generation in the last movement will be the individual with highest value in its fitness, because it is the individual that makes the final winning movement (if we consider that the team which is managed by the computer wins the game).

The information which is hold in the file of results is very useful, for example, to determinate the number of generations, or how many individuals are needed to find a valid solution for each level of the fitness function. It is also possible to study what happens with the individuals if too many generations are fixed (when the genetic algorithm finds the solution, all the individuals for all the generations from that moment, have the same fitness). On the other hand, if fewer generations than the necessaries are established, the characters will make bad movements, and the fitness will be low.

In conclusion, with the information contained in the file of results, we can study in depth how the behaviour of the individuals changes (and in what quantity) depending on the different configurations established (for the genetic algorithm), which is very important from an educational point of view.

3. THE TEN AND A HALF GAME

The ten and a half game is a card game based on a popular card game called "seven and a half" that is played with Spanish playing cards. Ten and a half is played with British playing cards. This game was selected in order to complete the genetic algorithms study that is initiated with the game explained in the previous section. In "the ten and a half" game we use different techniques to develop different genetic algorithms, so both games make this work more complete and richer in didactic experiences and contents.

3.1 Game description

The objective of the game for each player (computer or human) is to get 10.5 points or the nearest possible, without going further. At the end of each round, the player that reaches the nearest sum to 10.5, but does not overtake it, is the winner. Anyway, there are some special cases that may modify this rule and that we explain below.

The game is played with British cards, with the four card suits (hearts, clubs, diamonds and spades), 13 cards each. In each suit, there are cards numbered from 1 to 10, plus a Jack, a Queen and a King. Each numbered card scores the number it has. J, Q and K scores 0.5 points.

To get points, one of the players asks for one card after another to an automatic croupier pressing a button in the interface. In each turn the player can ask for as many cards as he/she wants (one is the minimum) or until he/she goes over 10.5 points. If this happens, he/she has to tell the other player that he/she went over 10.5. If he/she is below 10.5, the cards stay hidden on the table, waiting for the other player to play his/her turn. The turn to ask for cards is randomly assigned before each round. When a round is over, the following rules are evaluated to decide who the winner is. The order of the rules is relevant:

1. If only one player has a punctuation of 10.5, he/she is the winner.
2. If both players have a punctuation of 10.5, the winner is the player who took cards first.
3. If not, if both players have a punctuation below 10.5, the winner is the player with the greatest punctuation below 10.5. If they both have the same number of points, the winner is the player who took cards first.
4. If not (both players went over 10.5), the winner is the player who took cards first.

This game is a two player game. One of the players is human and the other is controlled by the computer by means of genetic algorithms. The genetic algorithm looks for a good playing strategy before the game starts. The game also has a didactic value because it includes the following features:

1. The ability to adjust the genetic algorithm to generate a good playing strategy for the ten and a half game.
2. The ability to log *and analyze* the genetic algorithm execution.
3. A counter of the rounds won by each player to evaluate the goodness of the strategy obtained with the genetic algorithm.

The main application window is shown in figure 18-10. The following elements are present:

- Information about the current game status, on the top of the window.
- At the bottom and in the middle of the window there is the rounds counter (which also counts how many rounds the human player has won and lost).
- The playing zone in the centre of the window. Cards are always in the playing zone. They appear while the players ask for them.
- User controls, below the playing zone. The application has buttons to: run the genetic algorithm, play (start a new round, ask for a card, and stop asking for cards), get some useful information (how to play, analyzed genetic algorithm execution results and the about dialog) and exit the application.

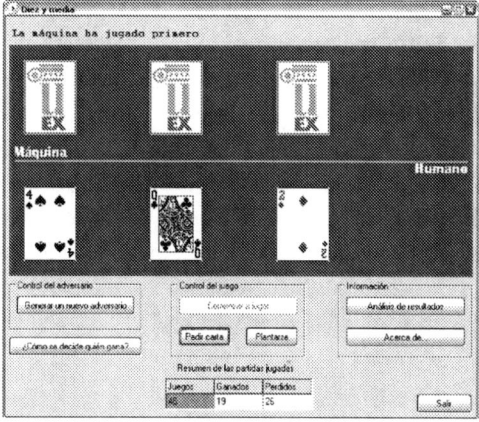

Figure 18-10. Application main window.

3.2   Genetic configuration of the game

As in "the rabbit and the dogs" game, before the game starts, it is compulsory to generate an opponent. The window shown in figure 18-11 has the necessary controls to do that.

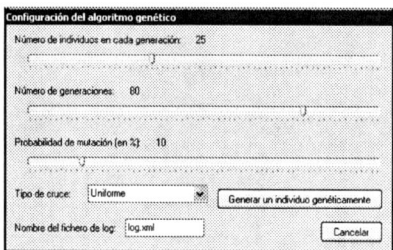

Figure 18-11. Genetic algorithm configuration window

The following parameters can be configured (fig. 18-11):

- The number of individuals per generation, between 2 and 100. Default value is 25.
- The number of generations, between 1 and 100. Default value is 80.
- The mutation probability (in %). Default value is 10%.

- The crossover. The user can choose uniform crossover, one point crossover or two point crossover.
- The name of the XML log file that stores the data generated from the genetic algorithm execution. This feature is an improvement in the log system of the previous game. Now the results are in a XML file, which is more standard than the text file used in "the rabbit and the dogs" game. However, both log files have the same purpose: analyze and help to understand and improve the genetic behaviour of the games.

3.3   Description of the individual

The genome of the individual has a length of 21 bits; each bit represents a boolean value. The individual can decide to ask for another card or to stop asking for cards during a game by querying its genome. Each bit in the genome relates to a possible accumulated score in that game. The first bit is required by the individual to decide if it wants another card when its score is 0, second when its score is 0.5, third when its score is 1 and so on. The 21st bit is queried when the score is 10 (since it makes nonsense to ask for another card when you have scored 10.5!). Figure 18-12 is a graphical representation of an individual's genome.

A good player has true boolean values in the first cells of the genome (when the score is low) and false values in the last cells (it refuses to take more cards when it has a considerable score, because if it goes over 10.5, he/she can lose the game easily).

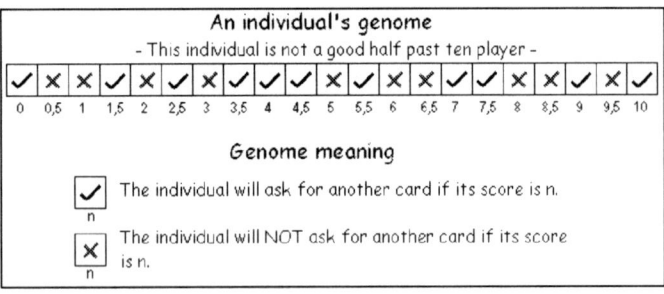

Figure 18-12. An individual's genome

3.4   Description of genetic operations

There is a simple statistical model to calculate how the perfect ten and a half player should behave. We could have calculated this individual and design a fitness function that somehow measures the "distance" between this perfect individual and a given one. But instead, we decided not to employ any external information to evaluate players. We use a tournament selection method. In each generation, each individual plays several games against every individual in that generation. Each individual has a counter of how many rounds it won and how many it lost (actually, a counter that counts victories minus defeats). This is a good measure of how good a player is in its own generation, so, we choose the parents for the next generation taking into account that counter. We also introduce elitism (parents survive from a generation to the next one) to ensure that if a good player arises in early generations it survives until it can not win its own offspring any more. The crossover can be chosen among random (bits are taken randomly from mother or father), in one, or two points crossover; so we can evaluate the results with each of them. Finally, there is also a chance for the mutation in each individual. A mutation consists in switching randomly the boolean value of a concrete gene (chosen randomly too).

3.5   Results

This game not only logs the results of a game, but also analyzes them. As we told in 3.2, when a new player is generated by the genetic algorithm, a XML log file is created. This file logs the algorithm configuration and tracks each generation by logging each individual, its genome, and its fitness function value. The log file can be analyzed with any XML parser, but the application has a simple built-in tool to do it. The dialog window which analyzes the results from the XML file generated in a game is shown in figure 18-13. Using this window, the user can load an XML file generated by the application to browse the data contained on it.

As it is shown in figure 18-13, on the left side there is a list with every generation which was generated during the execution. Clicking on a concrete generation, more detailed information is obtained. This information is shown on the right side of the window, and it consists in a list with every individual of the generation and the value of the fitness function for each. This list is also graphically displayed, with each individual represented by a bar. The more fitness the individual has, the higher its bar is. Clicking on an individual also it is shown its genome at the top of the window. Finally, at

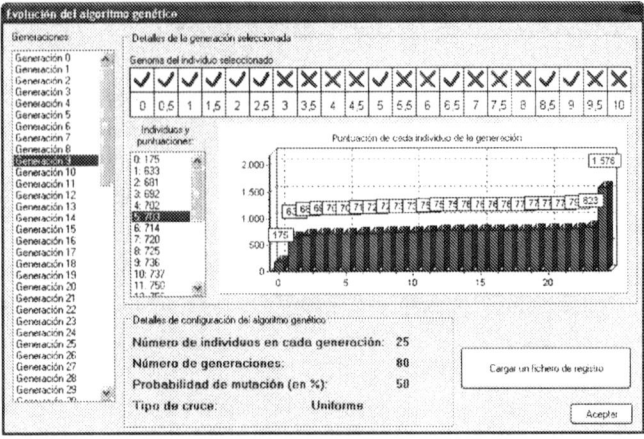

Figure 18-13. Results analysis window.

the bottom, the configuration parameters are situated. These parameters were the ones used in that concrete execution of the genetic algorithm (and they were selected using the window in figure 18-11).

4.   CONCLUSIONS

The work expounded in this chapter describes both the main features of the games our students build and the educational experience we get with their development. It is possible that the inner characteristics of the chosen applications do not take all advantages that genetic algorithms offer, because genetic algorithms are used in problems where their solution is difficult to reach, and in our case, the developed games have quite easy solutions, and maybe other techniques of artificial intelligence would have been better to solve them. However, the development of this type of applications has, what we can consider, educational advantages. The implemented programs are quite simple, but students have to understand complex concepts to build them. So, if we propose an interesting, easy to understand and funny activity to a student, we will probably get better results than the obtained ones with a boring or hard activity. The reason is clear: motivated students (or motivated people in general) get involved in which they are studying (Cordova and Lepper, 1996; Lepper and Cordova, 1992), and they will probably obtain better results that the students that learn something because they have the obligation to do it. If a student, not only studies something, but also understands it, uses it in practice and besides, he/she does it in an entertaining way, he/she is motivated and learns much more.

So we can conclude that this kind of practices is a very interesting pedagogical experience that makes the study of genetic algorithms (in our case) going from theory assimilation to good understanding of how these algorithms work. Therefore, the implementation of games as a practical usage of artificial intelligence problems based on genetic algorithms motivates the students to go further when they build a first version of the program, because probably the behaviour of the automatic player will not be as good as the students want. Then, the students will analyze the results obtained with the program, they will try different configurations, they will change the algorithms used and, at the end, they will change the classical learning process into an amusing and entertaining sort of game that gives them much more satisfaction that any other theoretical lesson.

REFERENCES

Aznar, F.; Suau, P.; Compañ, P.; Rizo, R. Aprender Jugando: ¿Qué Opinan los Alumnos?. XII JENUI, Bilbao, Spain, pp. 199-206, July 2006. (in Spanish)

Cordova, D.I.; Lepper, M.R. Intrinsic Motivation and the Process of Learning: Beneficial Effects of Contextualization, Personalization, and Choice. Journal of Educational Psychology, vol. 88, no. 4, pp. 715-730, 1996.

Gallego, F.; Satorre, R.; Llorens, F. Computer Games Tell, Show, Involve,... and Teach. 8th Int. Symposium on Computers in Education, León, Spain, pp. 157-165, October 2006.

Garris, R.; Ahlers, R.; Driskell, J.E. Games, Motivation and Learning: A Research and Practice Model. Simulation & Gaming, vol. 33, no. 4, pp. 441-467, 2002.

Goldberg, D.E. Genetic Algorithms in Search, Optimization and Machine Learning. Addison-Wesley, January 1989.

Granado-Criado, J.M.; Vega-Rodríguez, M.A.; Ballesteros-Rubio, J.; Sánchez-Pérez, J.M.; Gómez-Pulido, J.A. Teaching Reconfigurable Computing in the New EHEA by means of the Multicycle MIPS Machine Implementation. 6th International Workshop on Microelectronics Education, Stockholm, Sweden, pp. 104-107, June 2006.

Lepper, M.R.; Cordova, D.I. A Desire to be Taught: Instructional Consequences of Intrinsic Motivation. Motivation and Emotion, vol. 16, pp. 187-208, 1992.

Martens, R.L.; Gulikers, J.; Bastiaens, T. The Impact of Intrinsic Motivation on E-Learning in Authentic Computer Tasks. Journal of Computer Assisted Learning, vol. 20, no. 5, pp. 368-376, 2004.

Mitchell, M. An Introduction to Genetic Algorithms. The MIT Press, February 1998.

Overmars, M. Teaching Computer Science through Game Design. IEEE Computer, vol. 37, no. 4, pp. 81-83, 2004.

Paredes-Juárez, R.G.; Ramírez-Morales, A.A.; Saito-Vázquez N. A. http://www.cs.tcu.edu/people/professors/asanchez/cosc40503/RasGA/index.html, 2006.

Vega-Rodríguez, M.A.; Sánchez-Pérez, J.M.; Gómez-Pulido, J.A. An Educational Tool for Testing Caches on Symmetric Multiprocessors. Microprocessors and Microsystems, vol. 25, no. 4, pp. 187-194, June 2001.

Chapter 19

INSTRUCTIONAL THEORIES TO MODEL EDUCATIONAL CONTENT: A CASE STUDY

Diego Bodas Sagi[1] and Miguel Rodríguez-Artacho[2]
[1] Ingeniería Técnica en Informática de Sistemas CES Felipe II 28300 Aranjuez, Spain [2] Dept. de Lenguajes y Sistemas Informáticos, UNED University 28040 Madrid, Spain

Abstract: This paper describes an experience to apply instructional design theories using formal specifications to model educational content. Our aim is to extend learning content specifications to cover instructional theories in the current trend of learning technologies standards to provide a formalization framework for templates and instructional patterns. We use LODAS (Learning Object Design and Sequencing Theory) to define the theoretical instructional framework in combination with PALO modelling language. LODAS use Learning Objects and provides instructional methods to create and apply them within sequencing and classification models. PALO is a formal specification to model educational material based on instructional templates and ontology-based repositories of Learning Objects. Our work shows a case study to use PALO formal specification to provide instructional templates based on LODAS methods that could be incorporated into an authoring tool.

Key words: Instructional theory, educational modelling language, learning object, instructional pattern.

1.   INTRODUCTION

The study of formal specifications to model educational content is one of the main issues in learning technologies (LT) research. The variety of specifications developed so far strongly facilitate the creation of reusable learning objects providing structure, packaging and sequencing attending to

225

B. Fernández-Manjón et al. (eds.), Computers and Education: E-learning, From Theory to Practice, 225–233.

pedagogical and instructional patterns, including the definition of complex instructional tasks. This complexity includes the development of software interfaces attached to the learning object to achieve software interoperability with the Learning Management Systems (LMS) and Run Time Environments (RTE).

However, in the framework of LT specification development there is currently a need to structure and link with instructional patterns the recent specification paradigms obtained from the LT research (Paquette 1999) (Leo et al., 2004). In this context some of the results in LT -as the notion of Learning Object- have been extrapolated from a variety of well known computational paradigms like *reusable component* as a software engineering concept, providing structured reusable elements labeled with metadata (Duval et al. 2001), and also from knowledge engineering, allowing content organization using knowledge-based structures like ontologies or semantic web development. On the other hand, from the cognitive sciences perspective, the adoption during the 50s and 60s of some instructional theories based on cognition have obtained useful abstractions to specify appropriate methods and situations in which those are to be applied during learning process. But, instructional theories (IT) have not evolved so far away from the original cognitive scope to the computational environment in which they are applied. Only recently has this need been noticed to combine cognitive sciences and representational mechanisms based in learning technologies (Concannon 2003) (Wiley 2000) or to create explicit instructional patters for LT specifications.

This paper applies specification patterns in the scope of LT and presents a case study to create templates based on an instructional theory using an educational modelling language. This theoretical framework has been pointed out as one of the three necessary components to model instructional objects along with instructional theory and a taxonomy of learning objects (Wiley 2000).

The aim is to provide instructional meaning to the learning object as a complex content description in the sense of the definition of *unit of study, which* differs from a simple aggregation of LO (as in a clip-art model). In this sense, EMLs allow not only to overcome that problem but also to define and apply instructional patterns with instructional components such as tasks, sequencing, tools, roles, etc. Additionally, this is a test bed of the expressiveness of PALO to create instructional templates and also in its capacity to represent knowledge domains based on topic maps and explicit conceptualizations.

This paper is structured as follows: section 2 describes formalization issues of instructional theories using EMLs. Section 3 describes LODAS formalization using PALO and proposes a case study and finally section 4 presents the conclusions.

2. INSTRUCTIONAL DESIGN AND CONTENT SPECIFICATIONS

Instructional Design Theories (IDT) research looks for instructional methods to enhance knowledge acquisition and new skills in the student, as well as provide descriptions of how to apply these methods to obtain the desired results (G. Soto et al. 1997).

1. Preliminary Activities
    1.1 Determine appropriateness
2. Analyze and Synthesize Content
    2.1 Principled skill decomposition
    2.2. Synthesize work models
    2.3 Identify the dimensionality of the domain
    2.4 Place work models on scales
    2.5 Synthesize integrated work models
    2.6 Expose domain map to expert review
3. Design practice and information presentation
    3.1 Classify the work models and constituent skills
    3.2 Design information presentation
4. Select and / or Design Learning Objects
5. Design Learning Object Sequencing
6. Loop Back for Quality Improvement

Figure 1: Blocks and LODAS methods

An IDT must provide means to analyze learning needs and schedule realistic goals as well as describe instructional methods and the situations in which these methods are applied, based on instructional design principles. From a computational point of view, methods are suitable to be implemented in a learning environment and provide students with mechanisms to accomplish the scheduled goals and facilitate the learning process.

These systems need not only to scaffold the learning processes in a given IDT, but the authoring process must also replicate the instructional methods and situations as instructional templates in order to create the appropriate content according to the theory (Concannon et al. 2003). In this respect, this paper focuses on LODAS, *Learning Object Design and Sequencing Theory* (Wiley 2001) as IDT because it is based on the notion of LO and it is suitable for implementation using learning technology formalisms. As mentioned in (Wiley 2001) for purposes of implementation, LODAS can be divided into two large sections: instruction design prescriptions and learning object design prescriptions. The first one considers a set of methods to decompose content into specifications; the second one proposes a sequencing of content depending on a unidimensional scale of expertise, among others. In the scope of this experience, we focus on content matter knowledge decomposition in terms of skills (to achieve) and expertise (to be accomplished). We cover the process to transform a given knowledge domain into the instructional components of the theory using an educational modelling language to describe both learning objects and sequencing.

The design process is divided into two steps. On the one hand we consider a conceptualization level of the LODAS process to reflect it in an instructional template. On the other hand, there is an instantiation level in PALO, an EML developed at UNED. PALO allows us to model units of study made up of modules and sequenced with prerequisite-based scheduling. External knowledge based on ontologies can be retrieved using a query sublanguage of the PALO structures. Additionally, the specification is defined on the basis of instructional templates based on XML schemas that define a subset of PALO language capabilities depending on the instructional purpose (Rodriguez-Artacho et al. 2004).

Entities of the language are scaffold in 6 levels: content, activities, structure, schedule, pedagogy and management. Design process is structured in two parallel steps. The first one, conceptualization level, consists of the definition of the ontology and the instructional template of PALO. The second one, the instantiation level, creates a conceptual map based on the ontology and a course based on the instructional template.

3.   BUILDING AN INSTRUCTIONAL TEMPLATE BASED ON LODAS

This section develops an instructional template in PALO to carry out LODAS methods. For clarification purposes, and based on the experience of one of the authors, we have selected a very simple content domain of *second degree equations* at secondary school. The example will be developed following the steps described in Figure 1.

The main skill to be acquired can be defined as "To identify and solve second degree equations". This global skill (1) is divided into five secondary skills: (1.1) "Solving first degree equations", (1.2) "Operating with second degree equations", (1.3) "Interpreting equations", (1.4) "Formalizing second degree equations" and (1.5) "Notation for second degree equations". Some of these skills can be grouped on the basis of common characteristics. These groups are synthesized into Work Models (WMs). As stated by LODAS, WMs are collections of individual objectives. The goal of these WMs is to develop the acquisition of certain skills through concrete tasks. According to our example we can find three clearly differentiated WMs: "First degree equations" (WM1), associated with skill 1.1. "Basic operations with second degree equations" (WM2), associated with skills 1.2 and 1.5. And finally, "Interpreting and formalizing second degree equations", (WM3) associated with skills 1.3 and 1.4.

As other instructional theories, LODAS suggests content insertion to activate knowledge required for the lesson. Consequently, sometimes we'll need a WM as a group of certain skills that (despite not being obtained from the initial decomposition) are needed anyway, like prerequisites to keep the new knowledge that we have obtained. For example, in our lesson about second degree equations it is useful to insert a WM called "Basic operations with integer and rational numbers" (WM0) as a way to make sure that students know the most essential mathematical operations.

The following step will set the dimensions of the domain where each WM has to be placed on one and only one of the dimensions of the domain. Our example is short enough to consider only the three following dimensions: Operations (calculus), Reasoning (application of mathematical laws) and Abstraction (to express a sentence in natural language into a mathematical expression). Following the steps we distribute WMs among the dimensions, thus we place WM0 in the Operations Dimension, WM1 and WM2 in the Reasoning Dimension (in addition, WM1 is a prerequisite to be able to study WM2), whereas WM3 is placed in the Abstraction Dimension. Next, we must find a scale in which we will display the different WMs by increasing the level of complexity, which represents one of the cognitive grounds of the theory. In this example, WM0 and WM1 are considered a basic content, WM2 is a medium content, and WM3 is high/difficult content. In general, the instructional designer has the choice to determine this scale and to place WMs in it.

The next step is to integrate the Work Models into the goal to assure certain pedagogical and educational goals are met. In this case, we can consider that the Operations level is easier than the Reasoning level and the last one easier than the Abstraction level. When considering aggregation of WMs, we need to take into account the intrinsic complexity of each one of them and each one of the previously created scales. In these conditions, we would not group WM0 *"Basic operations with integer and rational numbers"* with WM3 *"Interpreting and formalizing second degree equations"*, as they have different and non-consecutive difficulty levels. Instead, we will consider three WMs as WM containers, the "root" is the top-most WM called "course", where "course" contains the WMs "initiation" and "development". At the "initiation" WM we first study the WM0 "Basic operations with integer and rational numbers", and then the WM1 "First degree equations". WM2 "Basic operations with second degree equations" and WM3 "Interpreting and Formalizing second degree equations" are included in the "development" WM. So far, we have a bi-dimensional axis using one dimensionality of the domain and the complexity scale that provides the WM sequencing.   The rest of the process includes the design and arrangement of the Learning Objects used in each WM.

LODAS formalization using PALO needs to establish some valid concepts and relations to model the theory and work with its elements. Table 1 shows the concepts and relationships used:

Table 1. LODAS concepts and LODAS relations.

Entity (Concept)	Attributes	Relationship	Related entities
Skill	-	composed_by	Skill
Primitive Work	Scale	develops	Skill
Model (PWM)	(difficulty)	belongs_to	Dimension
		uses	Learning Object
		Precede_in_scale	PWM
		Precede_in_NPWM	PWM
		scope	Knowledge Domain
Non primitive work model (NPWM)	-	Contains	PWM
Dimension	-	-	-
Knowledge subdomain	-	-	-

Elementary (primitive) work models (PWM) can be grouped in "non primitive WMs" (NPWM) as shown in Table 1.   Thus, PWM are those which are no longer divisible. Relationships between entities are generally self-explained. The relation "precede_in_scale" organises work models of a given dimension increasingly, according to its difficulty. The relation "precede_in_NPWM" orders PWN of a given NPWM (the relationship also serves to link the last PWN of a NPWN with the first PWN of the next NPWN in a course sequence).

According to the previous analysis, modelling content using PALO can be carried out using the equivalence of Table 2.   The process includes creating learning objects and associating them to the different WMs according to its knowledge domain. PWM will be associated to a PALO *module* and PWM precedence will be sequenced using module prerequisites according to the precede_in_MPWM relationship. Additionally, pedagogical domains in PALO can be used to hold the conceptualization of the LODAS precedence scale. A PWM is placed on one and only one of the dimensionalities of the domain, therefore, the PWM will be related to a concrete part of one domain.

At the end of this process, the corresponding LODAS components of our example can be expressed in PALO as follows:

- External repository continues using the tag *element* to retrieve LOs, included in modules.
- Skills are included in the structure of *modules* and *sections.*
- A *module* is the main structure and corresponds to a Primitive Work Model.
- Sequencing is scheduled using precedence (according to the scale) and groups of PWM and NPWMs.
- The *course* level defines the top hierarchical element of the template

The authoring process lacks effective PALO tags to cover LODAS complexity. In this respect an enhanced template is needed, and accordingly, a new compiler to process LODAS templates must be developed. However, the rest of the methods can be implemented using PALO structure tags and external domains (See Table 2). Once modules have been defined for each one of the WMs, PALO domains can be used to instantiate WM hierarchy and dimensions. Two external domains can be defined: "LODAS" (to describe the instructional schema associated to LODAS theory), and "DIMENSIONS" (to describe knowledge associated to LODAS domain dimensions).

LODAS concept	PALO entity
SKILL	(implicit) element of a MODULE
PWM	MODULE
NPWM	Not available, can be simulated using MODULE sequence
DIMENSION	DOMAIN attribute of each ELEMENT
SUBDOMAIN	(implicit) ELEMENT sequence

Table 2: Elementary equivalences LODAS – PALO

PWMs are thus defined as the lower granularity reusable components and are implemented in PALO as elements of the external conceptualisation that can be retrieved using the *element* tag. Hierarchy of NPWM is implemented using relationships of the conceptualisation that refers to the equivalent structure of *modules*, which is not currently present in the language.

4.   CONCLUSIONS

This work describes an experience to model LODAS instructional theory, using formal content specification as an approach to extend learning content specifications to formalize instructional theories.   In order to illustrate the instructional process of the theory we have modelled a simplified study domain analyzed according to the LODAS dimensions and created a PALO specification.

Some lack of expressiveness has been noticed when describing WM structures. We have mitigated it by using PALO basic ontology for Learning Objects to describe and structure Primitive Work Models (PWM), and using relationships to describe composition hierarchy. Our LODAS model has not been able to completely formalize the skills and WM analysis, but those could be described in the ontology and referenced from the language using module attributes.

Hopefully, the work shows that we are not so far from applying LODAS methods to create a course description based on a content specification that could formalize all the steps of the theory as an instructional pattern. Taking this into consideration, the work introduces a valuable theoretical framework for the authoring process based on instructional patterns with the following principles:

- Providing instructional meaning to learning content and creating technology independent content. In this respect LT specifications are a first step.
- As an instructional theory, LODAS assures an educational process based on the principles of instructional design. Accordingly, authoring could be assisted and structured in WMs rather than in *modules* or *sections*.
- Skills are associated both to *course* and to PWMs, consequently we increase reusability, as reusing skills is easier than reusing tasks, despite the fact that the process of analyzing a content domain and identifying skills is more difficult.
- Formalizing the LODAS analysis of a given content matter can provide us with a useful analysis pattern on other similar domains.

Our future work could focus on applying these principles to an authoring tool based on PALO templates and LODAS patterns. However, more work is needed in the study of how current LT specifications facilitate the instructional design process based on IDTs.

REFERENCES

Concannon F., Byrne M., Shields J., (2003) Instructional Design and its implications for eLearning technologies. 2003 On Line: http://www.ilta.net/EdTech2003/papers/byrne_concannon_shields.doc

Duval E. and R. Robson. (2001) Guest Editorial on Metadata. Interactive Learning Environments, Special issue: Metadata, Volume 9-3, December 2001, pp. 201-206

González Soto A.P., Jiménez J.B.,et al. (1997) Grupo Educación y Telemática de la Universidad Jaime I de Castellón. Informe Preliminar TEL96-1383 (diciembre 1997) (Capítulo 6) On Line: http:// get.fcep.urv.es/publica/informe/indi6.html#i7

Leo, D.H.; Perez, J.I.A.; Dimitriadis, Y.A. (2004) IMS learning design support for the formalization of collaborative learning patterns in Advanced Learning Technologies, 2004. Proceedings. IEEE International Conference on Volume , Issue , 30 Aug.-1 Sept. 2004 Page(s): 350 - 354

Paquette G., Aubin C., & Crevier, F. (1999). MISA: A knowledge-based method for the engineering of learning systems. Journal of Courseware Engineering , 2.

Rodriguez-Artacho M. and Verdejo, M. F. (2004) Modeling Educational Content: The Cognitive Approach of the PALO Language in Journal of Educational Technology & Society (Vol. 7 # 3, 2004)

Wiley, David. (2001) Connecting learning objects to instructional design theory. Book: The Instructional Use of Learning Objects. http://reusability.org/read.

Willey David, Learning Object Design and Sequencing Theory. (2000) Brigham Young University. June 2000. On Line: http://wiley.ed.usu.edu/docs/dissertation.pdf

AUTHOR INDEX

235

SUBJECT INDEX

Printed in the United States
97374LV00003B/180/A